Windows® 2000 Hardware and Disk Management

ISBN 0-13-089104-5

90000

9 780130 891044

PRENTICE HALL PTR MICROSOFT® TECHNOLOGIES SERIES

NETWORKING

- Microsoft Technology: Networking, Concepts, Tools
  Woodard, Gattuccio, Brain

- NT Network Programming Toolkit
  Murphy

- Building COM Applications with Internet Explorer
  Loveman

- Understanding DCOM
  Rubin, Brain

- Web Database Development for Windows Platforms
  Gutierrez

PROGRAMMING

- The COM and COM+ Programming Primer
  Gordon

- Windows 2000 Web Applications Developer's Guide
  Yager

- The Visual Basic Object and Component Handbook
  Vogel

- Developing Solutions with Office 2000 Components and VBA
  Aitken

- Windows Shell Programming
  Seely

- The Visual Basic Style Guide
  Patrick

- Introduction to Windows 98 Programming
  Murray, Pappas

- Developing Professional Applications for Windows 98 and NT Using MFC, Third Edition
  Brain, Lovette

- Win 32 System Services: The Heart of Windows 98 and Windows NT, Third Edition
  Brain

- Multithreaded Programming with Win32
  Pham, Garg

- Visual Basic 6: Design, Specification, and Objects
  Hollis

- ADO Programming in Visual Basic 6
  Holzner

- Visual Basic 6: Error Coding and Layering
  Gill

- Visual C++ Templates
  Murray, Pappas

- Introduction to MFC Programming with Visual C++
  Jones

- MFC Programming in C++ with the Standard Template Libraries
  Murray, Pappas

- COM-CORBA Interoperability
  Geraghty, Joyce, Moriarty, Noone

- Distributed COM Application Development Using Visual Basic 6.0
  Maloney

- Distributed COM Application Development Using Visual C++ 6.0
  Maloney

- Understanding and Programming COM+: A Practical Guide to Windows 2000 DNA
  Oberg

- ASP/MTS/ADSI Web Security
  Harrison

- Microsoft Site Server 3.0 Commerce Edition
  Libertone, Scoppa

- Building Microsoft SQL Server 7 Web Sites
  Byrne

ADMINISTRATION

- Windows 2000 Hardware and Disk Management
  Simmons

- Creating Active Directory Infrastructures
  Simmons

- Windows 2000 Registry
  Sanna

- Configuring Windows 2000 Server
  Simmons

- Tuning and Sizing NT Server
  Aubley

- Windows NT Cluster Server Guidebook
  Libertone

- Windows NT 4.0 Server Security Guide
  Goncalves

- Windows NT Security
  McInerney

- Supporting Windows NT and 2000 Workstation and Server
  Mohr

- Zero Administration Kit for Windows
  McInerney

- Designing Enterprise Solutions with Microsoft Technologies
  Kemp, Kemp, Goncalves

PRENTICE HALL PTR MICROSOFT® TECHNOLOGIES SERIES

SIMMONS

Windows 2000 Hardware and Disk Management

Prentice Hall PTR, Upper Saddle River, NJ 07458
www.phptr.com

Editorial/Production Supervision: MetroVoice Publishing Services
Acquisitions Editor: Jill Pisoni
Editorial Assistant: Justin Somma
Development Editor: Ralph Moore
Cover Design Director: Jerry Votta
Cover Designer: Anthony Gemmellaro
Buyer: Maura Goldstaub
Series Design: Maureen Eide
Marketing Manager: Bryan Gambrel
Art Director: Gail Cocker-Bogusz
Project Coordinator: Anne Trowbridge

© 2000 by Prentice Hall PTR
Prentice-Hall, Inc.
Upper Saddle River, New Jersey 07458

Prentice Hall books are widely used by corporations and government agencies for training, marketing, and resale. The publisher offers discounts on this book when ordered in bulk quantities. For more information, contact:

Corporate Sales Department,
Prentice Hall PTR
One Lake Street
Upper Saddle River, NJ 07458
Phone: 800-382-3419; FAX: 201-236-7141
E-mail (Internet): corpsales@prenhall.com

Printed in the United States of America

10 9 8 7 6 5 4 3 2 1

ISBN 0-13-089104-5

Prentice-Hall International (UK) Limited, *London*
Prentice-Hall of Australia Pty. Limited, *Sydney*
Prentice-Hall Canada Inc., *Toronto*
Prentice-Hall Hispanoamericana, S.A., *Mexico*
Prentice-Hall of India Private Limited, *New Delhi*
Prentice-Hall of Japan, Inc., *Tokyo*
Pearson Education Asia Pte. Ltd.
Editora Prentice-Hall do Brasil, Ltda., *Rio de Janeiro*

CONTENTS

PREFACE   *xv*

Who This Book Is For   *xv*

What's in the Book?   *xvi*

    Part One: Installing and Configuring Windows 2000 Hardware   *xvi*

    Part Two: Windows 2000 Hard Disk Management   *xvii*

    Part Three: Windows 2000 Storage Features   *xvii*

    Part Four: Windows 2000 File Management   *xviii*

ACKNOWLEDGMENTS   *xix*

PART ONE   Installing & Configuring Windows 2000 Hardware

ONE   Managing Hardware in Windows 2000   *3*

Understanding Plug and Play   *3*

Checking the HCL   *5*

Adding New Hardware to Your System   *5*

    Using the Add/Remove Hardware Wizard to Add New Hardware   *6*

    Using the Add/Remove Hardware Wizard to Troubleshoot a Device   *9*

    Using the Add/Remove Hardware Wizard to Uninstall/Unplug a Device   *10*

Using Device Manager   *11*

Hardware Configuration Options in System Properties   *17*

Understanding System Resources   *20*

Summary   *21*

Q&A   *22*

TWO   Configuring Modems   *25*

How Modems Work   *25*
Installing Modems   *27*
Configuring Dialing Rules   *28*
Configuring the Modem   *30*
Configuring a Dial-Up Connection   *33*
    Using HyperTerminal   37
    Using the Phone Dialer   37
Summary   *38*
Q&A   *39*

THREE   Managing Network Adapter Cards and USB
        Devices   *41*

How Network Interface Cards Work   *41*
Installing Network Interface Cards   *42*
Configuring Network Interface Cards   *42*
Binding the Network Adapter to Protocols   *44*
Installing and Configuring Universal Serial Bus Devices   *46*
    Understanding USB Controllers and Hubs   46
    About USB Devices   48
Summary   *49*
Q&A   *49*

FOUR   Setting Up Printers   *51*

Printing Overview   *51*
    New Windows 2000 Print Features   52
Installing Printers   *53*
    Configuring the Printer   55
Setting Up Client Computers to Access Shared Printers   *61*
Printing to Macintosh and UNIX Servers   *62*
Managing Print Documents   *63*
Summary   *64*
Q&A   *64*

FIVE   Video and Sound Cards   67

Installing Video Cards   *67*

Configuring Display Settings   *69*

> *General   69*
>
> *Adapter   70*
>
> *Monitor   71*
>
> *Troubleshooting   72*
>
> *Color Management   72*

Solving Problems with a Video Card   *74*

Using Multiple Video Cards and Monitors   *75*

Installing Sound Cards   *76*

Configuring Sound and Multimedia   *76*

> *Sounds   76*
>
> *Audio   77*
>
> *Hardware   77*

Summary   *79*

Q&A   *80*

SIX   Other Peripherals   *81*

FAX   *81*

> *User Information   82*
>
> *Cover Pages   83*
>
> *Status Monitor   83*
>
> *Advanced Options   83*

Scanners and Cameras   *85*

Game Controllers   *87*

Mouse and Keyboard   *88*

Power Options   *88*

Summary   *89*

Q&A   *89*

SEVEN   Troubleshooting Hardware Devices   *91*

Windows 2000 Troubleshooting Tools   *91*

Hardware Problems and Solutions   *93*

    Modems   93

    Network Adapter Cards   94

    USB Devices   94

    Printers   94

    Video Card   95

    Sound Card   95

    Other Peripherals   95

Summary   *96*

PART TWO   Windows 2000 Disk Management

EIGHT   Windows 2000 Hard Disk Basics   *99*

How Hard Disks Work   *99*

Windows 2000 File Systems   *100*

    FAT   100

    FAT32   101

    NTFS   101

The Disk Management Console   *102*

Summary   *107*

Q&A   *107*

NINE   Dynamic Disks in Windows 2000   *109*

Dynamic and Basic Disks   *109*

    Upgrading a Basic Disk to a Dynamic Disk   112

Writing Disk Signatures   *115*

Returning to a Basic Disk   *116*

Understanding Disk States   *117*

Adding a New Disk   *118*

Removing a Disk   *119*

Examining Disk Properties   *119*

Summary   *120*
Q&A   *120*

TEN   Configuring Dynamic Volumes   *123*

Creating a New Simple Volume   *123*
Mounting a Simple Volume to an Empty Folder   *127*
Extending a Volume   *129*
Creating Spanned Volumes   *132*
Creating Striped Volumes   *134*
Common Volume Tasks   *137*
Dynamic Volume States   *137*
 Configuring Volume Properties   138
Summary   *139*
Q&A   *140*

ELEVEN   Configuring Windows 2000 Fault Tolerance   *143*

What is Fault Tolerance?   *143*
Configuring Mirrored Volumes   *145*
 Creating a Mirrored Volume   145
 Resynchronizing the Mirrored Volume   148
 Breaking a Mirror   149
 Removing a Mirror   149
 Repairing a Mirrored Volume   149
 Booting From a Mirror   150
Configuring RAID 5 Volumes   *150*
 Creating a RAID 5 Volume   151
 Repairing a RAID 5 Volume   152
Summary   *153*
Q&A   *153*

TWELVE   Windows 2000 Backup   *155*

Backup Options in Windows 2000   *155*

    Backup Types   156

    Using Windows Backup   157

Summary   *168*

Q&A   *168*

THIRTEEN   Windows 2000 Disk Tools   *171*

Disk Cleanup   *171*

Error Checking   *173*

Disk Defragmenter   *174*

Scheduled Tasks   *177*

Event Viewer   *179*

Summary   *181*

Q&A   *181*

FOURTEEN   Troubleshooting Disk Problems   *183*

Troubleshooting Specific Disk Problems   *183*

    Problems with a SCSI Hard Disk   184

    Check for Access to the Boot Partition   185

    Tape Devices and Floppy Disk Drive   185

    Using More than Two IDE or ESDI Devices   185

    Test the Drive on Another Computer   185

    Check the Drivers   185

General Troubleshooting   *186*

Summary   *188*

PART THREE Windows 2000 Storage Features

FIFTEEN   Remote Storage   *191*

Remote Storage Concepts   *191*

How Remote Storage Works with Removable Storage   *193*

Setting Up and Using Remote Storage   *193*

    Volume Management   195

    Managing Media   198

Summary   *199*

Q&A   *199*

SIXTEEN   Removable Storage   *201*

Understanding Removable Storage   *201*

    Understanding Media Pools   202

    Understanding Media States   202

Using Removable Storage   *203*

    Configuring and Managing Libraries   203

    Configuring Media Pools   207

    Configuring and Managing Physical Media   208

    Configuring Queued Work and Operator Requests   209

    Configuring Removable Storage Security   212

    Using Removable Storage Command Line   213

Summary   *215*

Q&A   *215*

SEVENTEEN   Additional Storage Technologies   *217*

Using Compression   *217*

Using Encrypting File System (EFS)   *221*

Using Disk Quotas   *224*

Summary   *226*

Q&A   *227*

EIGHTEEN   Distributed File System   *229*

Understanding Dfs   *229*

Configuring a Stand-Alone Dfs   *233*

  Creating Dfs Links   235

Configuring a Domain-Based Dfs   *238*

Summary   *240*

Q&A   *241*

NINETEEN   Troubleshooting Windows 2000 Storage
  243

Remote Storage   *243*

Removable Storage   *245*

Disk Quotas   *246*

Encrypting File System and Compression   *247*

Distributed File System   *248*

Summary   *249*

PART FOUR Windows 2000 File Management

TWENTY   File and Folder Management and Security
  253

NTFS Permissions   *253*

  Assigning NTFS Permissions   255

  Advanced Access Permissions   258

Managing Shared Folders   *261*

Synchronization Manager   *263*

  Setting Up Your Computer to Use Offline Files   263

  Making a File or Folder Available Offline   264

  Setting Up Synchronization Manager   264

Summary   *269*

Q&A   *269*

TWENTY-ONE   Indexing Service   *271*

Indexing Service   *271*

    Installing the Indexing Service   272

    Configuring the Indexing Service   272

    Creating a New Catalog   274

    Performing Manual Catalog Scans   275

    Checking Indexing Service Performance   275

    Retrieving a List of Unindexed Documents   277

    Preventing an NTFS Directory or Document from Being Indexed   277

Summary   *278*

Q&A   *278*

APPENDIX   Using the Microsoft Management Console
              281

What is the MMC?   *281*

Adding Snap-ins   *283*

Choosing an MMC Mode   *287*

Using Multiple Windows   *288*

Summary   *290*

INDEX   *291*

Welcome to *Windows 2000 Hardware and Disk Management*. This book is designed to be your Windows 2000 companion to help you install and configure your hardware devices and take advantage of Windows 2000's new disk management and remote/removable storage features. In the past, managing your hardware and hard disks was an often tedious and frustrating task. Fortunately, Windows 2000 provides a plug-and-play operating system with many new features and support for hardware. Additionally, disk management is completely different in Windows 2000, with new technologies and features. With this book, you can get your Windows 2000 Professional or Server computer configured and operating in peak condition.

Who This Book Is For

This book is written for two diverse groups of people. First, if you are an IT professional faced with the responsibilities of configuring and managing Windows 2000 Server as well as Windows 2000 Professional, this book serves as a handy reference tool for hardware installation and configuration as well as disk management. You can use this book to support the many tasks you need to perform. Second, this book is written for all users of Windows 2000 Professional. Whether you are working in an office that is implementing Windows 2000 or if you have purchased Windows 2000 Professional as an upgrade to your home PC, you can use this book to help you configure your hardware devices and make use of the new disk configuration options provided in Windows 2000.

This book examines the installation and configuration of hardware devices and disk management for both Windows 2000 Professional and Windows 2000 Server. This is because the hardware and disk features of Professional and Server are essentially the same. Throughout the book, I refer to Professional and Server as simply "Windows 2000." When there are differences between the two operating systems, I note those so you can stay on track.

I have written this book in a clear, concise manner so you can easily get the information you need whether you are an IT professional or an enduser. You will see a lot of step-by-step instructions and screen prints to help you along the way.

What's in the Book?

This book is divided into three major sections. First, you learn about hardware installation and configuration. In this section, you can learn all about Windows 2000 hardware tools, plug-and-play compliance, and how to install and configure devices such as modems, network adapter cards, printers, USB devices, and a host of others.

Next, the book explores the new disk configuration options and management features of Windows 2000. In this section, you learn about dynamic disks, disk states, creating volumes, and using Windows 2000 fault-tolerant solutions. You also learn about Windows 2000 disk tools, including backup.

In Part Three, you learn about the new remote and removable storage features of Windows 2000. Remote and removable storage allow you to take advantage of tape drives, zip disks, writeable CD, and other media to extend your hard drive to remote and removable storage. You also examine other storage features, such as the Distributed File System, the encrypting file system, and disk quotas.

Finally, Part Four examines file management in Windows 2000, where you learn about offline files, file and folder security options, and Windows 2000's indexing service.

The following tells you what you can expect to see in each chapter.

Part One: Installing and Configuring Windows 2000 Hardware

Chapter 1: Managing Hardware in Windows 2000. In this chapter, you learn all about the new hardware features in Windows 2000, such as plug-and-play support, the Add/Remove Hardware wizard, Device Manager, and a number of related topics.

Chapter 2: Configuring Modems. In this chapter, you learn how to install and configure modems, area code rules, and how to create modem connections.

Chapter 3: Managing Network Adapter Cards and USB Devices. In Chapter 3, you learn all about network adapter cards, which give your computer access to a local area network, and you also explore the new Universal Serial Bus (USB) support in Windows 2000.

Chapter 4: Setting Up Printers. This chapter explores the new printing features of Windows 2000 and shows you how to install and configure your printer for local or network use.

Chapter 5: Video and Sound Cards. Video and sound cards can be tricky devices that can cause you some problems. In this chapter, I explore the installation issues and configuration of video and sound cards in your Windows 2000 system.

Chapter 6: Other Peripherals. This chapter examines a number of additional peripheral devices now supported in Windows 2000, such as scanners, digital cameras, game controllers, and so forth.

Chapter 7: Troubleshooting Hardware Devices. This chapter provides a handy reference location for common problems you could experience with your hardware and their solutions.

Part Two: Windows 2000 Disk Management

Chapter 8: Windows 2000 Hard Disk Basics. This chapter introduces you to disk management in Windows 2000 and shows you the new management features.

Chapter 9: Dynamic Disks in Windows 2000. This chapter examines the configuration of dynamic disks and explores the online/offline features as well as configuration options.

Chapter 10: Configuring Dynamic Volumes. This chapter shows you how to configure volumes on dynamic disks and the volume options that are available to you.

Chapter 11: Configuring Windows 2000 Fault Tolerance. Windows 2000 offers fault-tolerant solutions to protect your data in case of a disk failure. This chapter shows you how to configure and manage fault tolerance.

Chapter 12: Windows 2000 Backup. The importance of data backup cannot be understated. This chapter shows you how to devise a backup plan and how to use the Windows Backup tool.

Chapter 13: Windows 2000 Disk Tools. A number of new tools are available in Windows 2000 to help you manage your hard disks. This chapter shows you how to use these tools.

Chapter 14: Troubleshooting Disk Problems. This chapter serves as a reference where you can examine a number of common disk problems and solutions.

Part Three: Windows 2000 Storage Features

Chapter 15: Remote Storage. Remote storage allows you to store data in a remote location, yet your system continues to manage it as though locally stored. This chapter shows you how to install and use remote storage.

Chapter 16: Removable Storage. Removable storage allows you to use zip drives, CD-ROM drives, etc. to store data on removable storage media. This chapter shows you how to use this feature.

Chapter 17: Additional Storage Technologies. This chapter shows you how to configure and implement two new Windows 2000 features, disk quotas and encrypting file system.

Chapter 18: Distributed File System. Are your network clients having problems finding shared folders on your network? Then Distributed File System may be the easy answer you need.

Chapter 19: Troubleshooting Windows 2000 Storage. This chapter offers you a number of potential problems and their solutions concerning Windows 2000 storage technologies.

Part Four: Windows 2000 File Management

Chapter 20: File and Folder Management and Security. This chapter examines offline files, file and folder management, and configuring NTFS security for files and folders.

Chapter 21: Indexing Service. This chapter shows you how to install and configure Windows 2000's indexing service.

ACKNOWLEDGMENTS

I would like to thank everyone at Prentice Hall, especially Jill Pisoni, for taking this one on. I owe a huge debt of gratitude to my agent, Margot Maley, who keeps book opportunities coming my way. Special thanks to Jim Kelly who brought his technical expertise to the table. I would also like to thank my wife, Dawn, for her constant support.

Installing and Configuring Windows 2000 Hardware

In This Part

▶ **CHAPTER 1**
Managing
Hardware in
Windows 2000

▶ **CHAPTER 2**
Configuring
Modems

▶ **CHAPTER 3**
Managing Network
Adapter Cards and
USB Devices

▶ **CHAPTER 4**
Setting Up Printers

▶ **CHAPTER 5**
Video and Sound
Cards

▶ **CHAPTER 6**
Other Peripherals

▶ **CHAPTER 7**
Troubleshooting
Hardware Devices

In Part One, you learn about installing and configuring Windows 2000 hardware. Windows 2000 provides a plug-and-play compliant system, which makes hardware management, configuration, and installation much easier than in previous versions of Windows. Part One contains the following chapters:

Chapter 1: Managing Hardware in Windows 2000
Chapter 2: Configuring Modems
Chapter 3: Managing Network Adapter Cards and
            USB Devices
Chapter 4: Setting Up Printers
Chapter 5: Video and Sound Cards
Chapter 6: Other Peripherals
Chapter 7: Troubleshooting Hardware Devices

Managing Hardware in Windows 2000

In previous versions of Windows, managing hardware could be a time-consuming, frustrating task. You had to know a thing or two about IRQ settings and hardware resource allocation—such things you would rather avoid. In Windows 2000, you are provided a plug-and-play compliant system, which places most of the burden of handling hardware on the computer instead of on you. This does not mean that you do not have to configure and manually install hardware from time to time, but Windows 2000 certainly leaves the legacy of difficult hardware configuration behind.

In this chapter, you learn about the new features of hardware management in Windows 2000, and you learn how to use the hardware installation management tools, Add/Remove Hardware and Device Manager.

Understanding Plug and Play

Plug and play, often called "plug and pray" in the past, allows your computer to automatically detect and install hardware devices without intervention from you. Plug and play first came onto the scene with Windows 95. The goal of plug-and-play (PnP) technology is to allow users to easily add and remove hardware without having to know a lot about hardware configuration or troubleshooting. A PnP system is designed to take care of the hardware needs with very little intervention from the user. A PnP system automatically detects new hardware and attempts to install it.

PnP has changed a lot since Windows 95. Windows 95 achieved PnP operation through the use of Advanced Power Management (APM) BIOS (Basic Input Output System) or a plug-and-play BIOS. Both of these were designed for Windows 95 PnP, and we know the design was less than perfect. PnP is much more stable now due to an OnNow design initiative called Advanced Configuration and Power Interface (ACPI) which defines the system board and BIOS interface and allows not only PnP, but also power management and other configuration capabilities. In Windows 2000, you can expect to see the following PnP features:

- Automatic adaptation to hardware changes. Windows 2000 Server automatically detects hardware changes in your system and seeks to install or remove those devices as the changes occur.
- Automatic hardware resource allocation. In times past, installing a new piece of hardware required you to have a good handle on the resources the hardware might need, such as DMA channels, IRQs, I/O ports, and so forth. PnP handles all of these issues for you and assigns the new hardware resources it needs while preserving the resource allocation of other devices.
- Automatic driver loading. PnP systems automatically load appropriate drivers for PnP devices.
- Hardware Wizard. Windows 2000 Server provides a hardware wizard so that adding and removing hardware is an easy task.

When new hardware is added to the system, Windows 2000 gives you a dialog box stating that Windows has found new hardware and is attempting to install it. If Windows can install the appropriate driver for the device, it will do so automatically. If not, the system will prompt you for help to provide a driver for the device.

Generally, installing new hardware requires three basic steps:

1. Attach the device to your computer, either internally or externally. You should follow the manufacturer's guidelines so that you attach the device to the correct port or slot.

2. Install device drivers and software. If the device is plug-and-play, Windows will be able to take care of this task automatically. In the case of older legacy hardware that is not plug-and-play aware, you can use the new Add/Remove Hardware Wizard described in the next section to install the hardware.

3. Configure the device and settings. This action involves accessing the properties sheet for the device and configuring it as needed. A later

section in this chapter shows you how to access various properties sheets.

Checking the HCL

When you are installing Windows 2000 on a computer, or any time you decide to purchase a new piece of hardware, one of the best actions you can take is to check the Windows 2000 Hardware Compatibility List (HCL). The HCL provides you with an extensive list of device manufacturers and models that have been tested with Windows 2000 and are approved for use with the operating system. Checking the HCL is a simple step you can take to make certain you do not have hardware problems due to an unsupported device. A copy of the HCL is available on your installation CD-ROM, but the list is being constantly updated, so you should check it out on the web at http://www.microsoft.com/hwtest/hcl.

Adding New Hardware to Your System

In most cases, Windows 2000 can automatically detect new plug-and-play hardware attached to your system. For example, let's say you just purchased a new modem. You can power-down your system, install the modem, then power up your system. When the system reboots, the computer can detect that a new device has been added to the system, and a message, such as the one in Figure 1.1, appears.

At this point, Windows will check its own database of drivers and attempt to find a driver suitable for the device. If it can find one, Windows installs the device without any intervention from you. If Windows cannot find a suitable driver, it will prompt you for help. In this case, you hopefully have the driver from the manufacturer of the hardware on a diskette or CD-ROM. Windows can then copy the driver from the location you specify and install the driver for the device.

FIGURE 1.1 Windows 2000 automatically detects plug-and-play devices.

A *driver* is a piece of software that allows Windows 2000 to interact and communicate with a hardware device. All hardware devices on a Windows 2000 computer have a driver that allows the system to operate them. Windows 2000 contains an extensive database of drivers so it can automatically install a driver for a hardware device without your help. When you purchase a hardware device, drivers are normally provided with the product on a floppy disk or CD-ROM.

As I mentioned, Windows 2000 can normally detect and automatically install plug-and-play devices. However, in some cases the system may fail to detect a device, or you may wish to install a "legacy" device, which is a device that does not support plug-and-play. In this case, Windows 2000 provides a handy wizard—the Add/Remove Hardware wizard.

First introduced in Windows 98, the Add/Remove Hardware wizard is a tool that allows you to install, remove, and even troubleshoot hardware devices on your system. It is designed to systematically walk you through the necessary steps to complete these goals.

The wizard is easy to use and generally self-explanatory, but the next few sections give you a walkthrough for using the wizard. Screen prints are included with the sections so you can use this as an easy guide to using the Add/Remove Hardware wizard.

Using the Add/Remove Hardware Wizard to Add New Hardware

You can use the Add/Remove Hardware wizard to install hardware Windows 2000 did not automatically detect and install, or to install legacy devices. The following steps walk you through the wizard when installing new hardware. Use these steps as a guide:

1. Click Start ➤ Settings ➤ Control Panel.
2. Double-click Add/Remove Hardware wizard.
3. Click Next on the Welcome screen.
4. At this point, you have either the option to Add/Troubleshoot a device or Uninstall/Unplug a device (Figure 1.2). Click the Add/Troubleshoot radio button, then click Next.
5. Windows performs a search for new plug-and-play devices to install. If it finds a new device, installation continues. If not, you are given the Choose a Hardware Device (Figure 1.3). You can select a device for which you are having problems, or you can click the Add option, then click Next.
6. Windows prompts you to either let Windows search for the device again or select the device from a list. If you allow Windows to search for the device again, Windows performs an exhaustive examination of the system, then still gives you the device list if it doesn't find the device. Click either Yes or No, then click Next.

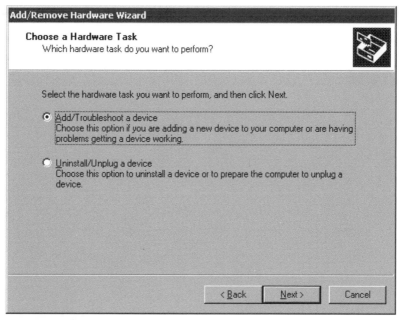

FIGURE 1.2   Use this window to select the desired task.

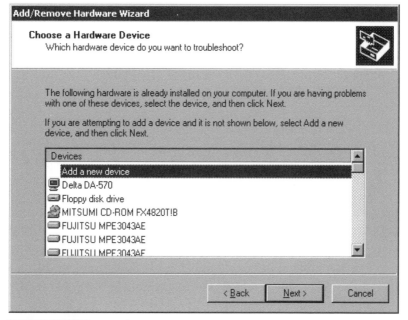

FIGURE 1.3   Use this window to choose a hardware device to troubleshoot, or click the Add option.

7. If Windows does not find the device, click the kind of device you want to install from the provided list (Figure 1.4), then click Next.

8. Depending on the device you select, Windows either provides you with a list to choose from, or launches another wizard to help you install that particular device. In most cases, Windows provides you with a model and make list, from which you simply select the manufacturer of your device and the modem (Figure 1.5). If your manufacturer or model is not listed, but you have an installation diskette or CD-ROM, click the Have Disk button. This action opens another window where you specify the location of the installation files, such as a diskette or CD-ROM, so Windows can copy the installation files (Figure 1.6). Make your selection, then click Next.

9. After making your selection, Windows either uses default settings for the device or uses the information from the disk you may have provided to complete the installation. Click Next.

10. Depending on the device you installed, other instructions may appear. Follow the instructions as necessary.

11. Click the Finish button to complete the wizard.

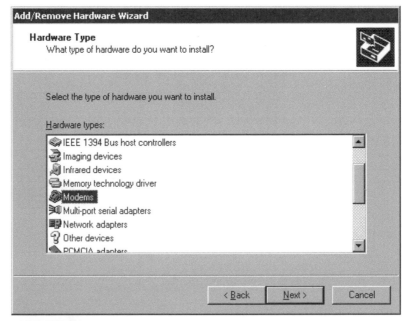

FIGURE 1.4 Select the kind of device you want to install.

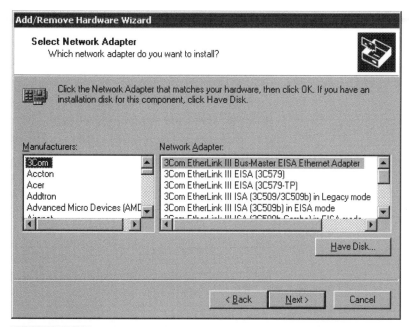

Select the manufacturer and model of the hardware device.

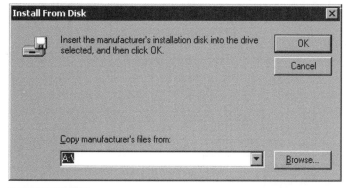

If you have an installation diskette or CD, enter the location so Windows can copy the setup files.

Using the Add/Remove Hardware Wizard to Troubleshoot a Device

The Add/Remove Hardware wizard includes a helpful feature that allows you to troubleshoot a device on your system that is not working properly. There are also other helpful Windows features that allow you to troubleshoot devices that are not working properly that you can learn about in this chapter and in Chapter 7. To use the Add/Remove Hardware wizard to troubleshoot a device, follow these steps:

1. Click Start ➤ Settings ➤ Control Panel.
2. Double-click the Add/Remove Hardware wizard.
3. Click Next on the Welcome screen.
4. Click the Add/Troubleshoot a device radio button on the Choose a Hardware Task window, then click Next.
5. Windows searches for any new plug-and-play hardware. In the Choose a Hardware Device window that appears, select the device from the list for which you are having problems, then click Next.
6. The final window of the wizard appears, listing information about the device and what might be causing the problem (such as a missing or corrupt driver). If the window does not report a problem with the device, then the problem is most likely incorrect configuration. Click Finish to end the wizard.

Using the Add/Remove Hardware Wizard to Uninstall/Unplug a Device

Windows 2000 allows you much control over the system hardware by allowing you to manually add, troubleshoot, and configure devices, but it also allows you to uninstall or unplug a device. If you choose to uninstall a device, the software and drivers for the device are removed from the system. You can then physically remove the device from your system. Of course, if the device is plug-and-play and you restart Windows without physically removing the device, Windows will redetect it. You can also "unplug" a device. This simply means that the device is still installed on the system, but it is disabled. This is a helpful feature if you are having problems with one device and you want to temporarily disable it. This feature allows you to leave a device installed on your system, but stop it from functioning or interfering with other devices. To use the Add/Remove Hardware wizard to uninstall or unplug a device, follow these steps:

1. Click Start ➤ Settings ➤ Control Panel.
2. Double-click Add/Remove Hardware.
3. Click Next on the Welcome screen.
4. On the Choose a Hardware Task window, click the Uninstall/Unplug a device radio button, then click Next.
5. On the Choose a Removal Task window, select either the Uninstall a device or Unplug/Eject a device radio button, then click Next (Figure 1.7).

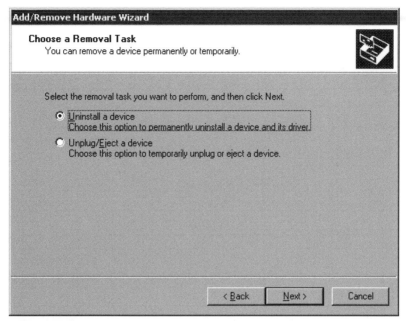

FIGURE 1.7   Choose to uninstall or unplug a device by clicking the desired radio button.

6. Depending on your selection, a window appears allowing you to uninstall or unplug a device. Make your selection, then click Next.

7. A window appears asking if you are sure you want to uninstall/unplug the device. Click either the Yes or No radio button, then click Next.

8. Click the Finish button to complete the wizard, then the selected hardware is either uninstalled or unplugged.

Using Device Manager

Device Manager in Windows 2000 is a tool that allows you to view all the hardware devices installed on your computer and manage them in a number of ways. You access Device Manager by clicking Start ➤ Programs ➤ Administrative Tools ➤ Computer Management. Expand the System Tools option in the left pane, then click Device Manager, which opens in the right pane (Figure 1.8).

If you expand the desired category, you can see the devices that are installed in that category. For example, in Figure 1.9, the CD-ROM drive installed on this computer appears under the DVD/CD-ROM Drives category.

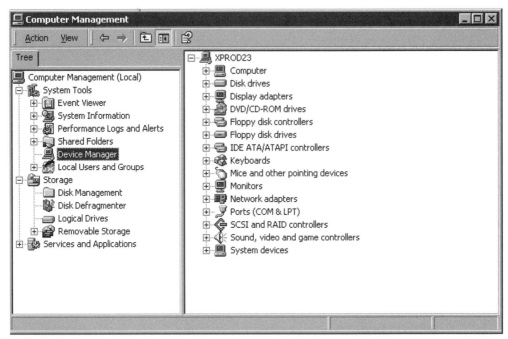

FIGURE 1.8 Device Manager gives you a single interface for device management.

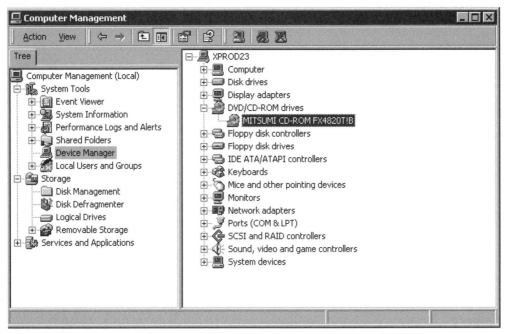

FIGURE 1.9 Expand the desired category to select a device.

If you select a desired device, then click the Action menu, there are four different actions you can perform, as described in the following list:

- Disable—allows you to disable the device. The device is still installed and configured on your system, but cannot be used when this option is selected.
- Uninstall—allows you to uninstall the device. This action causes the device and the driver files to be removed from your system.
- Scan For Hardware Changes—scans your system for any hardware changes. If Windows detects any hardware changes, the Add/Remove Hardware wizard appears if required.
- Properties—opens the generic properties sheets for the device.

If you click Properties, the properties sheets for the device opens. The available tabs will vary, depending on the device you select, but I do want to mention three generic tabs you will find useful.

First, you have General tab (Figure 1.10). The General tab gives you information about the device and provides you with a Device Status window.

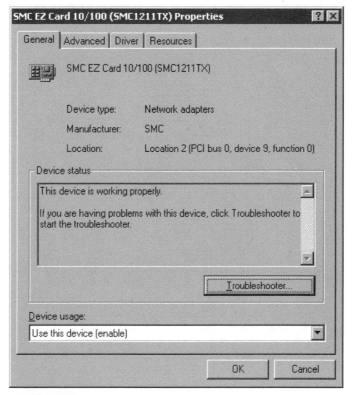

FIGURE 1.10 Use the General tab to gain information about the device, use or disable it, or access troubleshooting help.

The Device Status window tells you if the device is working properly or not, and if it isn't, it normally tells you what is wrong with the device. A Troubleshooter button also appears, which opens the Windows 2000 Help files and walks you through a series of steps to help you resolve any problems you may be having. See Chapter 8 for more information on troubleshooting. Finally, you also have the option on the General tab to either use the device or disable it by making your selection using the drop-down menu.

Next, a generic tab you see for each device is the Driver tab, shown in Figure 1.11. The Driver tab gives you information about the driver installed for the particular hardware device, such as the provider, the driver's date, version, and the digital signer. You can also click the Driver Details button to gain additional information, such as the storage location in Windows 2000, the provider, file version, and copyright date.

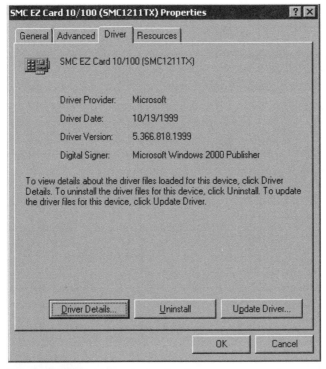

FIGURE 1.11 The Driver tab allows you to update or remove a driver.

Notice on the Driver tab that there is a "Digital Signer." A digital signature is a piece of code installed with a driver that reports to the operating system "who" the driver is from. For example, in Figure 1.11, Microsoft is the digital signer. This lets the system know the driver is from a safe resource. The digital signature feature is particularly useful if you download new drivers from the Internet. The signature helps the system know the driver is from a reliable source, and not something that could harm your system (such as a hidden virus).

The most useful aspects of the Driver tab are the uninstall and update driver features. You can choose to uninstall a driver by clicking the Uninstall button. This action effectively removes the device from your system, and you are prompted to confirm your action before the system continues.

If you click the Update Driver button, the Upgrade Device Driver wizard appears. This wizard is provided by Windows 2000 so you can easily install or upgrade drivers as new drivers become available for your hardware devices. The following steps walk you through the wizard:

1. When you click the Update Driver button on the Driver tab, the wizard appears. Click Next on the Welcome screen.

2. In the Install Hardware Device Drivers window, you have the option to allow Windows to search for a new driver, or to view a list of drivers and select one from the list. The recommended action is to allow Windows to search for and find the best driver. Make your selection and click Next.

3. The Locate Driver Files window appears (Figure 1.12). Windows will search for a driver in its database and in any optional locations you select, such as your diskette or CD-ROM drive. Select any optional search locations and click Next.

4. Windows locates the most suitable device driver for your hardware. To use this device driver, click Next. If you want to select a different driver, click the check box at the bottom of the window and click Next.

5. If you choose to select a different driver, make your selection and click Next.

6. Click Finish to complete the wizard.

Finally, another generic tab you are likely to see for most hardware devices is a Resources tab, shown in Figure 1.13.

The Resources tab gives you the settings, or resource allocation, for a particular hardware device, such I/O range, memory range, and IRQ. These resources are allocated automatically by the system when a new device is installed. In some circumstances, such as in the case of manually forced or legacy hardware, you can make adjustments to these. In Figure 1.13, which is a plug-and-play network adapter card, changes cannot be made to these

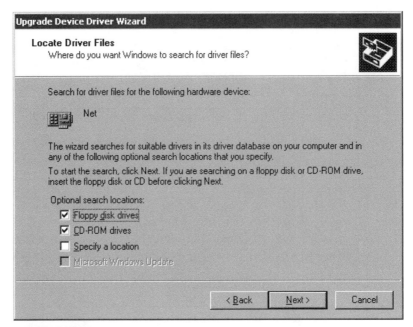

FIGURE 1.12 Select option search locations as desired.

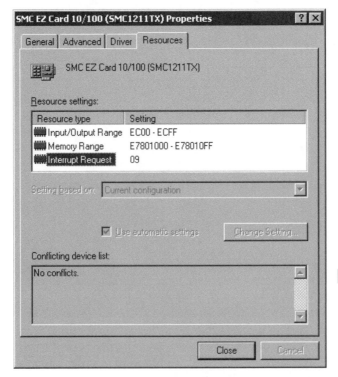

FIGURE 1.13

Use the Resources tab to manage or troubleshoot system resources used by the hardware.

settings. See the "Understanding System Resources" section later in this chapter for more information.

An excellent feature of the Resources tab is the Conflicting Device List. This section, at the bottom of the window, tells you if there are resource conflicts with other devices. As you can see in Figure 1.13, there are no conflicts with this device. If there had been, the conflicting device and the problem with the device would have been listed as well.

Hardware Configuration Options in System Properties

In addition to your major tools of Add/Remove Hardware and Device Manager, you also have a Hardware tab in the System Properties. To access System Properties, right-click My Computer, then click Properties, then click the Hardware tab. On the Hardware tab, you have four buttons; Hardware Wizard, Driver Signing, Device Manager, and Hardware Profiles. Since we have already covered the Hardware Wizard (Add/Remove Hardware) and Device Manager, let's examine the remaining two.

The Driver Signing button opens a single window where you can configure how your system handles driver signing (Figure 1.14).

As mentioned previously, driver signing refers to digital signatures carried by device drivers. These signatures allow the system to know if the driver you are installing is from a reliable source or not. You use the Driver

FIGURE 1.14

Use the Driver Signing Options to configure your system for driver signing.

Signing Options window to determine how your system handles signed drivers. You have three options:

- Ignore—By selecting this option, your system installs all drivers, regardless of the signature.
- Warn—This option is set by default, and it provides you with a warning message before installing unsigned driver files.
- Block—This feature is the most secure, and it prevents you or another user from installing any unsigned driver files.

You also have a check box at the bottom of the window that allows you to apply the setting you select as the system default. This feature is used if you are logged on as the administrator for your computer. You can make your option selection, then select the check box so the setting is in effect for any other user that logs onto your computer. In other words, when an administrator sets this option, a user logged onto the computer cannot change it.

Also on the Hardware tab, you see a button for Hardware Profiles. If you click this button, the Profiles window opens, as shown in Figure 1.15.

You see a Profile 1 (Current listing). This profile contains your current hardware profile. You can use the Copy button to create an additional profile. When you do this, you receive a menu at boot up allowing you to select the profile you want to use. Then, once the system boots, you can

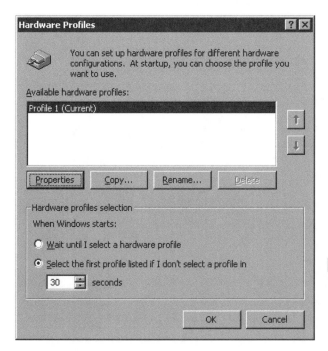

FIGURE 1.15

Use the Hardware Profiles tab to manage profiles on your computer.

make changes to your hardware that are saved in your profile. When you boot into the profile again, you see the new changes.

Hardware profiles are most often used on Windows 2000 computers that are laptops. You can have one hardware profile in use while you are docked or connected to the network, and a different one in use while you are mobile. For example, you could disable your network adapter card for your mobile profile as well as other devices that are not needed when you are not connected to the network. In fact, if you click the Properties button, you see that the single properties sheet allows you to specify the computer as a portable computer, as shown in Figure 1.16.

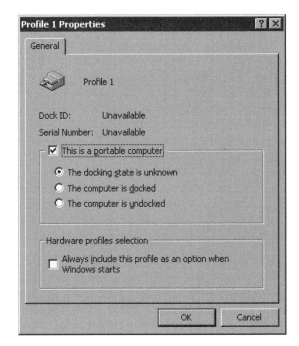

FIGURE 1.16

The Profile's Properties sheet allows you to specify the computer as portable.

Understanding System Resources

As you noticed on the Resources tab of a device's properties, each device attached to your computer is assigned unique system resources. These resources allow the device to operate within the system without conflicting with another device. Although for plug-and-play hardware, Windows automatically makes these assignments, there may be times when you need to manually configure system resources, in which case you should know what resources are allocated by the system. The following list explains each of these:

- Interrupt Request (IRQ) line—IRQs are hardware lines over which hardware devices can send and receive signals from the system processor. When a particular hardware device needs the processor to perform some action, the request is sent over an IRQ. This feature allows the processor to interact with and service the needs of hardware resources on your system. IRQs are numbered from 0 to 15, and each device must be assigned a unique IRQ.
- Direct Memory Access (DMA)—DMA is access to memory that does not involve the processor. DMA is most often used for data transfer directly between memory and a peripheral device, such as a hard disk.
- Input/Output (I/O) port—An I/O port is a channel through which data is transferred from a device to the processor. The port appears to the processor as one or more memory addresses that it can use to send and receive data.
- Memory Address Ranges—A portion of computer memory can be allocated to a device. Devices are allocated a range of memory addresses that can be used if memory usage is necessary.

Once again, the operating system handles all of this and allocates resources to hardware devices. The system can also dynamically change the allocation when necessary. Because of this, you should allow Windows 2000 to manage its own resource allocation. However, in the case of legacy devices, you will have to use the Resources tab on the device's properties sheets to manually assign an IRQ, I/O port, etc, which is a task you would rather avoid. It is also important to note that incorrect resource allocation can cause other devices to stop functioning and cause system-wide problems. Your best bet is to always use hardware that is compatible with Windows 2000 (listed on the HCL) and that is plug-and-play. This will give you the best performance while greatly reducing the likelihood of problems.

Windows 2000 includes a tool called System Information, which first appeared with Windows 98, so you can gain an overall look at your system allocation configuration. To access System Information, click Start ➤ Programs ➤ Administrative Tools ➤ Computer Management. In the left console, expand System Information, then expand Hardware Resources. You

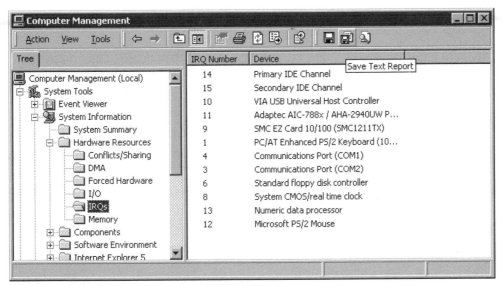

IRQ Number	Device
14	Primary IDE Channel
15	Secondary IDE Channel
10	VIA USB Universal Host Controller
11	Adaptec AIC-788x / AHA-2940UW P...
9	SMC EZ Card 10/100 (SMC1211TX)
1	PC/AT Enhanced PS/2 Keyboard (10...
4	Communications Port (COM1)
3	Communications Port (COM2)
6	Standard floppy disk controller
8	System CMOS/real time clock
13	Numeric data processor
12	Microsoft PS/2 Mouse

FIGURE 1.17 Use System Information to gain an overall look at resource allocation on your computer.

see categories for Conflicts/Sharing, DMA, Forced Hardware, I/O, IRQs, and Memory. You can select any one of these and see a report in the right-pane, as shown in Figure 1.17.

System Information is a particularly useful troubleshooting tool where you can get an overall look at the hardware resource allocation on your system and even see what devices may have conflicts or are sharing hardware resources.

■ Summary

Windows 2000 provides a rich hardware environment where you can easily install and configure the hardware devices you need to use. By providing a plug-and-play compliant system, Windows 2000 can automatically detect and install most plug-and-play devices. For legacy hardware or troubleshooting purposes, as well as to unplug or eject a device, you can use the Add/Remove Hardware wizard and you can further manage hardware by using Device Manager and System Information. Finally, Windows 2000 includes the New Driver wizard so you can easily update device drivers, and it allows you to configure your system for a desired level of driver signing.

Q&A

Review these questions and answers to resolve problems and to check your knowledge of this chapter's content.

Q: *Can Windows 2000 automatically detect hardware changes in my system?*

A: Yes. Due to the plug-and-play features of Windows 2000, your operating system can automatically detect and adapt to hardware changes. For example, if you connect an external modem to your computer, Windows automatically detects that a new piece of hardware is present and attempts to install it. This feature provides an operating system that is "hardware aware" and can adapt as you make hardware changes and additions.

Q: *What does a hardware driver do?*

A: A hardware driver is a piece of software that allows your operating system to communicate with a hardware device. Windows 2000 has an extensive database of drivers it can use to communicate with your hardware, and when you purchase a new piece of hardware, a disk or CD is normally included that provides the manufacturer's driver, which you can install on your system. The Update Driver wizard can help you easily update or install a new driver for a hardware device.

Q: *What is the purpose of the Add/Remove Hardware wizard?*

A: Windows 2000 can install plug-and-play devices automatically. However, for legacy devices, you can use the Add/Remove Hardware wizard to complete the installation. The wizard allows you to specify the type of device you are installing and provide the necessary driver. The Add/Remove Hardware wizard can also be used to troubleshoot problems you may be having with hardware devices.

Q: *How can I check to see if a hardware device is compatible with Windows 2000.*

A: You can check to see if a device is compatible with Windows 2000 by consulting the Hardware Compatibility List (HCL) found on your installation CD-ROM. Be advised that the HCL is constantly updated, so you should also check the most current version of the HCL found on Microsoft's web site at www.microsoft.com/hwtest/hcl.

Q: I want to force a device to stop working on my system, but I do not want to uninstall it. Can this be done?

A: Yes. Use the Add/Remove Hardware wizard to unplug the device. This action stops the device from functioning, but does not remove it from your system. You can also access the device's properties pages within Device Manager, then access the General tab. At the bottom of the window, use the Device Usage drop down menu and select Do not use this device.

Q: What is the easiest way to update a device driver?

A: If you need to update a device driver, access the device's properties sheets and click the Driver tab. Then, click the Update Driver button. This launches the Upgrade Device Driver wizard. Follow the wizard's steps to complete the upgrade.

Q: Several people use my computer. How can I make certain that any device drivers that are downloaded from the Internet are digitally signed before they are installed?

A: You can use the Driver Signing option to configure this. Access System Properties, then click the Hardware tab. Click the Driver Signing button. Click the Block radio button, then click the Apply setting as system default check box. You must be logged on as an administrator to complete this option. This forces the Driver Signing setting on all users who log on to your computer.

Configuring Modems

If you are one of those early Internet geeks like me, you know that configuring your modem and keeping it working was often less than easy. Indeed, many early users of modems eventually threw their hands in the air and gave up. Modems have come a long way in the past several years, and with the widespread use of the Internet and remote access to private networks, modems continue to be an important piece of hardware.

Modem configuration in Windows 2000 does not have to be a painful task. There are a number of features that make modem configuration much easier and provide you with more options. In this chapter, I show you how to install and configure modems.

How Modems Work

Modems are designed to transmit data over traditional phone lines. Phone lines were designed to transmit human speech using analog signals. Analog signals vary continuously along their length, like a wave. Computers communicate with each other using digital signals, which uses binary digits (1s and 0s). So for computer communication to travel over a phone line, the digital data must be converted to analog (called modulation), sent over the phone line, then reconverted to digital (called demodulation). The modem in your computer handles this task. The modulation and demodulation tasks are handled by the use of modem protocols, based on international standards. These international protocol standards allow different modems created by different manufacturers installed on different operating systems to communicate with one another.

A protocol is a communication standard, or rule of communication, that defines how two different computers on different networks, even running different operating systems, communicate with each other. The most popular protocol today is TCP/IP, which is used both on the Internet and in many private networks.

Aside from the typical modem, other kinds of "modems," or in more appropriate terms, "connection devices," are available today, such as cable modems, ISDN connections, and even DSL connections. The use of these types of connection devices is also supported in Windows 2000.

When you begin a dial-up connection, there are three separate components that determine the speed of your connection. First, you have a "local interface speed," which is the speed of the connection between your modem and the computer. This is also called the DTE rate, and determines how fast your computer and your modem communicate with each other.

Second, there is a "connection speed," which is the speed at which data is transferred between modems over the communication line. This is also called the DCE rate.

Finally, there is a "remote interface speed" which is the speed at which data is transmitted between the receiving modem and computer.

So, the actual speed you get depends on all three of these items. Most modems today offer "56 Kbps" speed, but your actual speed will be lower. Due to phone company controls, the highest speed you are likely to get with a standard analog modem is 53 Kbps, and depending on other factors, your speed will probably be somewhat lower.

Windows 2000 supports 56 Kbps modems. The international standard for 56 Kbps modems is the V.90 protocol, which is designed for use with Internet service providers. To increase the reliability of communication over phone lines, modems make use of three major technologies, which are described in the following list:

- Error correction—Modems use error correction technology, which helps reduce the interference that exists on public phone lines. The error correction feature detects corruption that may occur during transmission. All modems in a network must use the same error correction protocols, with the most common being the V.42 protocol. Error correction is configured automatically by Windows 2000 when you install a modem, but you can manually change it, as described in a later section.
- Data compression—Modems use data compression to reduce the amount of time it takes to transmit data. This feature allows you to gain transmission speeds beyond what is actually available.

■ Flow control—Modems also use flow control, which allows the system to control the flow of data. Because modem speeds may vary between two modems, flow control allows the operating system to speed up or slow down the flow of data depending on the connection speed.

You can configure these options as well as others so that your modem operates in a desired manner. Configuration is discussed later in this chapter.

Installing Modems

Modems are installed just as any other hardware device. You can purchase either internal or external modems. With an internal modem, you remove your computer's case and insert the modem into an internal slot. You should carefully follow the manufacturer's instructions when performing the physical installation. Also, you can purchase external modems that attach to a port on the back of your computer (such as a SCSI port). The modem then resides outside of your computer but communicates with your system just as though it were internally connected. Again, always follow the manufacturer's instructions.

Once the new modem is physically attached to your computer, boot your machine. For most plug-and-play modems, Windows 2000 automatically detects it and attempts to install it. You may be prompted to provide drivers if necessary.

If you remove a modem, or attach an external modem to your computer while it is booted, you can have Windows search for the modem without rebooting your machine. You can use either the Add/Remove Hardware wizard or the Install a New Modem wizard, a subset of the Add/Remove Hardware wizard, that is also included with Windows 2000. To use the Install a New Modem wizard, follow these steps:

1. Click Start → Settings → Control Panel.
2. Double-click Phone and Modem Options, then click the Modems tab.
3. Click the Add button. The Install a New Modem wizard appears. You can either allow Windows to detect the modem, or you can click the "Don't detect my modem; I will select it from a list" check box. Make your selection and click Next.
4. If you chose to allow Windows to detect the modem, the system is checked, and if the modem is found, a window appears reporting the find to you. The modem is automatically installed. Click Finish to complete the wizard.

In the case of legacy modems that are not plug-and-play compliant, you can use the Install a New Modem wizard to manually select the modem from a list or use your installation diskette to install it. Of course, with the advances in technology of the past few years, the likelihood of using a legacy modem is rather small. Most plug-and-play modems work well with Windows 2000, but when in doubt, examine the HCL. Modems listed on the HCL have been tested by Microsoft to work with Windows 2000, but modems that do not appear on the HCL may work just as well.

Configuring Dialing Rules

Once your modem is installed, you can use the phone and modem options in Control Panel to configure dialing rules. Access the Dialing Rules tab to configure these options. Dialing rules determine how your computer connects with the remote network. When you access the Dialing Rules tab, you see a default entry called My Location (Figure 2.1). This entry contains your area code, access to an outside line, and whether you use tone or pulse dialing.

You can make changes to the default entry by clicking the Edit button, or you can click the New button to create a new entry. When you click the New button, the New Location window opens so you can configure it.

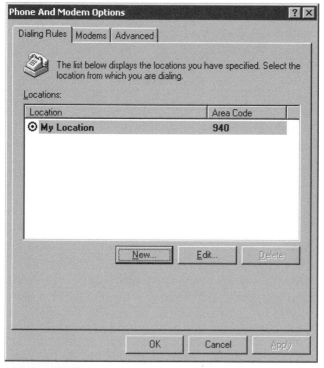

FIGURE 2.1   The Dialing Rules tab is used to configure rules for connecting to a remote network.

On the General tab, shown in Figure 2.2, you can name the location, select your country or region, and enter your area code. In the Dialing rules section, you can enter numbers, if required, to access an outside line or for a long-distance call. You can also disable call waiting and select either tone or pulse dialing.

The Area Code Rules tab (Figure 2.3) allows you to determine how your computer should handle various area codes. For example, you may have several area codes that are not considered long-distance. If you click the New button, you can establish a rule for a particular area code. This feature allows you to specify an area code, include prefixes necessary for the area code, and determine whether or not to dial a "1" in front of the area code.

The Calling Card tab allows you to select a calling card that you need to use, enter your account number, and enter your personal ID number (PIN). Calling cards are most often used by remote users who connect to private networks.

You can create several different dialing rules, which can then be used when calling from two different locations or for other connection needs.

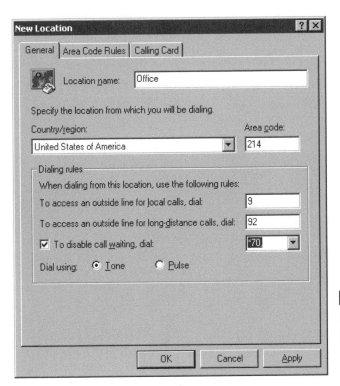

FIGURE 2.2

Use the General tab to configure standard dialing rules options.

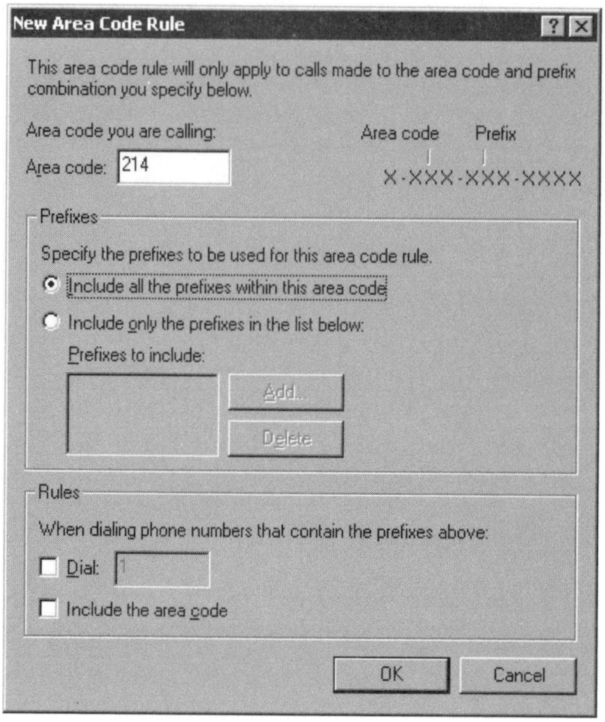

FIGURE 2.3

Create Area Code Rules necessary for your connections.

Configuring the Modem

You can also use the phone and modem options in Control Panel to configure your modem. Access the Modems tab and select your modem in the list. Click properties.

On the General tab (Figure 2.4), you have three options. First, you can adjust the modem's volume. This volume setting is the sound you hear when the modem is making a connection. Use the slider bar to make the modem softer or louder. In the middle of the window, you see a Maximum Port Speed setting with a drop-down menu which you can adjust. By default, your maximum port speed is much higher than the line speed you will obtain. This default setting allows your computer to communicate faster with the actual modem port, which helps your modem communicate more quickly with the operating system. You can change this setting, but under most circumstances the default setting is fine. Finally, you have a Dial Control option, which causes your computer to wait for a phone line dialing tone before actually making the call. You should keep this check box enabled.

The Diagnostics tab (Figure 2.5) allows you to query your modem in order to test it. This is an easy way to see if your computer is communicating with the modem. You can also choose to record a log file, then view the

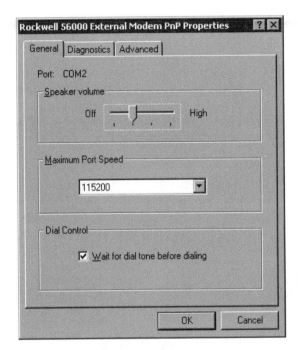

FIGURE 2.4

Use the General tab to configure basic connection properties.

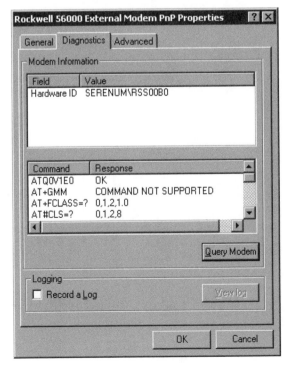

FIGURE 2.5

Use the Diagnostics tab to test your computer and modem communication.

log file if desired. If you are having problems with your modem, this should be your first troubleshooting step. With this tab, you can easily see if your operating system and the modem are communicating correctly.

On the Advanced tab, you have the option to enter additional initialization strings. Initialization strings allow you to further configure how your modem communicates with the modem at the remote network. In most cases, extra initialization strings are unnecessary; however, they may be required by your modem or the modem to which you are connecting. Your modem hardware documentation should give you initialization strings that can be used and information about when they should be used.

Also on the Advanced tab, you can click the Change Default Preferences button to further configure how your modem behaves.

Once you click the Change Default Preferences button, you see additional General (Figure 2.6) and Advanced (Figure 2.7) tabs. On these tabs, you can configure a disconnect time for your modem if it is idle for a certain period, and you can choose to disconnect if the call is not negotiated in a set amount of time. You can also make changes to data connection preferences and hardware settings. For example, you can choose not to use flow control, change the data protocol, choose not to use compression, and make basic changes to the hardware settings. Again, Windows 2000 does a good job of managing these settings and you normally do not need to make

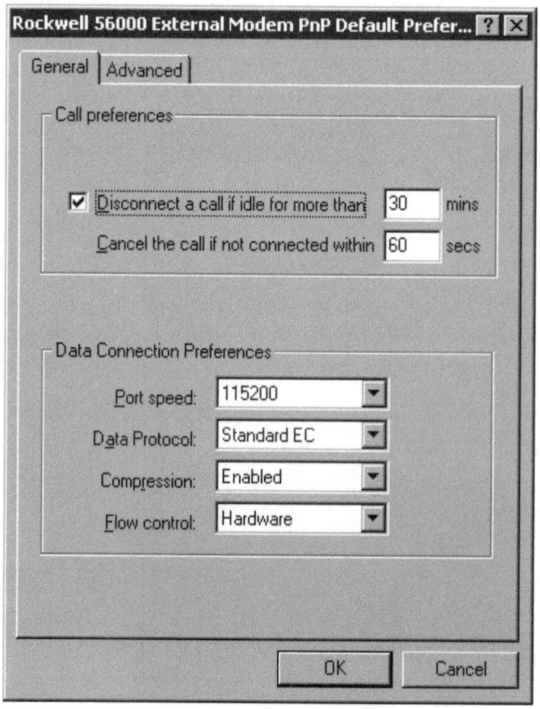

FIGURE 2.6

Use the General tab to set call and data connection preferences.

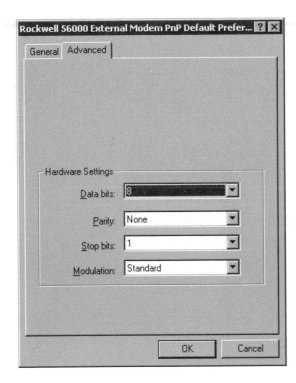

FIGURE 2.7

Use the Advanced tab to make changes to modem hardware settings.

configuration changes here. The options are available, however, if your modem documentation recommends a different setting. You should always refer to your modem documentation before making any of these changes since performance may be hindered if the modem is configured incorrectly.

Configuring a Dial-Up Connection

Once your modem is configured, you need to create a dial-up connection the modem can use to communicate with another modem at a remote location. In Windows 2000, you create dial-up connections by establishing a "new connection." Right-click on My Network Places, then click Properties. The Network and Dial-up Connections window opens. You can also access this Window by double-clicking Network and Dial-Up Connections in Control Panel. Within the window, you see the Make New Connection wizard. To create your dial-up connection, double-click the wizard's icon, then follow these steps:

1. Click Next on the Welcome screen.
2. In the Network Connection Type window (Figure 2.8), select the Dial-up to private network radio button, then click Next.

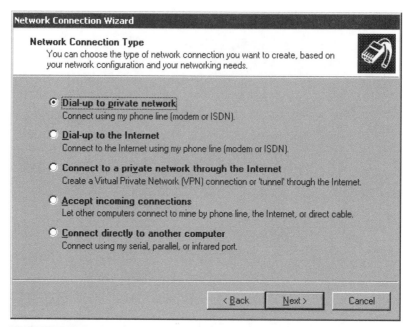

FIGURE 2.8 Select the dial-up option for a modem/adapter connection.

3. Enter the phone number the computer should dial to access the private network. You can also click the Use Dialing Rules check box in order to use any dialing rules you have configured. Click Next.

4. On the Connection Availability window, select either For all Users or Only For Myself. Click Next.

5. If you selected For all Users, the Internet Connection Sharing window appears. Windows 2000 allows you to share your Internet connections so that other users on your network can use your modem (or other adapter, such as ISDN) to access the Internet. If you select this option, you can also enable on-demand dialing, which allows your modem to automatically dial the connection when a user connects to the share (Figure 2.9). When you choose this option, your LAN adapter is set to an IP address of 192.168.0.1, which may cause it to lose connectivity with other computers on your network. Select the desired check boxes, then click Next.

6. Click Finish.

Once you create the new connection, you can right-click it in the Network and Dial-up Connections window and click Properties to further configure it.

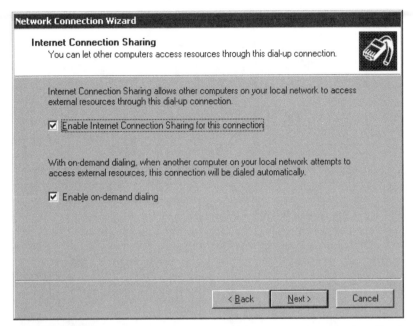

FIGURE 2.9   Click these boxes to enable Internet Connection Sharing.

On the General tab, you can click the Configure button to configure your modem; this option presents you with modem configuration settings discussed earlier in the chapter. You can also specify additional phone numbers, or alternates, that can be dialed if the primary phone number is busy or unavailable. You can also choose, once again, whether or not to use dialing rules.

On the Options tab (Figure 2.10), you can enable several dialing options, such as display progress while connecting, prompt for user name and password, etc. You can also configure dialing options, such as how long to wait before a redial and the amount of idle time that passes before the modem automatically hangs up the call. You also see an X.25 button where you can configure your settings if you are dialing into an X.25 network.

The Security tab presents you with logon options (Figure 2.11). By default, your connection is set to log on with an unsecured password. In some circumstances, such as connecting to a private LAN, you may need to use a secure password method. This option depends entirely on the configuration of your network, so you should contact a system administrator before attempting to use any type of secure logons. For a dial-up connection to an ISP, the default settings are typically all you need.

The Networking tab lists the kinds of networking components in operation for the dial-up connection. Typically, you do not need to change any-

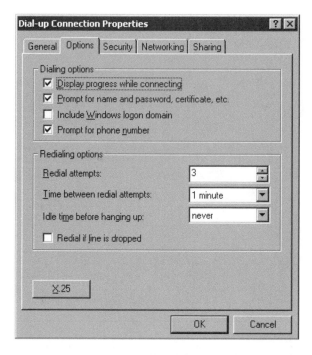

FIGURE 2.10

Use the Options tab to configure general dialing options.

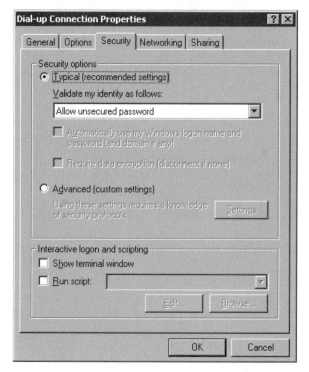

FIGURE 2.11

The Security tab allows you to configure secure logon, if in use.

thing here unless you have specific instructions from a network administrator. The Sharing tab presents you once again with the option to share the Internet connection or not.

In addition to a direct, dial-up connection, Windows 2000 also supports the use of modems with HyperTerminal and using the phone dialer. The following sections explain each of these options.

Using HyperTerminal

HyperTerminal is a utility you can use in Windows 2000 to connect to other computers, telnet sites, bulletin boards, and other online services. The utility can work with your modem to establish connections to remote locations. You can access HyperTerminal by clicking Start ➤ Programs ➤ Accessories ➤ Communication ➤ HyperTerminal. When you first access HyperTerminal, a window appears (Figure 2.12) where you can name a new connection and select an icon for it. Once you establish the connections for HyperTerminal, you can then use the interface to establish the connections desired by dialing them with your modem.

Using the Phone Dialer

The Phone Dialer, also available under Start ➤ Programs ➤ Accessories ➤ Communication ➤ Phone Dialer, is a simple utility you can use to dial phone numbers from your computer and connect to a variety of services, such as video conferencing. You use phone dialer in conjunction with your phone and modem connected to your computer. You can use the Phone Dialer interface, shown in Figure 2.13, to establish and configure access to conference calls and other similar services.

FIGURE 2.12

Use this HyperTerminal window to create a new connection.

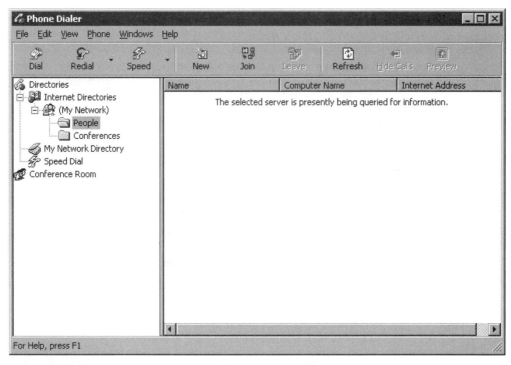

FIGURE 2.13 Use the Phone Dialer interface to configure access to conference calls and other services

■ Summary

Configuring modems in Windows 2000 is a relatively easy task. With plug-and-play modems, Windows can automatically detect and install the modem on your system; then you simply configure the desired dialing rules and connection objects. You can also use legacy modems on your Windows 2000 system provided you have appropriate drivers, but you see the greatest benefit and less problems with plug-and-play modems. Before purchasing a modem, remember to check the HCL and purchase a modem that has been tested with Windows 2000.

Q&A

Review these questions and answers to resolve problems or check your knowledge of this chapter's content.

Q: *What is the different between analog and digital communication?*

A: Analog signals vary continuously along their length, like a wave. Digital signals are a fixed pattern. Telephone lines function by sending analog signals, but computers function with digital signals. In order to send computer communication over the phone lines, the digital signals must be converted to analog, then reconverted to digital at the receiving computer (called modulation and demodulation). This process is performed by the modem.

Q: *What is the highest speed I am likely to get with a 56 Kbps modem?*

A: Due to certain telephone company restrictions, the highest speed you are likely to get with a 56 Kbps modem is about 53 Kbps, but in reality, your speed will probably be somewhat lower (such as 48 Kbps).

Q: *What is flow control?*

A: Flow control allows your system to control the flow of data over the phone line between two modems. This process allows modems to speed up or slow down the sending of data, based on traffic and the connection speed.

Q: *What is the purpose of dialing rules?*

A: Dialing rules enable you to configure your dial-up connections to perform certain connection procedures. Common examples are dialing a "1" in front of a long distance number or using a calling card to establish a long distance connection. Dialing rules enable you to configure your dial-up connections to meet your specific dialing needs.

Q: *Where can I configure dial-up connections in Windows 2000 computers?*

A: Access the Network and Dial-up Connections window, then use the Make New Connection wizard to configure your dial-up connections.

Q: *Can I use a legacy modem in Windows 2000?*

A: Yes. You can use a legacy modem, but you will need to provide the drivers for the modem so you can install it on your system. Use the Add/Remove Hardware wizard to install the modem. Due to the age of legacy modems and the likelihood of slow transmission speeds, your best option is to purchase a new modem that is compatible with Windows 2000 and provides plug-and-play installation. You will see the best performance and experience the least amount of problems.

Q: Do I have to configure plug-and-play modems in Windows 2000?

A: When you install a plug-and-play modem, Windows 2000 can handle most of the modem's configuration automatically. You should not change these settings unless your modem documentation specifically tells you to do so. This is a great feature of plug-and-play and one that allows you to spend less time configuring the modem for operation with Windows 2000.

Managing Network Adapter Cards and USB Devices

....

A network adapter card, or network interface card (NIC), is a piece of hardware that allows your computer to have connectivity on a local area network. The network cable connects to the NIC and allows you to send and receive data over the network. For the most part, NICs are easy to install and configure on your Windows 2000 computer. This chapter also explores the installation and use of the universal serial bus (USB) devices and hubs. In this chapter, I show you how to install and configure your NIC and I examine USB devices in Windows 2000. You can check out Chapter 7 for troubleshooting information on both of these topics.

How Network Interface Cards Work

A NIC card is your computer's interface with the network. Using a NIC, your computer can package data so it can be sent over the network cabling and received by another computer. That computer's NIC then interprets the data and passes it on to the system. You purchase a NIC based on your network's architecture, such as Ethernet or token ring. The NIC then manages data transmission, based on the architecture of your network. This is accomplished through the design elements of the NIC as well as protocols. Your

NIC uses a group of protocols appropriate for your network, such as TCP/IP, to package data and communicate with other computers on the network. For network communication to work, NICs must conform to the Open Systems Interconnect (OSI) model, which provides a standard for data communication on networks. This process involves a series of steps that packages data into frames so those frames can be transmitted over the network cabling. Frames contain error-checking mechanisms to make certain data is transmitted without errors. This entire process is invisible to users.

Installing Network Interface Cards

You install NICs in the same way you install other hardware components on your Windows 2000 computer. If the NIC is plug-and-play-compliant, your system will automatically detect and install the NIC, and in most cases, little or no intervention is required from you. If you want to install a NIC that does not support plug-and-play (legacy), then you should carefully examine the manufacturer's instructions. In some cases, legacy NICs contain jumper switches on the hardware itself that you must manually set. After inserting the NIC in an appropriate slot, you can restart your computer and use the Add/Remove Hardware wizard to install the legacy NIC. You will need drivers and, for some NICs, you will need an installation disk so the NIC can communicate with your system appropriately, and if you don't have these on hand, you may have a difficult time installing a legacy NIC in your Windows 2000 computer. Of course, when you are purchasing NICs, you should choose ones that are plug-and-play compliant and that are included on the HCL.

Configuring Network Interface Cards

Once the NIC is installed in your system, you can use Device Manager to further configure the NIC if necessary. Click Start ➤ Programs ➤ Administrative Tools ➤ Computer Management, or access Computer Management in your Administrative Tools folder in Control Panel. Click Device Manager, then expand the Network Adapters category to see the NIC installed on your computer (Figure 3.1).

If you right-click the NIC, you can click Properties to access the properties pages. You see General, Advanced, Driver, and Resources tabs. The General, Driver, and Resources tabs are the same tabs for each device, and there is an overview of them in Chapter 1. The Advanced tab is used to configure specific NIC properties (Figure 3.2).

What appears on the Advanced tab will vary, depending on the NIC you have installed. The general rule is not to make changes to these settings

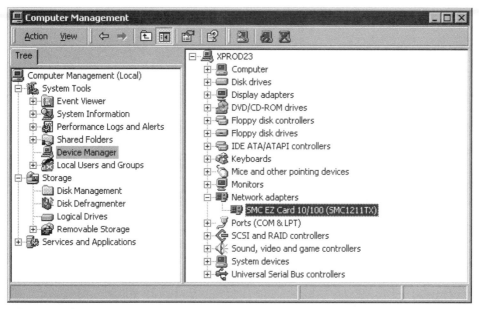

FIGURE 3.1 Use Device Manager to access your NIC's properties.

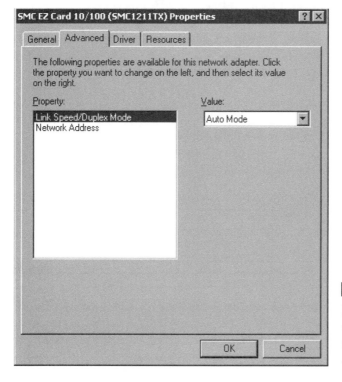

FIGURE 3.2

NIC configuration changes can be made on the Advanced tab.

unless your NIC documentation specifically tells you to do so. In most cases, Windows does a good job of configuring these settings without intervention from you.

As stated previously, the property and setting options are device-dependent, so check your documentation. Generally, for Ethernet adapters, you may see a property for the transceiver type, which is the device that connects a computer to the network as in Thicknet, Thinnet, twisted pair, etc. For token ring adapters, you may see the following:

- I/O Port Base Address: This value specifies the base memory address used by the adapter.
- Network Address: By default, the address burned into the adapter is used, but you can select a different network address by using the drop-down menu.
- Ring Speed: The ring speed is 4 or 16 megabits per second and is set by using the jumper on the adapter or through the use of the adapter's configuration utility.

Again, check your documentation before adjusting any of the settings on the Advanced tab.

Binding the Network Adapter to Protocols

Once a NIC is installed on your system, it must be bound to appropriate network protocol(s) in order for it to function on the network. This task must be performed for plug-and-play and legacy NICs. Windows 2000 automatically binds your NIC to TCP/IP. TCP/IP is the protocol of choice in Windows 2000 networks and predominates in networks today.

By default, TCP/IP is configured to receive an IP address automatically. This can be accomplished by leasing an IP address from a DHCP server, or Windows 2000 can automatically assign itself an IP address in the 169 class if a DHCP Server is unavailable.

 An IP address is a unique computer address on the network, such as 131.107.2.200. Each computer in a TCP/IP network must have a unique IP address and a default subnet mask. DHCP (Dynamic Host Configuration Protocol) is a server service that dynamically leases IP addresses to TCP/IP clients on a network. DHCP is widely used and removes the need for manual TCP/IP configuration for client computers.

You can access the TCP/IP properties sheet and make IP address changes for your NIC if desired. This is an action that should be performed only if you have instructions to do so from a system administrator. Right-click My Network Places and click Properties. The Network and Dial-up

Connections window opens. Right-click your Local Area Connection and click Properties. Select Internet Protocol (TCP/IP) in the window, then click Properties, shown in Figure 3.3.

Notice that the NIC card is listed at the top of the window with a Configure button. If you click the button, the same properties sheets appear as described in the previous section.

The Internet Protocol Properties window is configured to obtain an IP address automatically as well as DNS server information automatically. You can enter this information manually by clicking the Use the following... radio button, then entering the IP addressing or DNS addressing information. Again, consult your system administrator before making any changes on this properties sheet.

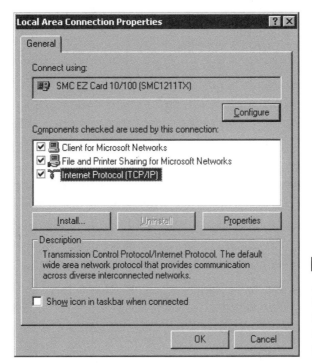

FIGURE 3.3

Access Local Area Connection properties to make changes to the components used by the LAN connection.

Installing and Configuring Universal Serial Bus Devices

The Universal Serial Bus (USB) is now supported in Windows 2000. Support for USB was first introduced in the Windows operating systems with Windows 98. USB is an external bus in your computer that supports plug-and-play. The best thing about USB is you can connect and disconnect devices without having to shut down or restart your computer. From a single USB port, you can connect up to 127 peripherals, such as scanners, CD-ROMs, speakers, telephones—you name it.

Understanding USB Controllers and Hubs

USB functions by using a "tiered" topology approach. There can be up to 127 devices attached to the bus at the same time through the tiered approach. There are three types of USB components that make up this tiered approach:

- Host—the Host, also called the root hub, is built onto your computer's motherboard or is installed as an adapter card in the computer. The host controls all of the traffic on the bus and functions as a hub.
- Hub—USB hubs provide a port to which you can attach USB devices. Hubs have the job of detecting devices attached to them. Hubs can either be self-powered, which means they have their own power source, or they can be bus-powered, which means they draw their power directly from the bus. A bus-powered hub cannot be connected to another bus-powered hub, and it cannot support more than four downstream ports.
- Device—a USB device connects to a hub, which is connected to a bus. USB devices can also function as hubs so that other USB devices can be attached to them

There can be up to five tiers, and each device can be located up to five meters from its hub. These specifications and features make certain that all hubs and devices have a power supply able to service the needs of the hub or device.

In Device Manager, you can expand Universal Serial Bus Controllers to see the USB Root Hub and USB Universal Controller (if installed on your system), as shown in Figure 3.4.

If you access the root hub's properties, you see the typical General and Driver tabs as well as a Power tab. If you click the Power tab, you can gain information about the power of the hub, such as whether the hub is self-powered or not, the amount of power available, and the devices attached to the hub (Figure 3.5).

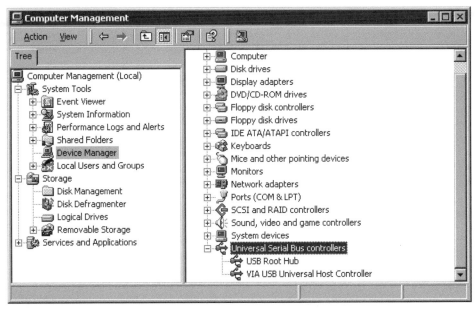

FIGURE 3.4 Universal Serial Bus hub and controller.

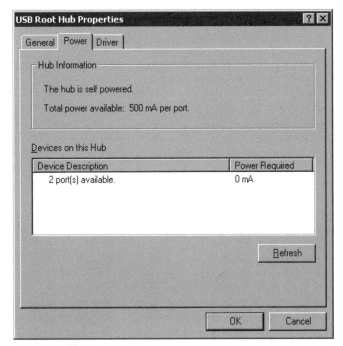

FIGURE 3.5 Use the USB hub Power tab to examine the hub's power configuration.

You can also access the Host Controller's properties sheets, where you see the typical General, Driver, and Resources tabs. If you click the Advanced tab, you are presented with information about the bandwidth used by each device. Since all USB devices are connected to one bus, bandwidth on that bus must be shared. This tab is a handy place to examine the bandwidth usage by your USB devices, as shown in Figure 3.6.

About USB Devices

USB devices are installed just as any other device in Windows 2000. Because of USB plug-and-play, each hub reports new devices to the operating system so they can be installed. Devices can be removed and reattached without having to reboot your computer. There are many, many devices that are now USB-enabled and supported in Windows 2000. Check the HCL as always to ensure compatibility. Also, see Chapter 7 for more information about troubleshooting USB devices.

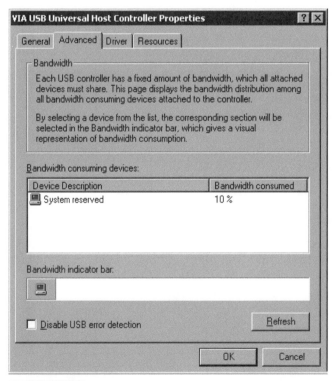

FIGURE 3.6   Use the USB host controller Advanced tab to view bandwidth usage.

■ Summary

This chapter examined the installation and configuration of Network Interface Cards and USB devices on your Windows 2000 system. Both of these components are typically easy to install and configure. As with most devices in Windows 2000, make certain you are using plug-and-play compliant devices that are supported by Windows 2000 to reduce the possibility of problems.

Q&A

Review these questions and answers to resolve problems and to check your knowledge of this chapter's content.

Q: *What configuration do I need to perform for my network adapter card?*

A: For plug-and-play network adapter card's, you most likely will not have to configure any of the settings manually. Windows 2000 can configure the NIC for operation when it is installed. In the case of legacy network adapter cards, you may need to configure certain settings, such as ring speed for token ring cards. Always consult the network adapter card's manufacturer's documentation for specific configuration information and instructions.

Q: *Are NICs automatically bound to any protocols in Windows 2000?*

A: Windows 2000 automatically binds network adapter cards to TCP/IP, which is the protocol of choice in Windows 2000.

Q: *How is TCP/IP automatically configured for the NIC?*

A: In Windows 2000, TCP/IP is configured to automatically receive an IP address. The IP can be provided by a DHCP server, or it can be self-assigned by the operating system. If the IP address is self-assigned, the operating system will give itself an IP address in the 169 range.

Q: *How many peripherals can be connected using USB?*

A: In Windows 2000, you can have up to 127 USB devices connected.

Q: *What is a bus-powered USB hub?*

A: A bus-powered USB hub gets its power from the USB bus. In other words, the bus-powered hub does not have a power supply of its own.

Setting Up Printers

It was once thought that computers would create a paperless office; information would be exchanged over the network and printed documents would become obsolete. We all know that never happened, and printing continues to be a very important function for both network computers and home computers. Windows 2000 provides several new printing features so you can install and support both local and network printers. In this chapter, I examine how to install and configure this very common hardware device.

Printing Overview

Windows 2000 supports a variety of network printing options that allow you great flexibility and more ease of administration concerning printers. In Windows 2000, you can share printer resources across the network. You can use a Windows 2000 Server as a dedicated print server—a wide variety of network client operating systems can print to Windows 2000. Windows 2000 even supports printing across the Internet. Except for the new features in Windows 2000, the printing process remains virtually the same as in Windows NT.

If you have worked with Windows at all, it is important to keep in mind the Microsoft definition of a printer. This helps reduce any confusion when learning about Microsoft printing. A "print device" is the actual physical hardware—the printer sitting on a table somewhere on the network. A "printer" is defined as the software interface. So, when you "set up a printer," you are actually configuring the software on your server that runs the print device.

Let's consider an example of what happens when a Windows client prints a document in order to review the process. Diane, a typical user, needs to print a Microsoft Word document she has been writing. When she clicks Print, Word calls the Graphics Device Interface (GDI), which calls the printer driver for the printer. Word, the GDI, and the driver render the print job in the printer language, and the print job gets passed to the client spooler. The client spooler then makes a Remote Procedure Call (RPC) to the print server. After negotiation, the document is sent over the network to the print server's spooler. The server then queries the print processor concerning the print job. The print processor recognizes the job's data type and accepts the print job. The print server service determines if modifications to the job are needed to make it print correctly, then the print job is passed to the print monitors. A two-way communication between the print monitor and the actual print device occurs and the print job is passed to the port which connects to the actual print device. The printer receives the print job, converts it to a bitmap format, then prints Diane's Word document.

New Windows 2000 Print Features

There are several new printing features available in Windows 2000. Most of these features are designed to make printing easier for clients (regardless of operating system used), and to enable more printing options for network environments. The following list explains the new printing features:

- Remote Port—Windows 2000 makes printer administration easier by including remote port administration. Printers connected to any Windows 2000 computer can be configured and administered remotely without having to walk to the physical server.
- Standard Port Monitor—Using the new standard port monitor, a Windows 2000 print server can print to network interface printers using TCP/IP. This feature replaces LPRMON for TCP/IP printers connected directly to the network with a network adapter. This new port monitor feature is fifty percent faster than LPRMON.
- Internet Printing—Windows 2000 integrates printing with the Internet. Client computers running Windows 2000 can print to Windows 2000 print servers using a URL, just as they would contact a website. You can pause, resume, and delete print jobs over the Internet as well.

- Active Directory—Printers can be stored in the Active Directory so users can easily find which printer they want to use. You can also perform Active Directory searches to find specific printers, such as color printers or laser printers.
- Additional User Settings—Users can change document defaults more easily and even change printers when they click on Print.
- Monitoring—Performance Monitor now includes a Print Queue object that allows you to set up various counters to closely monitor printing performance.
- Macintosh and Unix—New Windows 2000 features support printing to Macintosh- and Unix-attached printers.

Installing Printers

As with all hardware devices, check the HCL to make certain that any print device you plan to buy is compatible with Windows. Windows 2000 supports most major types of printers, but it is better to be safe then sorry. Follow the manufacturer's guidelines to assemble the printer and attach it to the correct port on your computer. Your print device may come with an installation CD-ROM which you can use to install the printer. If not, you can use the Add Printer wizard, found in Start ➤ Settings ➤ Printers, or by double-clicking the Printers icon in Control Panel. The following steps walk you through the wizard:

1. Click Next on the Welcome screen.
2. Select either the Local printer or Network printer radio buttons, depending on which type of printer you are installing. For these steps, it is assumed you are installing a local printer attached to your computer. Click Next.
3. Windows attempts to automatically detect your printer. If it can detect it, a window appears listing the printer name and model. If it cannot, Windows gives you a message telling you the printer was not found and that you can click Next to manually install it. Click Next.
4. Select the port you want to use (Figure 4.1). In most cases, your printer will be connected to LPT1. You can use this window to configure additional printer ports as well. This feature allows you to select the port you want to use from the list, or you can use the Create a new port radio button. If you want to create a new port, click the Create a new port radio button, then select either TCP/IP port or local port.
5. If you decide to create a TCP/IP port, another wizard begins—the Add Standard TCP/IP Printer Port wizard. Click Next to continue.
6. In the Add Port window (Figure 4.2), enter the printer name or IP address and the port name, then click Next.

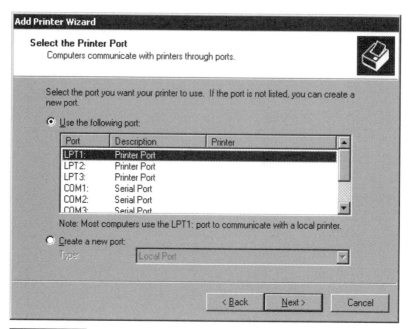

FIGURE 4.1 Select the local port, you can create a new local or TCP/IP port.

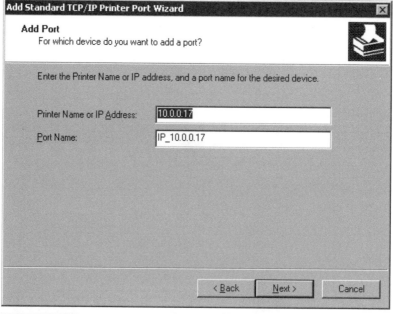

FIGURE 4.2 Enter the name of the print device.

7. The TCP/IP address is checked and installed if correct. Click Finish. This returns you to the Add Printer wizard.

8. If Windows did not detect your printer, you are prompted to select the manufacturer and model of the printer (Figure 4.3). If you have an installation disk or CD-ROM, you can click the Have Disk button and install the printer that way. Make your selections and click Next.

9. Enter a name for the printer, then click Next.

10. Choose the desired radio button to either share the printer or not. Click Next.

11. If you chose to share the printer, you can enter a description if desired. Click Next.

12. Click Yes or No to print a test page. Click Next.

13. Click Finish. The printer now appears in the printer folder.

Configuring the Printer

Once you install printers on your server, an icon for each printer appears in the Printers folder. You can access the properties pages for the printers by right-clicking on the printer icon and clicking Properties. The following sections explain what you can configure on each page.

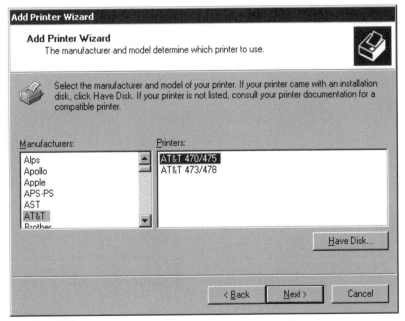

FIGURE 4.3 Use this window to manually install your printer.

GENERAL

On the General properties page, shown in Figure 4.4, you can enter location information and comments if desired. The page lists the features of the printer. You can use the Print Test Page button to print a test page on the printer, and you can also click the Printing Preferences button to adjust the page layout (either portrait or landscape) and the color (either color or grayscale).

If you click the Printing Preferences button, then click the Advanced tab, you are provided with a tree structure of color advanced options, shown in Figure 4.5. You can click on a feature and a drop-down menu will appear so you can adjust the feature as desired.

SHARING

The Sharing tab, as shown in Figure 4.6, allows you to either share the printer or not by clicking the appropriate radio button. If you share the printer, you can click the List in the Directory check box to add the printer to the Active Directory. In Active Directory environments, printers can be

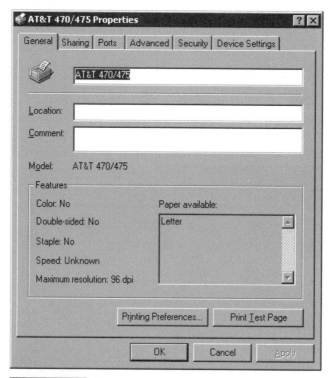

FIGURE 4.4 General properties

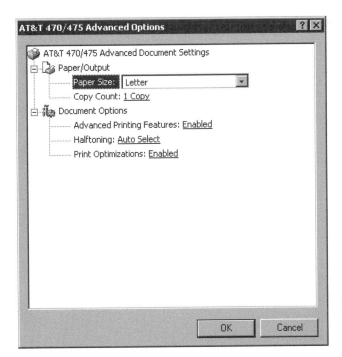

FIGURE 4.5

Color Advanced
options

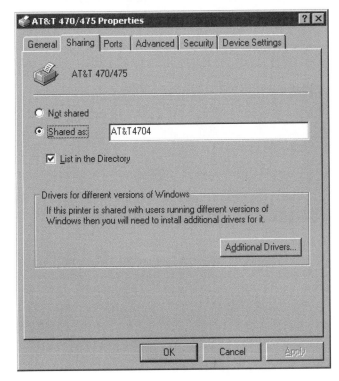

FIGURE 4.6

Sharing properties

listed in the directory so users can find shared printers on the network and connect to them. Windows 2000 computers can automatically publish their printers in the Active Directory without intervention from an administrator. In most cases, if you are sharing a printer on a Windows 2000 computer in an Active Directory environment, you should choose this option; however, you should first check the rules for printer sharing as established by your network administrators.

If you click the Additional Drivers button, you can install additional drivers for the printer so that users on other operating systems can download the drivers automatically and connect to the printer. For example, if you have Windows 95 or 98 computers on your network, you can choose to also install the drivers for those operating systems so those computers can download the drivers and use the printer, shown in Figure 4.7. Simply select the system you want to be able to download the drivers and click OK. You need your Windows 2000 CD-ROM to complete this action.

PORTS

On the Ports tab, shown in Figure 4.8, you can select which ports the server should use to print to the device. You determined this setting during installation, but you can use this tab to make changes to the port as needed. Documents print to the first free port that is checked. You can select additional ports for use, add a new port, delete a port, or click the Configure Port button. You also have the option to enable bi-directional printing, for printers that support it, and you can enable printer pooling. Printer pooling allows you to com-

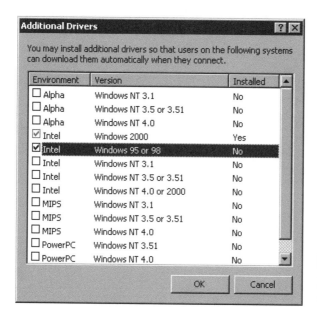

FIGURE 4.7

Install additional drivers as needed.

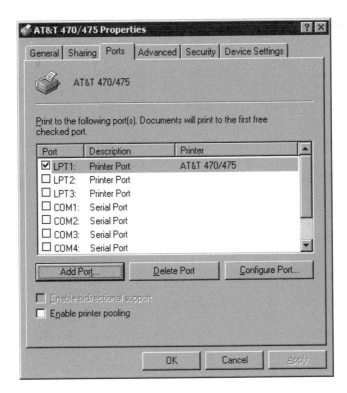

FIGURE 4.8

Ports properties

bine two or more identical printers together so they appear as one printer to users. This feature is a useful way to manage printing with several print devices while reducing possible user confusion about which printer to use.

ADVANCED

The Advanced Properties, as shown in Figure 4.9, allow you to configure several actions that determine how the printer behaves. First, you can allow the printer to be always available or available only during certain hours of the day, which you set by using the scroll boxes. You can also adjust the priority. The priority range is 1 to 99 with one being the lowest and 99 being the highest. Higher priority documents print before lower priority documents. With multiple printers connected to the same port, a printer that has a priority of 2 will always print before the printer with a priority of 1. This feature allows you to send critical documents to a certain printer with a higher priority and less critical documents to the lower-priority printer.

You can use the New Driver button to configure a new driver for the printer. This action launches a wizard that helps you select the correct driver for your print device. In this window, you can adjust how documents are spooled. You can choose to spool the documents so the program finish-

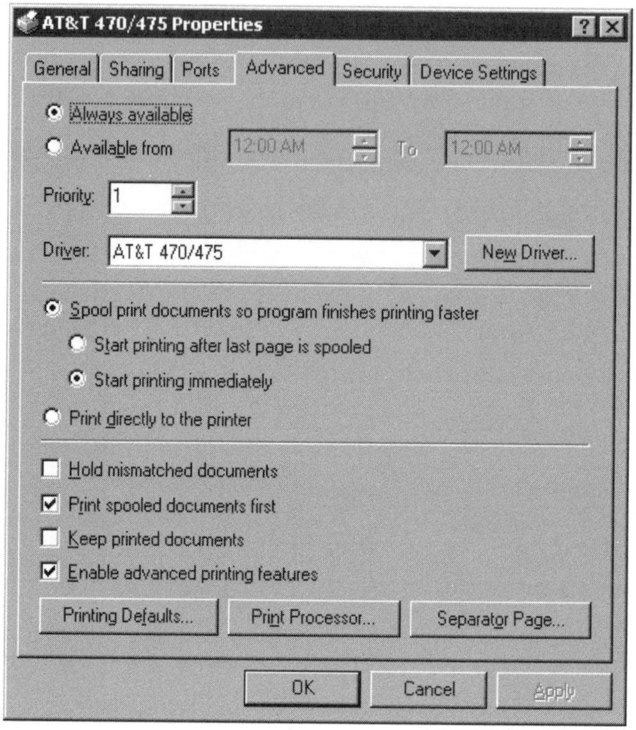

FIGURE 4.9

Advanced
properties

es printing faster, then you can choose to either start printing after the last page is spooled or start printing immediately. You can choose to print directly to the printer, but this action may slow performance.

The check boxes at the bottom of the screen allow you to select other options, such as hold mismatched documents, print spooled documents first, keep printed documents, or enable advanced printing features.

The Printing Defaults button allows you to adjust the print layout, as you saw on the General properties sheet. The Print Processor button allows you to select from a list a different print processor, if one is available. Finally, the Separator Page button allows you to set a separator page to be printed between each document.

SECURITY

The Security properties page (Figure 4.10) is the same page you have seen in other Windows 2000 components. The permissions are print, manage printers, and manage documents. You can use the Add button to select users and groups from the Active Directory that you want to manage the printer. By default, the Everyone group has print permission. This can also be changed if you only want specific users or groups to access the printer.

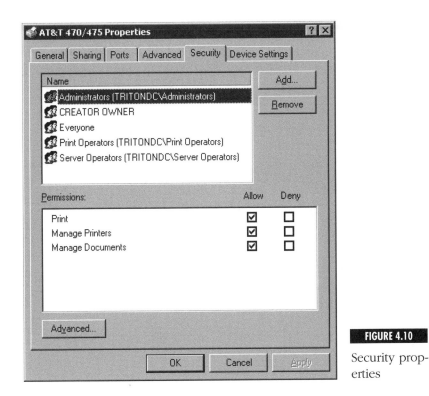

FIGURE 4.10

Security properties

Depending on the print device you installed, additional tabs may be available as well. For example, some print devices provide a Color Management tab where you can make changes or adjustments to color printers. These tabs are device-specific, so check your documentation for configuration instructions for these tabs.

Setting Up Client Computers to Access Shared Printers

In order to print to network printers, client computers must be set up to connect to the desired printer, and the correct printer drivers must be installed. For Windows 2000, Windows NT, Windows 95 and 98, you only need to make a connection to the shared printer. Windows 2000 Server will automatically download the appropriate driver for the printer to the client, assuming that the appropriate print drivers are on the server. Client computers running older Microsoft operating systems must manually install the print drivers on the computer. For non-Windows clients, such as NetWare,

UNIX, and Macintosh, various tasks must be performed in order for the clients to connect, as explained in the following list:

■ NetWare—FPNW (File and Print Services for NetWare) services must be installed on the server. FPNW is an optional component not included with Windows 2000 Server.

■ UNIX—UNIX requires TCP/IP printing (also called Line Printer Daemon). This service is included in Windows 2000 but must be installed.

■ Macintosh—Service for Macintosh must be installed for Macintosh clients to connect to network printers.

Clients can connect to network printers in a variety of ways. First, clients can use the Add Printer wizard and select the network printer they want to install. Client Computers running Windows 2000 can use the Active Directory to find the desired printer or UNC naming convention, or they can simply browse the network. Windows 2000 clients can use a web browser by typing `http://server_name/printers`. Clients running Windows NT 4.0, Windows 95, or Windows 98 can connect to a printer using the UNC naming convention or the Add Printer wizard. Clients running older Microsoft operating systems can use the Print Manager feature or the Net Use command line feature to connect.

Printing to Macintosh and UNIX Servers

In Windows 2000, you can now print to Macintosh and UNIX servers. To use this feature, you need to install the service(s) on a Windows 2000 Server by using Add/Remove Programs in Control Panel, clicking Add/Remove Windows Components, double-clicking Other Network File and Print Services, then selecting either Print Services for Macintosh or Print Services for UNIX, or both.

Once the Print Services for Macintosh is installed, you can use the Add New Printer wizard in the Printers folder. Select Add a New Local Printer, click Next, then click the Create New Port button and select AppleTalk Printing Devices. The wizard will search for AppleTalk printing devices on the network and allow you to install the printer. Then Windows clients can print to the Macintosh server.

The same process applies to UNIX. Instead of selecting the AppleTalk Printing Device for the new point, configure a TCP/IP port for the connection to the UNIX server that the printer is attached to.

Managing Print Documents

As documents are printed to your printer, there arise situations where you need to manage those documents that are waiting to be printed, which are in the print queue. To perform this action, double-click on your printer in the Printers folder. This opens the print queue where you can see a list of documents waiting to be printed, shown in Figure 4.11.

You can use the Printer menu to pause printing or cancel all documents that are waiting to be printed. This action is sometimes necessary if you are having problems with the printer. You can also use the Document menu to pause, resume, or restart a print job. Simply select the desired document in the print queue and use the Document menu to perform the desired action.

For Windows 2000 Servers acting as print servers, you can use Group Policy in Windows 2000 to further define how users access and use printers, and you can also use Performance Monitor to examine the performance of printers. While these topics are outside the scope of this book, be certain to check the Microsoft documentation when setting up a print server so you are aware of all of the features available to you.

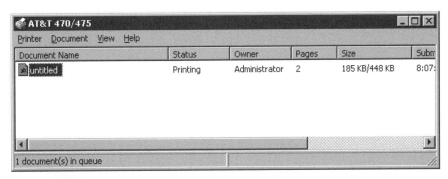

FIGURE 4.11 Print queue

■ Summary

Windows 2000 provides a full range of printing features that make network printing easier to manage and easier for clients to use. Client computers using Windows 2000 have the additional options of finding the printers they want to use in the Active Directory or by using a web browser. Windows 2000 Server also supports printing over the Internet. A wide variety of drivers and support for various printer vendors makes the installation, configuration, and management of network printers easier and more flexible than in previous versions of Windows.

Q&A

Q: *What is the advantage of remote ports in Windows 2000?*

A: Remote port is a feature of Windows 2000 printing that allows you to remotely manage printer devices connected to Windows 2000 computers without having to physically visit the print device.

Q: *What is the standard port monitor in Windows 2000?*

A: The standard port monitor in Windows 2000 replaces LPRMON for TCP/IP printers connected directly to the network with a network adapter card. Standard port monitor allows computers to print to the print device using TCP/IP, and is fifty percent faster than LPRMON.

Q: *Which computers can store print device information in the Active Directory?*

A: Any computer can have its print device published in the Active Directory. Windows 2000 computers can automatically publish their print devices to the Active Directory while other operating systems, such as Windows 95 and 98 and Windows NT must have their print devices manually added to the Active Directory by an administrator.

Q: *On a Windows 2000 computer, how can I have my print device automatically published to the Active Directory?*

A: When you share the printer, click the List in the Directory check box provided. This action causes the Windows 2000 computer to send the printer information to a domain controller for publication in the Active Directory.

Q: *On a Windows 2000 computer, I want to share a print device, but I want the drivers for Windows 95 computers to be available to those clients. How can I configure this?*

A: On the Sharing tab of the printer's properties sheets, click the Additional Drivers button, then select the Windows 95 or 98 check box. You will need your installation CD-ROM to complete this action. When the printer is published to the Active Directory, the additional drivers will be made available so that the Windows 95 computers can automatically download the drivers and use the printer.

Q: *I want to configure my network printer on a Windows 2000 computer so that a separator page is printed between documents. Where can I configure this?*

A: Access the printer's properties and click the Advanced tab. Click the Separator Page button and select the separator page you want to use.

Q: *I want NetWare clients to be able to access a printer on a Windows 2000 Server. What do I need to do to allow this to occur?*

A: You need to install FPNW services on the server. FPNW is an optional component available from microsoft.com.

Q: *What is a printer pool?*

A: A printer pool groups two or more identical printers together so they appear as one printer to network users. This feature makes management easier and increases printer availability.

Video and Sound Cards

In this chapter, you learn about two major system components, video cards and sound cards. As you may be aware, there are many video and sound cards available for purchase from different manufacturers. Depending on your needs and desires, you may choose to change the video and sound cards that initially came with your computer for more exciting models. For those of you who enjoy games, the quality of your video and sound cards certainly affect your game playing. Also, with the intensive graphics now available on the Internet, most people demand a high-quality graphics card. This chapter examines video and sound cards and shows you how to configure them on your system.

Installing Video Cards

Video cards provide the display you see on your monitor. Depending on the type of video card, you may have basic graphics with minimal colors. On the other hand, you may use a video card that supports a virtually unlimited number of colors as well as 3D. There are a lot of video cards available from different manufacturers, and choosing the one that is right for you can take a little homework. However, you should first begin by checking the Windows 2000 HCL to make certain you select a video card that is compatible with

Windows 2000. Windows 2000 supports a lot of them, but be sure to check the HCL before buying one.

Once you purchase a video card, your next task is to install it on your system. Turn off the power to your computer and open the case, then follow the manufacturers guidelines for installing the video card into an appropriate Peripheral Component Interconnect (PCI) or Accelerated Graphics Port (AGP). Once the card is securely in place, replace your computer's cover and attach your monitor to the new video card. Boot your Windows 2000 computer, and Windows will automatically detect the new card.

Your operating system always needs a VGA device. The computer's basic input/output system (BIOS) detects the VGA device based on slot order, unless the BIOS offers an option for choosing which device is treated as the VGA device. So, if you are using multiple video cards, do be aware that the first VGA device will be used when booting the system.

Once your video card is installed, you can manage it just as you would any other device—by using Device Manager and accessing its properties sheets, shown in Figure 5.1. You can access the troubleshooter, use the Driver tab to update the driver, and see what resources are in use by accessing the Resources tab.

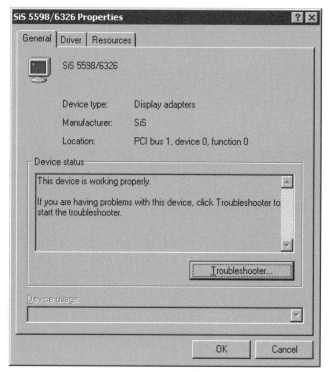

FIGURE 5.1

Video card properties sheets

Configuring Display Settings

Once your video card is installed, you can configure how your system interacts with it by double clicking Display in Control Panel, or by right-clicking on the desktop and clicking Properties. You can use the properties sheets to configure the appearance of your desktop, icons, background, and screen saver. You can also adjust the settings of the adapter using the Settings tab.

On the Settings tab, shown in Figure 5.2, you can adjust the colors used by the system and also the screen area. You can also launch the Troubleshooter from this location by clicking the button. Finally, the Advanced button allows you to configure a number of additional settings. When you click the Advanced button, a properties sheet with five tabs appears. The following sections describe what you can configure on each tab.

General

On the General tab, shown in Figure 5.3, you can select the display font you want to use. By default, small fonts are selected, but you can choose to use large fonts or custom fonts if desired. In the Compatibility section of the screen, you have three options concerning the way Windows handles dis-

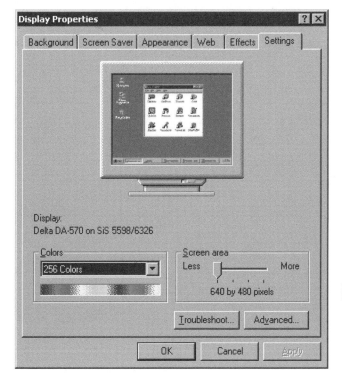

FIGURE 5.2

Use the Settings tab to configure the adapter settings.

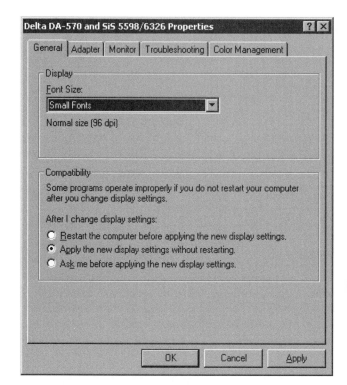

FIGURE 5.3

Use the General tab to make font changes and display change settings.

play changes. Windows does not need to restart your computer when you make changes to your settings. For example, if you change the number of colors in use, Windows can make the adjustment without having to restart. However, some applications that are open cannot handle this change without restarting. So, this tab gives you the options to restart the computer when changes are made, not to restart the computer, or to prompt you so you can make the decision at that time.

Adapter

The Adapter tab, shown in Figure 5.4, tells you what adapter is installed on the system. You can click the Properties button to open the adapter's properties sheets, which is the same as seen using Device Manager. If you click the List All Modes button, shown in Figure 5.5, all of the possible modes that are supported by the video card are selected. You can select the desired mode from this location, or it can be configured on the Settings tab as well.

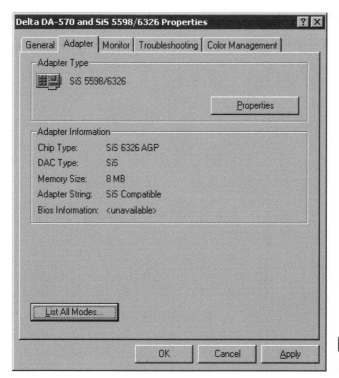

FIGURE 5.4

Adapter tab

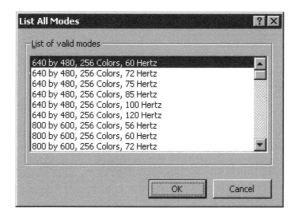

FIGURE 5.5

List All Modes option

Monitor

On the Monitor tab, shown in Figure 5.6, you can access the properties sheets for your monitor, which are also available in Device Manager. You can also adjust the refresh fre-

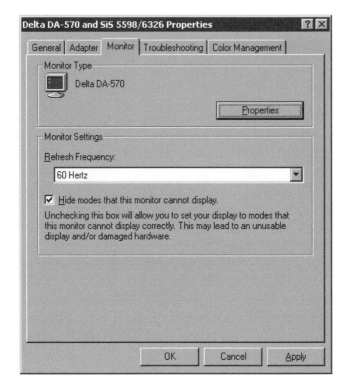

FIGURE 5.6

Use the Monitor tab to adjust the refresh frequency.

quency. The refresh frequency is the speed at which your monitor is refreshed. In some cases, you can use the refresh frequency to solve problems you may be experiencing with your adapter and monitor; however, you may experience problems with a refresh frequency that is set too high. See the Solving Problems with a Video Card section to learn more about the refresh frequency. Also, you can choose to hide modes that are not supported by your adapter and monitor. By default, this option is selected.

Troubleshooting

On the Troubleshooting tab, shown in Figure 5.7, you can make changes to the hardware acceleration. This feature allows you to manually control the level of acceleration and the level of performance of your video card. You should consult the Display Troubleshooter before making any changes on this tab, and you should not make any changes if you are not having problems with your video card.

Color Management

The Color Management tab, shown in Figure 5.8, allows you to change the color profile currently used by your monitor. If you click the Add button,

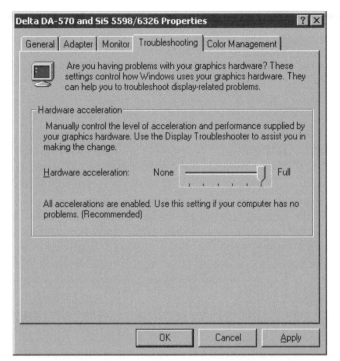

FIGURE 5.7

Use this tab to adjust the hardware acceleration if necessary.

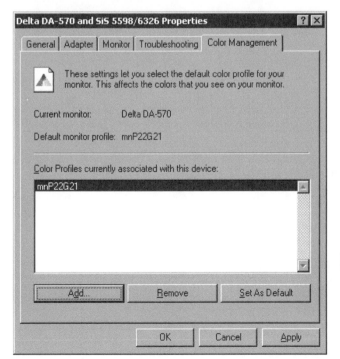

FIGURE 5.8

Use the Color Management tab to change your monitor's color profile.

you can select a color profile that is best suited for your display adapter. Be advised that not all color profiles work with all monitors, so you may have to experiment to find the color profile that works best with your monitor.

Solving Problems with a Video Card

Once you install your video card, it is possible that you will encounter problems. This can especially happen if your video is not listed on the Windows 2000 HCL. If this happens, you are likely to experience one of two problems. First, you can boot your computer, but your screen flickers or contains a garbled display that is essentially unreadable. If you can't see anything, you will need to restart your computer in safe mode. Pressing the F8 key at startup can do this. Safe Mode will give you a menu of safe mode options. Simply select Safe Mode, then click the ENTER key. This boots your system using the minimal amount of drivers, including a minimal VGA driver, shown in Figure 5.9. You can try to solve the problem once you are in safe mode.

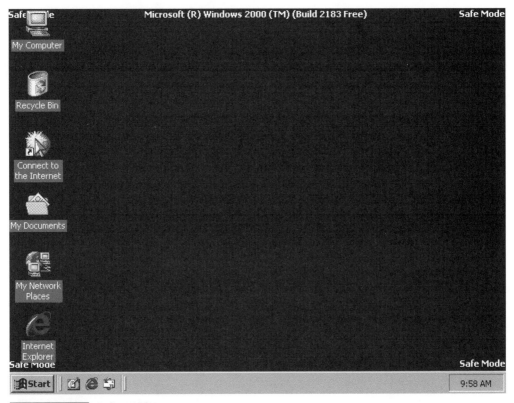

FIGURE 5.9   Safe mode

Once you are booted into safe mode, open Control Panel and double-click Display, then click the Settings tab. To attempt to solve the problem, try these different settings:

- On the Colors drop-down menu, select a color option that is less than currently used. For example, try 16 colors.
- Reduce the size of the desktop by using the slider bar under Screen Area.
- Click the Advanced button, then click the Monitor tab. Lower the refresh frequency by clicking the drop-down menu.

Some older monitors cannot handle a high refresh frequency. If you are using an older monitor and you set the refresh frequency too high, your monitor may be permanently damaged.

After making these changes, restart your computer in normal boot mode and see if the problem has been resolved. If the problem is still not resolved, try reinstalling the display adapter driver and make certain you have the most current driver available.

The second problem you could experience is simply no video at all, or a Stop message appears telling you the driver is missing or corrupt.

A Stop message halts the operating system. In the case of a problem video driver, the Stop message will read 0x000000B4 VIDEO_DRIVER_INIT_FAILURE.

When this Stop message occurs, you need to reboot your computer in safe mode, then uninstall and reinstall your video driver. If your video card is supported in Windows 2000, this action normally solves the problem.

Using Multiple Video Cards and Monitors

Windows 2000 supports the use of multiple monitors and multiple display adapters. Multiple monitor support was first introduced in Windows 98 and is designed to allow you to connect up to ten monitors to your Windows 2000 computer. This feature allows you to open different programs on different monitors and work with them all at the same time. You can move items between monitors and even stretch them across several monitors. When you set up this configuration, one monitor serves as the primary display and will contain the logon dialog box when you boot your system. Most programs will open in the primary monitor, but you can move them to different monitors as desired.

You install additional monitors by installing additional video cards and connecting monitors to them. You perform this task the same way you install a single video card, so see the first section of this chapter for specific information. Once the additional monitors are installed, access the Settings tab of the Display properties in Control Panel, select the monitor icon you want to use, then click the Extend my Windows Desktop onto this monitor check box, then click Apply and OK. You can then drag items from one monitor to the other as desired. You can also change the primary monitor by using the Settings tab. Click the desired monitor, then click the Use This Device as the Primary Monitor check box so that it becomes the primary monitor.

Installing Sound Cards

As with video cards, there are many different sound cards available from many different manufacturers. You have many options, ranging from basic sound cards to those that support stereo sound and even surround sound. As with video cards, check the HCL to ensure the sound card you want to install is compatible with Windows 2000.

Install the sound card in an available port inside your computer and check the manufacturers guide for specific instructions. Once the sound card is placed in a proper port, reboot your computer so that Windows can detect it. As with all other devices, you can use Device Manager to check the sound card and update the driver as necessary.

Configuring Sound and Multimedia

One you have a sound card installed on your system, you can access the sounds and multimedia properties by double-clicking the icon in Control Panel. There are three tabs, which are explained in the following sections.

Sounds

The Sounds tab, shown in Figure 5.10, allows you test the Windows sounds you would like to use for particular events that occur on your system. Once you select the desired sounds, you can save your settings as a sound scheme. You can also use this tab to adjust the overall sound volume.

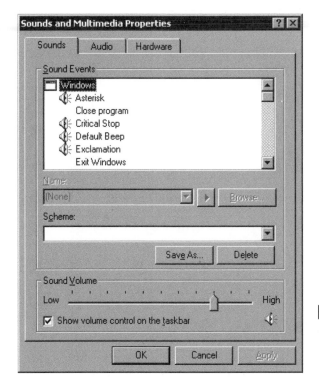

FIGURE 5.10

The Sounds tab is used to adjust system sounds and the volume.

Audio

The Audio tab, shown in Figure 5.11, presents you with three categories, Sound Playback, Sound Recording, and MIDI Music Playback. You can use the drop-down menus to select the desired devices that should be used for each category. The Volume tab for each allows you to individually control the volume, and the Advanced button, shown in Figure 5.12, allows you to change the hardware acceleration settings and conversion quality on Sound Playback and Sound Recording. Typically, there are not settings that you need to adjust unless you are having problems with the device. Note that when you set the preferred device for each category, Windows can still use other available devices unless you click the Use Only Preferred Devices check box at the bottom of the Audio tab. This setting forces Windows to use the devices you have selected.

Hardware

The Hardware tab, shown in Figure 5.13, lists all of your hardware that is used for various sounds. You can select the desired hardware device and click the Properties button to access the properties sheets, which are also available in Device Manager. The Troubleshooter button can also be used to

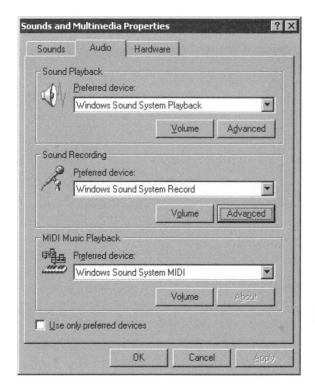

FIGURE 5.11

The Audio tab is used to select devices for different audio categories.

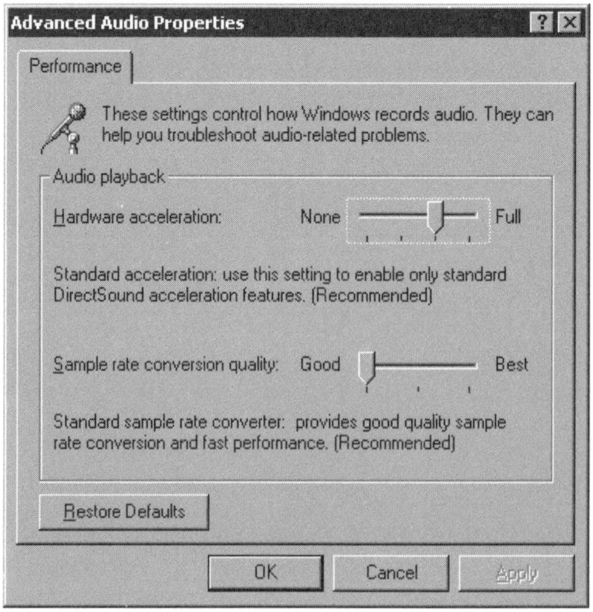

FIGURE 5.12

The Advanced button provides the option to change acceleration settings.

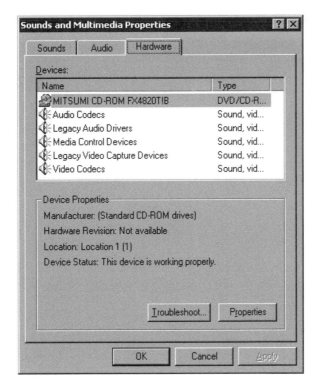

FIGURE 5.13

The Hardware tab provides you access to device properties or the troubleshooter.

open the Windows 2000 help files so you can resolve problems with any sound device. See Chapter 8 to learn more about troubleshooting sound problems.

■ Summary

Windows 2000 provides excellent support for the many video and sound cards available today. With high quality sound and video, you can experience rich multimedia and play your favorite games—as well as experience the graphics of the Internet. Windows 2000 also supports multiple monitors, where you can install additional video cards and monitors on your system. These qualities make Windows 2000 an effective multimedia system to meet whatever multimedia needs you may have.

Q&A

Q: *Can I use any sound or video card with Windows 2000 as long as I have the drivers?*

A: Most sound and video cards work well with Windows 2000. You should, however, check the HCL to ensure compatibility. This does not mean that a sound or video card not found on the HCL will not work under Windows 2000, it simply means that the sound or video card has not been tested. In order to avoid potential problems, purchase sound or video cards found on the HCL.

Q: *Do I need to select a color profile for my monitor?*

A: A color profile is selected for your monitor by default. You can change it on the Color Management tab if desired, and depending on your monitor, you may see better quality by selecting a more suitable profile.

Q: *I want Windows to reboot the system whenever I make a display setting change. Where can I configure this?*

A: You can have Windows automatically reboot your system when you make a display settings change by selecting the appropriate check box on the General tab under Advanced Settings.

Q: *How many monitors can I use with Windows 2000?*

A: Windows 2000 supports the use of up to ten multiple monitors.

Other Peripherals

It never ceases to amaze me how quickly things in the computer world change. It was only a few years ago that the idea of a "desktop scanner" was introduced, and now the device, as well as digital cameras and other devices, are quite commonly used. Fortunately, Windows 2000 keeps pace with these constant developments and provides rich support for a great number of additional peripherals. Many of these are now available as USB devices, which you can learn more about in Chapter 3. In this chapter, I examine the installation and configuration of a number of additional peripheral devices you may choose to use.

FAX

Your Windows 2000 computer can fax a text document or graphics file by using a fax modem. Fax also supports scanned graphics images and will automatically convert those images to a .tif file. You can also use email to send mail and fax messages at the same time. To fax a document or picture, you need a fax device, such as a fax modem. In many cases, newer modems automatically support fax, so you probably already have the capability in your system through your modem. You cannot, however, share a fax printer with other users on your network.

Windows 2000 automatically detects fax-capable devices, such as a modem, then installs the fax service and fax printer. You can send and receive faxes using more than one fax device, but all faxes are filtered through one fax printer using the printer port. You can create multiple copies of the fax printer so that you can assign different preferences to each.

To configure your fax operations, double-click Fax in Control Panel. There are four tabs, which are explained in the following sections.

User Information

The User Information tab, shown in Figure 6.1, allows you to enter information about yourself which can be used to identify you when sending faxes. You can enter your name, address, email address, and office. You can also enter a billing code. This feature is useful for environments that track fax usage.

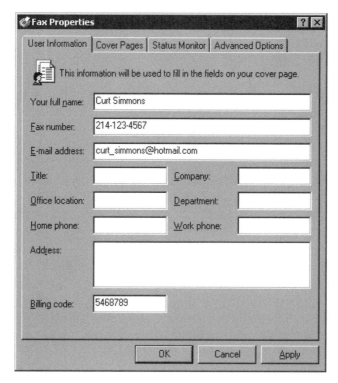

FIGURE 6.1

User Information tab

Cover Pages

The Cover Pages tab, shown in Figure 6.2, allows you to configure and use different fax cover pages. If you click the New button, a text editor window opens where you can create a desired fax cover page. If you click Add, you can select a fax cover page that already exists.

Status Monitor

The Status Monitor tab, shown in Figure 6.3, allows you to configure how the fax status monitor behaves. It has a series of check boxes which allow you to display the status monitor, have the status monitor always on top, display an icon on the taskbar, play a sound, and enable manual answer for the first device. The last option prevents the fax device from automatically answering a fax call.

Advanced Options

The Advanced Options tab, shown in Figure 6.4, provides you with three buttons so you can access the Fax Management console, fax help, or add a fax printer. The Fax Management console, shown in Figure 6.5, is an MMC snap-in where you can configure fax devices and also configure fax logging.

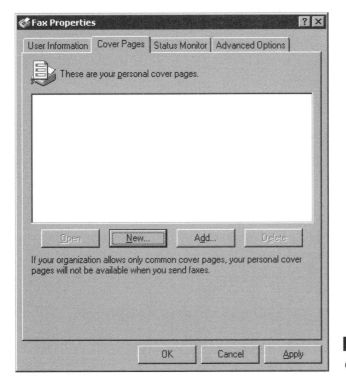

FIGURE 6.2

Cover Pages tab

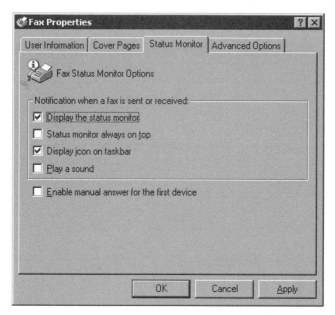

FIGURE 6.3

Status Monitor tab

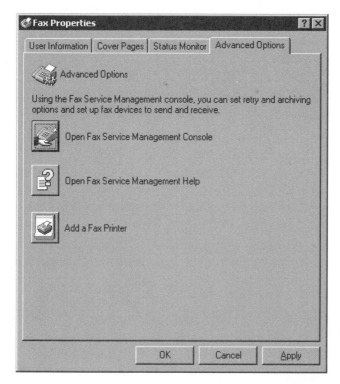

FIGURE 6.4

Advanced
Options tab

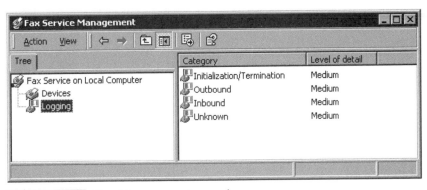

FIGURE 6.5 Fax Management console

Scanners and Cameras

As mentioned in the introduction of this chapter, scanners and cameras have become very popular in the past few years, and Windows 2000 supports them as well. With scanners, you can scan documents, photographs—virtually anything—and digital cameras allow you to take pictures, then directly load the digital image into your computer. Like all hardware devices, you simply attach the device to the correct port on your computer and Windows 2000 will detect it. You also find a Scanners and Cameras icon in Control Panel.

If you double-click Scanners and Cameras in Control Panel, a Devices tab appears, shown in Figure 6.6, which lists any scanners or cameras installed on your computer.

You can use the Add or Remove buttons to add a new device or remove one from the list. If you click Add, the Scanner and Camera Installation wizard appears, which searches for your scanner or camera or allows you to choose it from a list. You can also select the desired device and click the Properties button. The properties sheets, which vary according to device, allow you to make basic configuration changes, such as port settings, color management, and the like. Figure 6.7 shows you an example of a properties sheet for a digital camera.

If you click the Troubleshooter button, you are taken to the Windows 2000 Troubleshooter in the help files. You can learn more about the troubleshooter and about solving problems with scanners and cameras in Chapter 7.

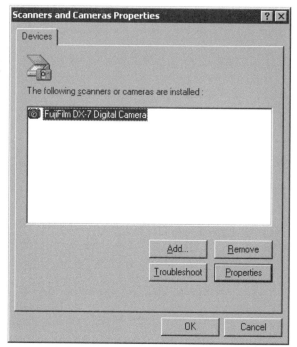

FIGURE 6.6

Scanners and Cameras properties

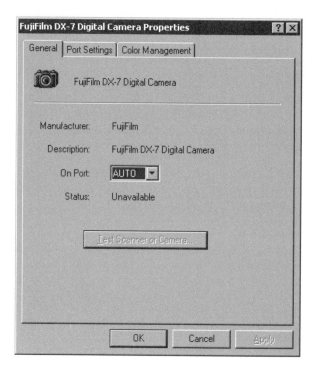

FIGURE 6.7

Camera properties

Game Controllers

Windows 2000 supports the use of game controllers, attached to your system. You can configure the game controllers as desired by using the Game Controllers properties sheets, available in Control Panel. When you open the Game Controllers properties sheets, you see the same kind of Window as with Scanners and Cameras. You can Add, Remove, Troubleshoot, or access the properties for any game controller in the list. The Game Controllers properties page also has an Advanced tab, shown in Figure 6.8. On the Advanced tab, you can make changes to the controller ID and port. Consult the manufacturer's documentation concerning controller ID assignment and port numbers.

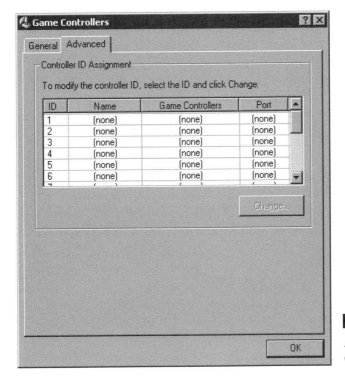

FIGURE 6.8

Advanced Game
Controllers tab

Mouse and Keyboard

Your mouse and keyboard require virtually no configuration from you, unless there are changes you would simply like to make. Your keyboard and mouse attach directly to ports on your computer and are detected by Windows 2000 upon installation. You have both a keyboard and mouse icon in Control Panel so you can make changes to the way they perform. By double-clicking Keyboard in Control Panel, you can adjust the keyboard's speed responsiveness, adjust language settings for your keyboard, and access the keyboard's properties sheets, such as those seen with other devices. The Mouse properties sheets, also available in Control Panel, allow you to change the mouse from right-handed to left-handed, use single or double-click to open items, adjust the speed, select a desired pointer, and access the mouse's properties sheets, which are the same as seen for other devices. Both your keyboard and mouse configuration options are very easy, and no further explanation is necessary here.

Power Options

You can also access the Power Options icon in Control Panel, which opens the properties sheets. With Power Options, you can select a power scheme. The power scheme tells your system how to operate during periods of inactivity. You can determine an amount of time that should pass before the system turns off your monitor and hard disks, or you can tell your system to never power down these components.

Power Options also provides "hibernate" support, which is configurable on the Hibernate tab, shown in Figure 6.9. When you click your Enable Hibernate Support, your computer goes into a hibernation state after a period of inactivity. When your computer hibernates, data that is currently in memory is stored on the hard disk. When the computer is brought out of hibernation, the data is placed again into memory and your computer returns to its previous state.

Finally, Power Options also provides a UPS tab. A UPS is an uninterruptible power supply. This device, which attaches to your computer, contains a battery that allows your system to continue running should there be a power failure. The UPS is designed to provide enough power to your system so that you can save your data and properly power down the system. In many networking environments, servers are provided a UPS so they can be properly powered down in case of a power failure. The UPS tab contains information about the UPS device and allows you to make any configuration changes that are available for the device.

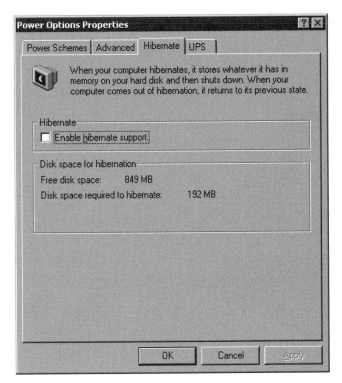

FIGURE 6.9

Hibernate tab

■ Summary

Windows 2000 supports a number of additional peripherals that enable you to use your Windows 2000 computer in a way best suited for you. You can use scanners and cameras, configure your computer as a fax machine, and even use game controllers. Windows 2000 also allows you to configure your keyboard and mouse settings as you desire, and if you want to use a UPS, these devices are supported. With these features of Windows 2000, you can configure your computer's peripherals in a desired manner, no matter if the computer is a server or a home PC.

Q&A

Q: *Which scanner models does Windows 2000 support?*

A: Windows 2000 supports an extensive selection of scanner and digital cameras, including SCSI devices. Before buying a scanner or camera, however, check the HCL and make certain the product you intend to buy is supported for use with Windows 2000. Also, many manufacturers' devices tell you on the box whether or not the device is supported by Windows 2000.

Q: *Can I attach an actual fax machine to my computer?*

A: Some fax machines on the market today support being linked to a computer. This allows the computer to send data directly to the actual fax machine, as well as receive faxes electronically as well. Consult your fax machine's documentation to see if this feature is supported.

Q: *I would like my mouse to automatically appear at the default location when I open a window, such as the OK button. Can this be configured?*

A: Yes. Double-click Mouse in Control Panel, click the Motion tab, then click the Snap to Default check box.

Q: *I have a disability that makes my keyboard difficult to use. Can I reconfigure it so it is easier for me?*

A: Yes. Although not discussed in this book, you can open Accessibility Options in Control Panel and configure several options, such as the use of Sticky Keys.

Troubleshooting Hardware Devices

The world of computing is far from perfect, and hardware devices, like any component of your computer, may give you some problems. Fortunately, with the Windows 2000 design, most hardware problems are much, much easier to fix than in the past. If you use plug-and-play devices and check the HCL for compatibility, the likelihood of problems is small, and when you do have problems, you can usually fix them in a short amount of time. This chapter shows you how to use the troubleshooting tools, then points out some common problems with the hardware previously discussed in this section of the book and their solutions.

Windows 2000 Troubleshooting Tools

You have three major tools to help you troubleshoot problems with hardware devices. First, you can use the Add/Remove Hardware wizard, as explained in Chapter 1. When you open the wizard, choose the Add/Troubleshoot a Device option and select the device that is causing you problems. The wizard will take a look at the device, and hopefully report to you what is wrong. You can then take the necessary steps to resolve the problem.

Second, you can use the General tab of the hardware device that is causing you problems. Open Device Manager, access the device's properties sheets, then check the General tab. The window on this tab may tell you what is wrong, and you can also click the Troubleshooter button. When you click the Troubleshooter button, the Windows 2000 help files, which walk you through a series of questions to attempt to help you find the solution to the problem, are opened, as shown in Figure 7.1.

If the troubleshooter can identify what is wrong, it gives you instructions for solving the problem.

Finally, you can use System Information to help you find problems. You can access System Information by clicking Start → Programs → Accessories → System Tools → System Information, or by typing `msinfo32` at the Run line. System Information is a tool first introduced with Windows 98 that provides you detailed information about your system hardware and processes. When System Information opens, click Hardware Resources, shown in Figure 7.2.

In the right pane, you see categories for Conflicts/Sharing, DMA, Forced Hardware, I/O, IRQs, and Memory. You can click each category to

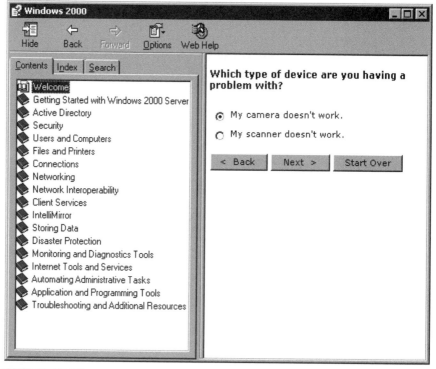

FIGURE 7.1 Use the Troubleshooter tool to resolve problems with your device.

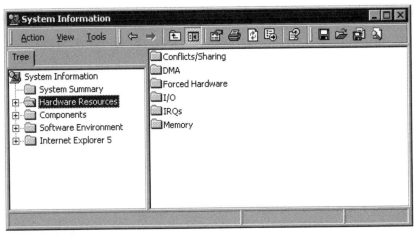

FIGURE 7.2   System Information

look for problems. For example, if you click Conflicts/Sharing, any devices that are conflicting with each other or sharing resources are reported. In IRQs, any conflicting IRQ settings are reported as well. As you can see, System Information can be an effective tool to help you find problems with your devices. You can use System Information, or the properties sheets for each device in Device Manager, to selectively disable different devices so you can resolve conflicts that may exist.

By using these tools, you can normally find the problem with your device and fix it. In many cases, the problem will either be a conflict with another device or a corrupt or incompatible driver. However, there are a number of problems that can occur with different hardware devices. The next section lists those devices and examines the problems you are most likely to encounter.

Hardware Problems and Solutions

In this section, I take a look at the hardware devices explored in the previous chapters. I point out the problems you are most likely to experience and the solutions to those problems. Use this section as a quick reference to resolve hardware problems on your system.

Modems

The most likely problem to occur with modems is detection. Once your modem is installed, the rest is simply configuration of a dial-up account and following your ISP's recommendations. If you have a plug-and-play modem and your computer cannot seem to detect it, Windows 2000 may not recognize the modem COM port. The other possible explanation is that the modem is in conflict with another device. You can check your COM ports by opening Ports in Device Manager to see if the port is recognized. For an internal modem, make certain the modem is completely inserted into the slot. Check the manufacture's documentation for installation instructions.

Network Adapter Cards

If you have problems with a Network Adapter Card, first and foremost, make certain your network adapter card is on the HCL. If you are using a legacy non-plug-and-play modem, you need the correct driver, and you still may have problems anyway. If this is not the case, sometimes your driver may be corrupted. In this case, remove the driver, which effectively removes the device from your system, and reinstall it. This may correct the problem. If this still doesn't work, take a hard look at the NIC itself. When it is connected to the network, do the lights on it blink? If not, you probably have a faulty NIC. Finally, check for hardware conflicts with other devices using System Information.

USB Devices

If you install a new USB device and it does not work, you may have conflicting drivers. USB devices should automatically install themselves, so if they don't, disconnect all of your USB devices and start your computer in safe mode. Then, in Device Manager, right-click the USB device and click Uninstall. Restart your computer, then connect the device directly to the USB port on the computer to test it. Also, make certain you do not have too many USB devices connected to one hub and that your USB hubs meet the power requirements. See Chapter 3 for more information.

Printers

As you can probably guess, printers can be one of your greatest sources of problems, and there are quite a few things that can go wrong. For most devices, you simply have to worry about installation and minor configuration, but printers can experience many problems, so I have outlined the most common ones in a problem-and-solution series:

Problem: The printer does not print.

Solution: This problem can be caused by hardware problems or by an application that is trying to use the printer. Check to make certain the printer is on and attached to the computer correctly, then try to print a test page. Then, try printing from Notepad. If you cannot print from Notepad, you most likely have a driver problem. Also, you could be short of disk space, which would interfere with the spooler. The key is to try one thing at a time to see if you can resolve the problem, and begin your troubleshooting steps with the most basic (like checking to see if the printer is attached to the computer).

Problem: On a network printer, users of Windows 95 or 98 cannot connect to the Windows 2000 printer.

Solution: The Windows 95/98 drivers are not installed. Use the Sharing tab for the printer and install the Windows 95/98 drivers so they can be download to the 95/98 clients.

Problem: An Access Denied message is displayed when trying to configure the printer.

Solution: You do not have appropriate permissions to configure the printer.

Problem: A document does not print or is garbled.

Solution: Garbled text always tells you there is a problem with the driver. The driver is either corrupt or not installed for the printer. Reinstall the driver to correct the problem.

Problem: Documents will not print and cannot be deleted.

Solution: The spooler has stalled. On the print server, stop and restart the Print Spooler service.

Video Card

If you are having a problem with your video card, the problem is most likely either a corrupt card or a card that is not supported in Windows 2000. If this is not the case, you can restart your computer in safe mode and access Display properties in Control Panel to make changes to your settings. This may solve the problem as well. Chapter 5 examines this issue, so refer to that chapter.

Sound Card

As with a video card, you are most likely to experience problems due to incompatibility with Windows 2000 or problems with the driver. Make certain the sound card is in the appropriate PCI or ISA slot in your computer. Check the manufacturer's guidelines to make certain the card is installed correctly. As with other hardware devices, also make certain there are no hardware conflicts. Use System Information to determine if hardware conflicts exist.

Other Peripherals

Your other peripheral devices, such as scanners, cameras, mice, etc., are all the same in terms of troubleshooting. First, make certain the device is attached to your computer correctly and make certain the correct driver is installed. Next, check the device's properties sheets and make any configuration changes that need to be made. In the case of game controllers, you may encounter problems with the controller depending on the game. Most games allow you to select the controller that will be used, so see the game's documentation for details. For mice and keyboards, you need to allow the system to detect them. Be wary of installing mice or keyboard software that worked under previous versions of Windows, as some of this software is not compatible with Windows 2000.

■ Summary

Troubleshooting hardware in Windows 2000, for the most part, does not have to be a highly difficult task. As long as you are using plug-and-play-compliant hardware that is compatible with Windows 2000, the problems you will experience are typically minimal. Use the troubleshooting tools provided for you in Windows 2000; due to Windows 2000's ability to manage system resource assignment and settings, difficult hardware problems are quickly becoming a thing of the past.

Windows 2000 Disk Management

In This Part

▶ **CHAPTER 8**
Windows 2000
Hard Disk Basics

▶ **CHAPTER 9**
Dynamic Disks in
Windows 2000

▶ **CHAPTER 10**
Configuring
Dynamic Volumes

CHAPTER 11
▶ Configuring
Windows 2000
Fault Tolerance

▶ **CHAPTER 12**
Windows 2000
Backup

▶ **CHAPTER 13**
Windows 2000
Disk Tools

▶ **CHAPTER 14**
Troubleshooting
Disk Problems

Windows 2000 provides many new features for configuring and managing hard disks. As you will learn in this part, these new features provide superior configuration and management options as well as performance. In this part, you learn about Windows 2000 hard disk management in the following chapters:

Chapter 8: Windows 2000 Hard Disk Basics
Chapter 9: Dynamic Disks in Windows 2000
Chapter 10: Configuring Dynamic Volumes
Chapter 11: Configuring Windows 2000 Fault Tolerance
Chapter 12: Windows 2000 Backup
Chapter 13: Windows 2000 Disk Tools
Chapter 14: Troubleshooting Disk Problems

Windows 2000 Hard Disk Basics

Before jumping into the configuration and management of hard disks in Windows 2000, there is some fundamental information you should know first. Depending on your level of technical expertise, you may be able to skip over this chapter and move directly into the new disk configuration features you begin to learn about in Chapter 10. If you don't know a lot about hard disks or file systems, then this chapter is what you need to get your feet on solid ground.

How Hard Disks Work

Every computer, whether it be a personal computer or a server, uses at least one hard disk to store information. The term "hard disk" is so common that we seldom give it much thought, and hard disks have been around since the 1950's. Hard disks function on your computer by using magnetic storage to read and write data. The hard disk stores the data you choose to save and, by accessing the hard disk, the computer can recall that data when it is needed. In essence, the hard disk is like the part of your brain that stores your memories and all of the information you learn over your lifetime.

Hard disks, which are also called "fixed disks," contain a platter that holds magnetic material. The platter is "hard" and is not flexible like the magnetic disk found in diskettes or magnetic tape. The magnetic material resides on the platter and is written to and read from by a head that hovers over the magnetic material. The hard disk spins (often at a speed of over 100 MPH) so that the data is read from the disk one byte at a time and sent to the CPU for processing. This design ensures that data can be read and written fast.

Typically, hard disks are sealed in an aluminum box with a controller attached to it. The computer uses the controller to move the read/write head and spin the disk so that information can be read or written. Depending on the hard disk, multiple platters and read/write heads may be used.

A blank platter cannot hold data. It has to be formatted so that data can be written and read. When formatting takes place, the platter is divided into sectors and tracks. Tracks run around the entire disk while sectors divide the disk into different sections. A sector contains a fixed number of bytes—either 512 or 256. Even with the disk being divided into sectors and tracks, data still cannot be written on the disk until formatting is complete and a file system is in place. The file system is a software feature that allows the operating system to store data on the hard disk. The file system determines how data is organized and stored. The next section explores the file systems that are available to you in Windows 2000.

Windows 2000 File Systems

Windows 2000 supports three file systems—FAT, FAT32, and NTFS. It also supports CDFS, which is the file system used by CD-ROMs, but since CDFS is not an option for your hard disks, it is not discussed here. To effectively format your disk and use a file system that is appropriate for your computer, you need to have a firm understanding of these three file systems. The following sections examine each of them.

FAT

FAT (File Allocation Table), or FAT16, is an older file system that was designed for use with small disks and implements a simple structure. The file allocation table is found at the beginning of a volume. There are always two copies of the file allocation table stored on the volume. If one table becomes corrupted, the other can be used. For both the Windows 2000 and the Windows NT systems, the maximum size of a FAT16 volume is 4,095 MB.

The cluster size of a FAT volume is determined by the size of the volume and can be as large as 64 KB. You learn more about cluster size and changing the cluster size in later chapters.

The important thing to remember is that FAT is not recommended for volumes larger than 511 MB (which is half of 1 GB) because FAT cannot use disk space efficiently on larger drives, and you cannot use FAT on drives larger than 5 GB, regardless of the cluster size. Obviously, FAT is provided in Windows 2000 for backwards compatibility. Considering the size of most hard drives today, FAT is not a file system you should intentionally choose to implement. It is supported in Windows 2000 in case you need to dual-boot Windows 2000 and an earlier version of Windows, such as Windows 95 or Windows 3.x. All Windows operating systems can read FAT, such as Windows 3.x, Windows 95/98, Windows NT, and Windows 2000.

 A dual boot system contains at least two operating systems. For example, you could have a computer that will boot either Windows 2000 or Windows 95. When you start the system, you receive a boot menu that allows you to choose the operating system you wish to load. In this scenario, if you format your disks with NTFS, which is only supported by Windows NT and Windows 2000, then the Windows 95 operating system will not be able to read your hard disks and data. This is why Windows 2000 still supports FAT.

FAT32

FAT32 is an enhancement to the FAT file system that was first supported in Windows 95 OSR2, and then in Windows 98. Windows NT does not support FAT32. FAT32 can theoretically support hard drives up to 2 terabytes in size. There are other differences between FAT and FAT32, but the major difference is that FAT32 breaks the drive size limitations of FAT. As with FAT, FAT32 is provided in Windows 2000 for backwards compatibility so that you can dual-boot other operating systems that use FAT32 with Windows 2000.

NTFS

NTFS is the file system of choice in Windows 2000, and Windows 2000's version of NTFS is an enhancement to the original NTFS provided in Windows NT. NTFS offers many security features and many of the security and disk configuration options available in Windows 2000 are only supported with NTFS. NTFS supports both file and folder security as well as fault tolerance and encryption features available in Windows 2000. As you continue working through this section of the book, you will see how limited your disk configurations are without NTFS. However, other than Windows NT, no other Windows operating system can read NTFS.

The basic rule you should follow, for both Windows 2000 Server and Windows 2000 Professional, is that you should format all disks with NTFS unless you need to dual-boot a computer with an earlier version of Windows. Beyond this fact, there is no advantage to using FAT or FAT32 over NTFS. Whenever you consider using FAT or FAT32, make certain you have a firm reason for doing so and that you are aware of limitations. The good news is that you can convert FAT and FAT32 drives to NTFS without losing any of your data with the Disk Management console, which you learn about next in this chapter.

The Disk Management Console

For all disk configuration in Windows 2000, you use the Disk Management console, which is somewhat similar to Disk Management found in Windows NT 4.0. The Disk Management console is now a snap-in that functions with a number of other snap-ins found on the Computer Management tool. Computer Management is available in your Administrative Tools folder. Open Computer Management, then click Disk Management in the left pane. The Disk Management console appears in the right pane, shown in Figure 8.1.

The Disk Management console, by default, contains two displays. The first display resides at the top right of the screen and contains your disk partitions (or volumes, which you learn about in coming chapters). For each partition listed, the following information is presented:

- Layout—Tells you the kind of partition/volume, such as simple volume, spanned volume, etc. You can learn more about volume configuration in Chapter 11.
- Type—Tells you if the disk is basic or dynamic. You can learn about dynamic and basic disks in Chapter 9.

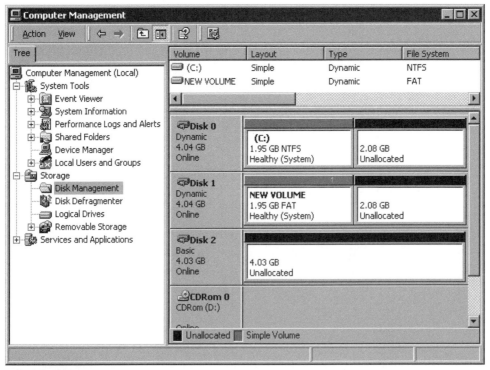

FIGURE 8.1 Disk Management Console within Computer Management

- File System—Tells you the type of file system in use, either NTFS, FAT32, or FAT.
- Status—Tells you the current status of the volume. You can learn more about volume status readings in Chapters 9 and 10.
- Capacity—Tells you the total storage capacity of the volume, such as 2 GB.
- Free Space—Tells you how much free space, either in GB or MB, there is available on the volume.
- % Free—Tells you the percentage of free space available.
- Fault Tolerance—Tells you whether or not the volume is a fault-tolerant volume. You can learn more about configuring fault tolerant volumes in Chapter 11.
- Overhead—Tells the percentage of the disk used for management overhead.

The second part of the Disk Management console (located in the lower right of the screen), by default, gives you a graphical representation of your hard disk(s). The display gives you each disk available on your system and tells you the partitions or volumes that reside on the disk. Under the disk number, you see whether the disk is dynamic or basic, its total size, and its status. The volumes tell you the drive letter or label, the size and file system, and the volume's status. Free space on the disk is displayed as unallocated. Depending on your disk configuration and the kinds of volumes you choose to implement, different volumes are displayed in different colors. You also see your CD-ROM drive displayed as well.

To exercise configuration or management options, simply use the graphical display to select the desired disk or volume, then click the Action menu and point to All Tasks to see the configuration options available for that disk or volume, shown in Figure 8.2.

Keep in mind that Disk Management is a Microsoft Management Console (MMC) snap-in. For all MMC consoles and snap-ins in Windows 2000, you can select what you want to configure and use the Action menu to select the desired option. Also, you can simply select the desired disk or volume and right-click it to get the same options, shown in Figure 8.3. If you are unfamiliar with the MMC and the use of snap-ins in Windows 2000, see Appendix A for a tutorial.

As mentioned previously, the default display of Disk Management is to give you the volume list in the top of the window and a graphical representation of disks and volumes in the lower portion. You can change this so that Disk Management displays your disks and volumes in a manner that is best for you. If you click the View menu, shown in Figure 8.4, you see that you can make changes to both the top and bottom portions of the window.

Using the View menu, you can change either the top or bottom parts of the Disk Management window, or both. For the top portion, you can choose to either display the Disk list, Volume list, or have the graphical

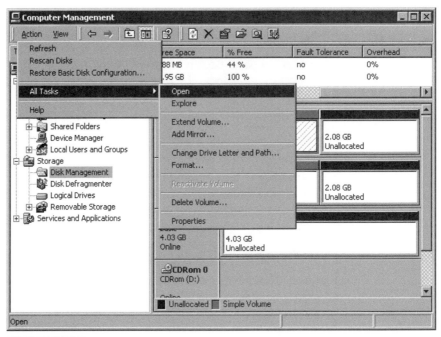

FIGURE 8.2   Select the desired disk or volume and click the Action menu to see the available tasks.

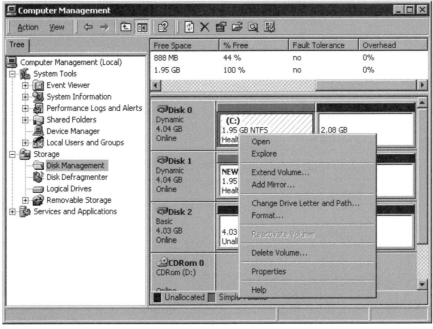

FIGURE 8.3   Right-click the desired disk or volume to see configuration options.

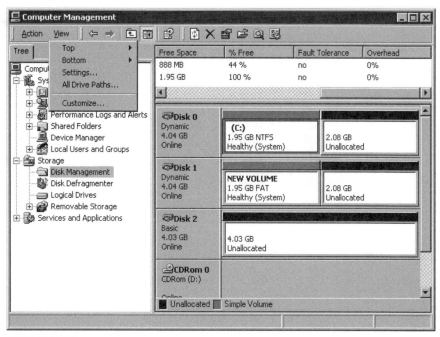

FIGURE 8.4   Adjust the display of Disk Management by using the View menu.

view displayed. By default, the Volume list is selected. For the bottom of the window, you can choose to display the Disk list, Volume list, graphical view, or you can hide it so that you only work with one display. By default, the graphical view is selected. As you can see in Figures 8.5 and 8.6, you can have Disk Management displayed in several different ways.

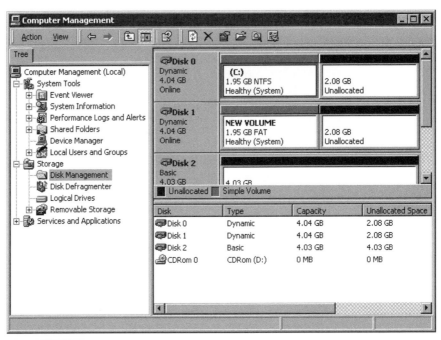

FIGURE 8.5 Graphical and Disk list display

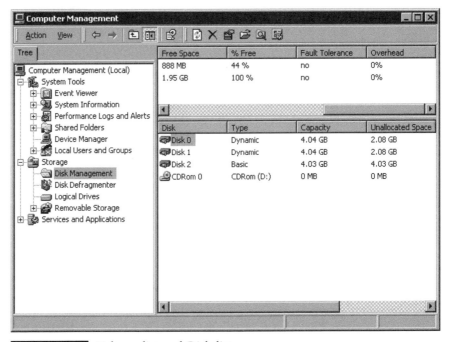

FIGURE 8.6 Volume list and Disk list

■ Summary

This chapter introduced you to disk management in Windows 2000. After an explanation of how hard disks work, this chapter explained the three file systems that are available in Windows 2000—FAT, FAT32, and NTFS. NTFS is the file system of choice for Windows 2000 computers, but FAT and FAT32 are provided for backwards compatibility in case you need to dual-boot Windows 2000 with previous versions of Windows, such as Windows 95/98. Finally, this chapter introduced you to Disk Management, the MMC console contained with the Computer Management tool. You use Disk Management to perform all disk configurations, which you learn about in the coming chapters.

Q&A

Use these questions and answers to resolve problems or to test your knowledge of this chapter's content.

Q: *How do hard disks read data?*

A: Hard disks write data using the file system and by physically writing the data in sector and tracks. The read/write head then uses the sectors and tracks to recall data it has written to the hard disk. The data is written in bytes and recalled in bytes, where it is sent to the computer's CPU for processing. The CPU processes the data, then displays it to you.

Q: *What is the difference between FAT and FAT32?*

A: FAT32 provides a number of enhancements to the original FAT file system, with the most important enhancement being support for large hard drives. Theoretically, FAT32 can support hard drives up to 2 Terabytes in size. However, FAT32 still does not provide the powerful security features of NTFS and is provided in Windows 2000 for backwards compatibility.

Q: *What is CDFS?*

A: CDFS is the file system used by CD-ROM drives. CDFS is supported in Windows 2000 for use with your CD-ROM drive, but it is not a file system you can use on a hard disk.

Q: *What is the MMC?*

A: The MMC is the Microsoft Management console. The MMC is a basic GUI interface that functions with the use of snap-ins. A snap-in is a management tool that is used within the MMC. For example, Disk Management is a snap-in used within the MMC. All administrative tools in Windows 2000 function as MMC snap-ins, which gives the operating system a streamlined look and helps reduce users' and administrators' learning curves. You can learn about the MMC in Appendix A.

Dynamic Disks in Windows 2000

In Chapter 8, you learned about hard disk basics and the types of file systems supported in Windows 2000. You were also introduced to the Disk Management console, which you continue to use throughout this section. At this point, we turn our attention to a fundamentally important aspect of hard disk configuration in Windows 2000—basic and dynamic disks. To make the most of Windows 2000, you will want to implement dynamic disks, a new technology that greatly improves disk management. In this chapter, you learn all about dynamic disks and how to configure your computer's hard disks for dynamic support.

Dynamic and Basic Disks

Windows 2000 Server now provides support for "dynamic" disks as well as "basic" disks. Before moving any further, it is important to understand the difference between a basic disk and a dynamic disk in Windows 2000.

A basic disk is simply partitions and logical drives (and volumes) that were created with Windows NT 4.0 or earlier, such as volume sets, stripe sets, mirror sets, and stripe sets with parity. In Windows 2000, these volumes are now called spanned volumes, striped volumes, mirrored volumes, and RAID-5 volumes. These storage and fault-tolerant solutions are also available in Windows 2000 Professional.

Windows NT Disk Solutions

In case you are a little rusty on the storage and fault-tolerant solutions provided in Windows NT, review the following points.

Volume Set. A volume set is a collection of partitions that are treated as one partition. This storage solution allows you to combine between 2 and 32 areas of unformatted free disk space to create one logical drive.

Stripe Set. A stripe set is like a volume set, but a stripe set combines unformatted free space on 2 to 32 physical drives to create one logical drive. Data is written across the disks in 64K blocks. This evenly distributes data on the disks and speeds performance. Stripe Sets, however, do not provide any inherent fault tolerance.

Mirror Set. A mirror set duplicates a partition and moves the duplicate copy onto another physical disk. In other words, a mirror set maintains two complete copies of the partition at all times. In this case, if one physical disk fails, the data remains on the other physical disk.

Stripe Set with Parity. A stripe set with parity (RAID 5) requires 3 to 32 physical drives. The data is written in rows across the disk with a parity bit. In the event of a single disk failure, the data can be regenerated using the parity bit.

Dynamic disks in Windows 2000 offer you more management flexibility without the partition limitation of basic disks. Dynamic disks do not contain partitions, logical drives, and so forth—they simply contain volumes, and you are not restricted to any volume limit per disk. Due to the growing gigabyte size of hard disks that are available today, dynamic disks allow you to be in control so you can section and manage your computer's hard disk in a way that is best for you. Also, with dynamic disks, you can make configuration changes to your disk (such as adding volumes) without having to reboot your computer. For Windows 2000 Servers, this is very advantageous.

If you are a little rusty on disk terms, the following list gives you the standard basic and dynamic disk terminology, and explains their meanings.

- Partition—A partition, now called a volume in dynamic disks, is a portion of a physical disk that acts as though it were a physically separate disk.
- System and Boot Partitions—System and boot partitions are now called system and boot volumes in dynamic disks. A system volume contains hardware-specific files needed to load Windows 2000. The boot volume contains the Windows 2000 operating system and support files. The boot and system volume can be the same volume, but do not have to be.
- Active Partition—The active partition, or active volume for dynamic disks, is the partition or volume from which the computer starts.

- Extended partition—In a basic disk, an extended partition is a portion of the disk that can contain logical drives. This solution gives you more than four volumes on the basic disk, but only one of the four partitions can be an extended partition. Dynamic disks do not use extended partitions; they are unnecessary because there is no volume number limit.
- Logical Drive—In a basic disk, a logical drive is a volume you create within an extended partition. Again, logical drives are unnecessary in dynamic volumes because there is not a volume limit per disk.

Also, once you upgrade to Windows 2000 Server from Windows NT Server, Windows 2000 Server further limits what you can do with a basic disk. The following list tells you what you can and cannot do with basic disks in Windows 2000 Server:

- You can check disk properties and run most administrative tools.
- You can view volume and partition properties.
- You can change drive-letters for disk volumes or partitions.
- You can share information and establish security restrictions.
- You can create new primary partitions or extended partitions.
- You can create and delete logical disks within an extended partition.
- You can format a partition and mark it as active.
- You can delete volume sets, stripe sets, and stripe sets with parity.
- You can break a mirror set.
- You can repair a mirror set or stripe set with parity.
- You cannot create new volume, stripe, mirror sets, or stripe sets with parity.
- You cannot extend existing volumes and volume sets.

Basically, Windows 2000 Server allows you to keep your disk configuration when you upgrade from Windows NT 4.0. You can manage your basic disks and make fault-tolerant repairs; however, you are limited to the current configuration. You really cannot make any significant changes to the disk or establish new volume or stripe sets, and you cannot implement new fault-tolerant solutions.

The logical question when considering basic or dynamic disks is whether to use a basic disk with your Windows 2000 system or a dynamic disk. The simple rule is to use a basic disk if you are dual-booting Windows 2000 with MS-DOS or a previous version of Windows, such as Windows 98 or Windows NT. Only Windows 2000 computers can access dynamic volumes, so if you upgrade your disk to dynamic, you will not be able to boot any previous versions of Windows or MS-DOS installed on your system. Also, if you are using Windows 2000 Professional, you may not need the features of dynamic disks, in which case a basic disk will work just fine. However, the best solution is to use dynamic disks unless you are dual-booting with MS-DOS or a previous version of Windows.

Upgrading a Basic Disk to a Dynamic Disk

Windows 2000 Server keeps your disk configuration if you upgrade from a previous version of Windows, so your disk will be a basic disk. If you install Windows 2000 on a blank machine, the system will also be configured with a basic disk. You can choose to upgrade the basic disk to a dynamic disk so that you have full access to the disk management tasks available in Windows 2000.

Any disk that you upgrade to dynamic must have at least 1 MB of unformatted free space at the end of the disk. If there is not at least 1 MB of unformatted free disk space at the end, the upgrade will fail. Disk Management uses this free space when creating partitions or volumes on a disk, but partitions or volumes created with Windows NT or Windows 95/98 may not have this free space readily available. Once you perform the upgrade, your basic partitions become dynamic volumes, which you cannot change back to partitions. If you have Windows NT volume sets, mirror sets, striped sets, or striped sets with parity on your disk, the upgrade will change those to Windows 2000's spanned volumes, striped volumes, mirrored volumes, or RAID-5 volumes. Remember that once the upgrade is complete, the disk cannot be accessed by operating systems other than Windows 2000. Also, before performing the upgrade, the following elements should be taken into consideration:

- Boot Partition: You can upgrade a basic disk containing the boot partition to a dynamic disk. The boot partition becomes a simple boot volume after the upgrade is complete.
- System Partition: You can upgrade a basic disk containing the system partition to a dynamic disk. The System partition becomes a simple system volume when the upgrade is complete.
- Removable Media: You cannot upgrade removable media to dynamic volumes.
- Volumes on multiple disks: If a basic disk contains any volumes that span multiple disks, as in a stripe set with parity, you must also upgrade the other disks that contain the parts of the volume.
- Disks with sector sizes larger than 512 bytes: You cannot upgrade a basic disk to a dynamic disk if the sector size of the disk is greater than 512 bytes.
- Revert to basic disk: You cannot change a dynamic disk back to a basic disk without deleting all of the volumes first. This action deletes all of the data on the disk. Once the volumes have been deleted, you can right click on the disk and choose Revert to Basic Disk.

To upgrade a basic disk to a dynamic disk, follow these steps:

1. Open Computer Management, available in Administrative Tools.

2. Expand the Storage tree and double-click Disk Management. The Disk Management interface appears in the right pane with a display of your disk(s), shown in Figure 9.1.

3. Select the disk you want to upgrade in the console (select the disk number—not a partition of the disk), then click the Action menu, point to All Tasks, then click Upgrade to Dynamic Disk, shown in Figure 9.2.

4. An Upgrade to Dynamic Disk window appears with the disk number selected for the upgrade. Click OK to continue, shown in Figure 9.3, then click the Upgrade button when it appears. A warning message appears telling you that you will not be able to boot previous versions of Windows once the upgrade is complete.

5. The upgrade takes place and you are prompted to reboot your computer. You must reboot your computer for the upgrade to complete the boot and system partition upgrades.

6. Once the upgrade is complete, Disk Management will display the disk as dynamic, as shown in Figure 9.4.

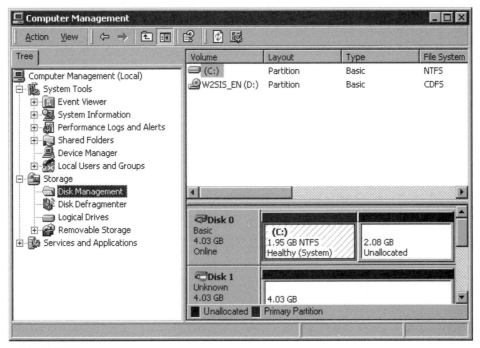

FIGURE 9.1   Use the Disk Management tool to upgrade your basic disk to dynamic.

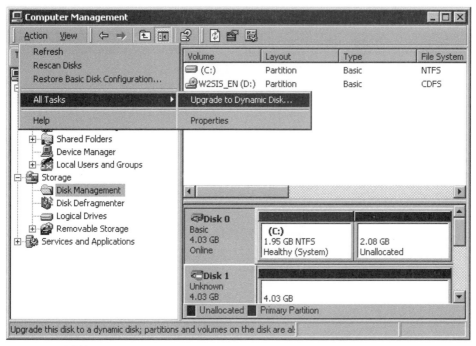

FIGURE 9.2   Select the disk and use the Action menu to start the upgrade.

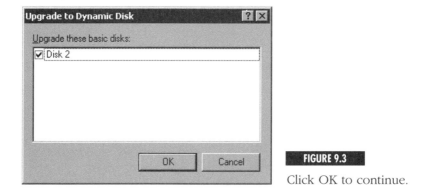

FIGURE 9.3

Click OK to continue.

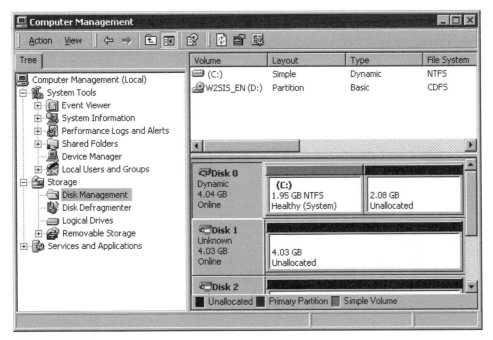

FIGURE 9.4 Dynamic Disk Upgrade

Writing Disk Signatures

In computers that have multiple hard drives, you may have formatted and installed Windows 2000 on the first disk, but the remaining disk(s) are not formatted. In this case, the disk is listed as "unknown" in the Disk Management console, which you can see for Disk 1 in Figure 9.4. In this case, before you can configure the disk, a signature must be written on it. If you have unformatted disks, a wizard appears when you launch Disk Management, prompting you to write the signature and upgrade the empty basic disk to a dynamic disk, shown in Figure 9.5.

You can cancel the wizard and perform the signature writing and dynamic upgrade by selecting the disk and using the Action menu, but the wizard is the easiest way to proceed. When you click Next, a window appears where you can select the disk(s) for which you want to write the signature and upgrade to dynamic. Select the desired check boxes, then click Next, then click Finish. The system writes the signature and upgrades the disk to dynamic. You do not have to reboot your computer for this operation.

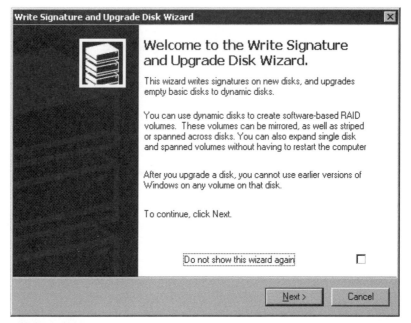

FIGURE 9.5   Write Signature and Upgrade Disk Wizard welcome screen

Returning to a Basic Disk

As mentioned previously, you cannot return to a basic disk from a dynamic disk without losing your dynamic disk configuration. Generally, returning to a basic disk is not a desirable task and you should carefully consider your reasons for returning to a basic disk. However, it can be done, but you will lose all of your configured volumes. The best way to return a disk to basic is to delete the volumes, then select the disk, click the Action menu, then click Restore Basic Disk Configuration. Windows provides you with a warning message (Figure 9.6), and then attempts to restore your dynamic disk to a basic disk using saved configuration information. Again, you should not have a need to return a dynamic disk to a basic disk (unless you want to install MS-DOS or a previous version of Windows on a different partition so you can dual-boot), so consider the action carefully before proceeding.

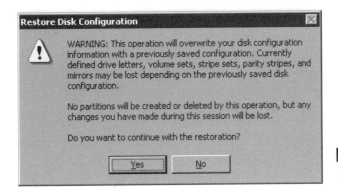

FIGURE 9.6

Restoration warning

Understanding Disk States

Windows 2000 dynamic disks have two fundamental states, either online or offline. Online means the disk is functioning as it should and no errors are present. Offline means there is some problem with the disk and it cannot be used or accessed. The state of the disk is always displayed in the Disk Management console under the Disk number. This feature allows you to easily see if a disk is online or if there is some problem. Aside from the online and offline status, there are a few other status indicators as well, as described in this list:

- Online (Errors)—I/O errors have been detected on a portion of the disk. Although the disk is still online and accessible, there may be read or write problems if the disk is not repaired.
- Offline/Missing—As stated previously, a disk Offline message tells you the disk is not accessible. This can be caused by corruption or a hardware problem. The status message may also tell you the disk is Offline/Missing, which means a disk that was once available on the system now does not appear to be present. This message can occur if the disk has been removed, has no power, is disconnected from the system, or possibly corrupted.
- Foreign—The Foreign message tells you that the disk has been moved from another Windows 2000 computer to your computer, but it has not been set up for use on your computer.
- Unreadable—the disk is not accessible due to failure, corruption, or I/O errors.
- Unrecognized—The disk has an original equipment manufacturer's (OEM) signature and Windows 2000 will not allow you to use the disk. This error is most often seen when you attempt to use a disk not compatible with Windows 2000, such as one from a UNIX system.

■ No Media—This error message appears for removable-media drives, such as Zip drives or CD-ROM drives. This message simply tells you that no media is present in the device.

Naturally, the next question concerning your hard disk state is what to do if there is a problem. In most cases, Windows 2000 can easily help you bring an offline or problematic disk back online. The following list tells you what action you should take for each status message you see in Disk Management.

■ Online—There are no problems with the disk and no action is necessary.

■ Online (Errors)—Right-click on the disk in the Disk Management console and click Reactivate Disk. This allows Windows 2000 to correct the disk's problems and bring it back online.

■ Offline/Missing—Check the disk's controller or cables and make certain it is plugged in or turned on and attached to the computer. Then right-click on the disk in the Disk Management console and click Reactivate Disk.

■ Foreign—If you want to use the disk on your system, you need to add the disk to your computer's configuration. Right-click on the disk and click Import Foreign Disk. The disk will be imported and any existing volumes on the disk become visible.

■ Unreadable—Select the disk, click the Action menu, then click Rescan disk. This action allows your system to rescan your disk configuration and bring it back online. You can also try rebooting the computer.

■ Unrecognized—This disk cannot be used with Windows 2000.

■ No Media—You simply need to insert the appropriate media into the removable media device to use it.

Adding a New Disk

At some point, you may decide to add a new internal or external hard disk. This process is no different from adding any new hardware to your system. Simply follow the manufacturer's instructions to physically attach the new disk to the system, then allow Windows to detect and install it (or use the Add/Remove Hardware Wizard). Once you are finished with the installation, open the Disk Management console, click the Action menu, then click Rescan Disks. This feature allows Disk Management to rescan your disk configuration so the new disk can be added to the console. After the scan is complete, you can write the signature on the disk and format it or create volumes/partitions as desired.

Removing a Disk

With multiple disks on your system, you may at some point need to remove a disk. If you need to remove a disk, you can easily do so in the Disk Management console by right clicking on the disk and clicking Remove Disk. This action removes the disk from your computer's disk configuration. Of course, any data on the disk will no longer be accessible once this action is performed.

Examining Disk Properties

A final option you may find useful from time to time concerning your hard disks, whether they are basic or dynamic, is the properties sheet. Your hard disk contains a single General tab that simply provides you with information, shown in Figure 9.7. You are given the disk number, the type (dynamic or basic), the status (either online or offline), the total capacity as well as any unallocated space, device type, hardware vendor, adapter name, and a list of the volumes that exist on the hard disk. You can select a desired volume and click the Properties button to see the Properties sheets for individual volumes on the disk. These properties and the configuration of volumes are explored in detail in the next chapter.

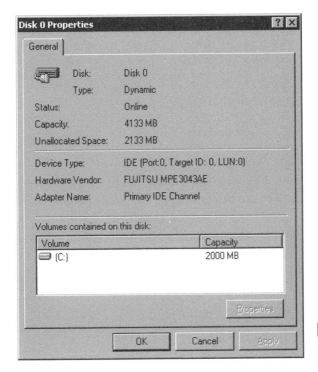

FIGURE 9.7

Hard Disk properties

■ Summary

Windows 2000 supports both basic and dynamic disks. Dynamic disks provide a number of management features in Windows 2000, with the option of unlimited volumes and configuration changes without reboot being two of the most important. Once you decide to upgrade your basic disks to dynamic disks, you can further configure the dynamic disk by creating volumes. You can learn all about volume creation in the next chapter.

Q&A

Review these questions and answers to resolve problems or to check your knowledge of this chapter's content.

Q: *How many disks are required to create a spanned volume?*

A: You need at least two physical dynamic disks to create a spanned volume, and you can have up to 32 physical dynamic disks.

Q: *Which disk solutions provided in Windows 2000 provide fault tolerance?*

A: Mirror sets and RAID-5 volumes provide fault tolerance. Spanned volumes and striped volumes provide effective storage solutions, but do not provide any inherent fault tolerance.

Q: *How do you configure logical drives on dynamic disks?*

A: Logical drives are unnecessary on dynamic disks. Dynamic disks do not limit you to a certain number of partitions, but are now simply disk volumes. There is no volume limit in dynamic disks, so you simply create the volumes you need instead of having to worry about partitions, extended partitions, and logical drives.

Q: *Aside from the unlimited number of volumes, what is another advantage of dynamic disks?*

A: One of the great advantages of dynamic disks in Windows 2000 is you can make configuration changes without having to reboot the computer. For example, you can create a new disk volume and format that volume without having to reboot the computer. This is a particular advantage for Windows 2000 Servers which need to remain online to service the needs of network clients.

Q: *A disk on my Windows 2000 computer displays the online (errors) status. What is wrong?*

A: The online (errors) status tells you that the disk is online and available, but I/O errors have been detected on this disk. Right-click the disk and click Reactivate Disk to repair the problem.

Q: *I moved a disk from another Windows 2000 computer to my computer. The status message reads "foreign." What do I need to do?*

A: The foreign status message tells you that you have imported a Windows 2000 disk from another computer, but the disk has not been set up for use on your computer. Right-click the disk and click Import Foreign Disks so that your computer can set the disk up for use on your system.

Configuring Dynamic Volumes

Once you upgrade your basic disk to a dynamic disk, you can then begin to configure volumes for the disk as desired. Remember that dynamic volumes replace partitions and extended partitions on basic disks. A volume, though a part of a physical hard disk, appears and acts as though it is an independent hard disk. This chapter shows you how to configure and manage dynamic volumes on your Windows 2000 computer.

Creating a New Simple Volume

You are not limited in the number of volumes you can create on a dynamic disk. The goal, of course, is to configure volumes that meet your needs. Keep in mind that each volume acts as if it is an independent physical disk, and you can create volumes in order to store different kinds of information, as needed. A simple volume is a single block of space and does not span multiple volumes or disks. Creating new volumes is easy in Windows 2000, and as with many components in Windows 2000, a wizard is provided to help you. To create a new volume on a dynamic disk, follow these steps:

1. Open Computer Management from your Administrative Tools folder in Control Panel, then click on Disk Management in the left pane.

2. Select the desired area of unallocated space on the desired disk, click the Action menu, point to All Tasks, then click Create Volume, shown in Figure 10.1. You can also right-click the unallocated space and click Create Volume.

3. The Create Volume wizard appears. Click Next.

4. On the Select Volume Type window, shown in Figure 10.2, click the Simple Volume radio button, then click Next.

5. On the Select Disks window, shown in Figure 10.3, the disk you selected appears in the right window, but you can change this if desired (if your system has more than one disk) by using the Add, Remove, and Remove All buttons. You select only one disk to create a simple volume. The total volume size that is available (in megabytes) is displayed. Use the Size dialog box to make changes to the volume size as desired, then click Next.

6. On the Assign a Drive Letter or Path window, a drive letter for the volume is already selected for you, but you can change it by selecting a different one from the drop-down box. You can also mount the volume to an empty folder, which you learn more about in the next section. You can also choose to not assign a drive letter or path at this time. Make your selection, and click Next.

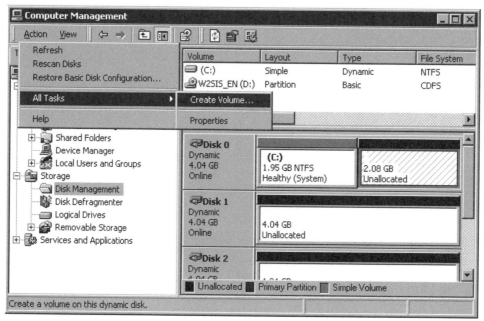

FIGURE 10.1   Use the Action menu to create a new volume.

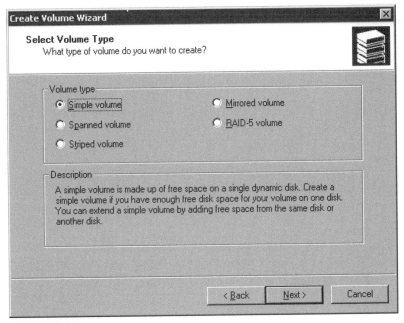

FIGURE 10.2 Select Simple Volume and click Next.

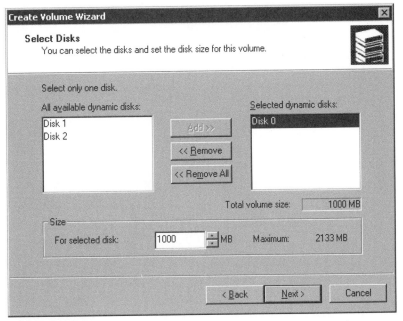

FIGURE 10.3 Select your disk and volume size in this window.

7. In the Format Volume window, shown in Figure 10.4, you can choose to either format the volume or not. If you choose to format the volume at this time, use the drop-down menus to select the desired file system and allocation unit size. You can leave the allocation unit size set to default. You can also enter a label for the volume in the provided dialog box. You can choose to perform a quick format and you can enable compression by clicking the check boxes. See Chapter 17 to learn more about compression. Make your selections and click Next.

All file systems used by Windows 2000 organize hard disks based on allocation unit size. The allocation unit size is the smallest amount of disk space that can be allocated to hold a file. The disk makes the best use of storage space if the allocation size is small. This helps prevent wasted space and fragmentation. If you do not select an allocation unit size when you configure a volume, Windows picks one for you based on the size of the volume.

A quick format removes existing files from the disk before formatting it, but it does not scan the disk for bad sectors. Unless the disk is new, it is best to not use the quick format option when creating the volume so that Windows can thoroughly check your disk.

8. In the Completion window, click the Finish button. The new simple volume is created and now appears in the Disk Management console, shown in Figure 10.5.

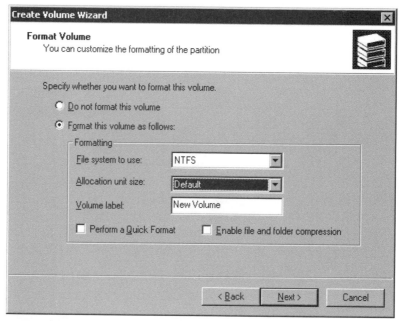

FIGURE 10.4 Select formatting options and click Next.

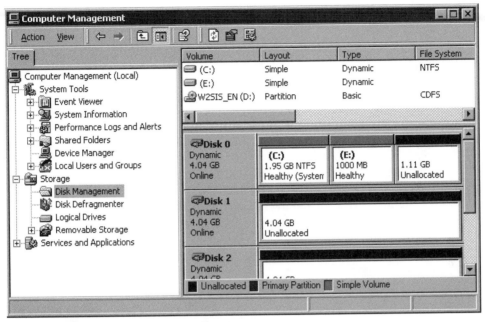

FIGURE 10.5 New volume now appears.

Mounting a Simple Volume to an Empty Folder

Windows 2000 includes a new feature that allows you some interesting management options concerning drive letters. In the past, partitions or extended partitions on basic disks were always labeled C, D, E, F, and so on. This, of course, limits you to the 26 letters of the alphabet. Windows 2000 provides a workaround for this limit as well as a different way to label your volumes by mounting the volume to an empty NTFS folder. The new volume you are creating is mounted on a folder on another local NTFS volume, but the new volume can be formatted with any file system supported by Windows 2000. This is accomplished by a drive path instead of a drive letter. For example, let's say you have a volume you want to create called "Company Documents." You want to use the volume for storage purposes, but you want it to appear on your C drive instead of its own drive. You simply mount the volume to an empty folder called "Company Documents" on your C drive (must be NTFS), and the new volume appears as C:\Documents instead of its own volume. This feature is designed to give you more management flexibility, and as you can imagine, there are a number of possible options. You can even mount your CD-ROM drive to your C drive so it appears as C:\CD-ROM.

To create a mounted volume, first create an empty NTFS folder on the desired drive (such as C). Remember that the folder must exist on an NTFS volume, but the new volume you are creating can be formatted with any file system supported by Windows 2000.

When you create the new volume using the Create New Volume wizard in Disk Management, select the "mount this volume at an empty folder that supports drive paths" radio button, shown in Figure 10.6, instead of the drive letter option on the Assign Drive Letter or Path window.

Then, enter the path to the shared folder, or click the Browse button. If you click the Browse button, you can select the desired folder from the desired drive, or you can click the New Folder button to create the new folder if you did not do so before starting the wizard. Make your selection and click OK, shown in Figure 10.7, then click Next to continue to the New Volume wizard.

Once you complete the wizard, you can open the volume where you mounted the new volume and see that it appears as a "drive within a drive," shown in Figure 10.8. As you work with the mounted volume option, you will see there are many possibilities that make information on your system more accessible.

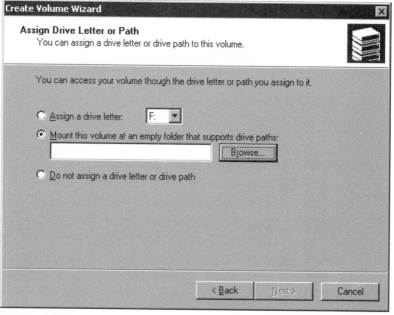

FIGURE 10.6   Select the Mount option.

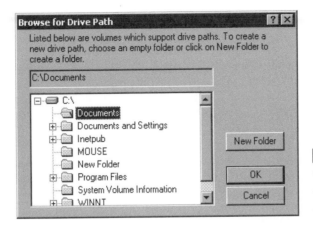

FIGURE 10.7

Use the Browse option to select a folder or create a new one.

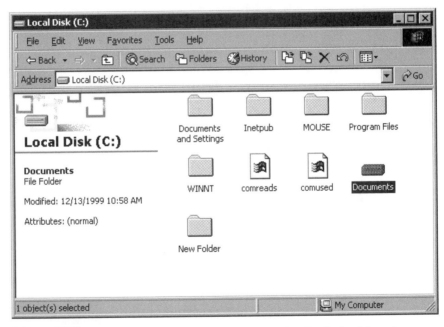

FIGURE 10.8 The mounted drive now appears in the desired location.

Extending a Volume

Once you create a simple volume, you can also later extend the amount of available storage space on the simple volume, if additional free space is still available on the disk. You can easily extend the volume without damaging any of the data on the volume or having to reboot your computer. For example, in Figure 10.9, a simple volume (F) on dynamic Disk 1 contains 1 GB of storage space; 3.06 GB of unallocated space are still available on Disk 1. I would like to extend that 1 GB on drive F to 2 GB. This can be easily accomplished using Disk Management.

To extend a drive, select it in Disk Management, click the Action menu, point to All Tasks, then click Extend Volume. This action opens the Extend Volume wizard. Follow these steps to extend a volume:

1. Click Next on the Extend Volume wizard welcome screen.

2. On the Select Disks window, make certain the correct disk is selected, then enter the amount (in megabytes) that you want to extend the volume in the Size dialog box. For example, in Figure 10.10, I want to extend the volume by 1 GB (1000 MB). Enter the amount and click Next.

3. Click Finish to complete the wizard. The extension to the volume appears in Disk Management with the same drive letter, shown in Figure 10.11.

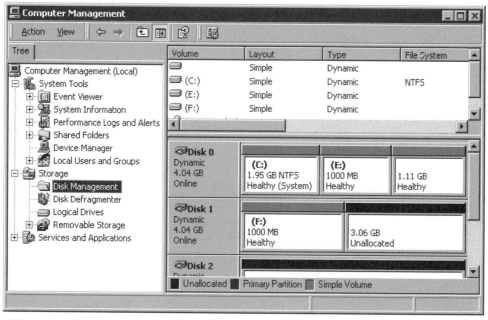

FIGURE 10.9   F Drive can be extended.

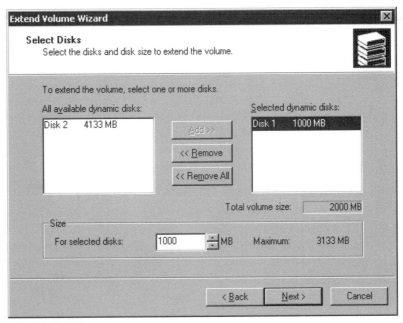

FIGURE 10.10 Select the extension amount and click Next.

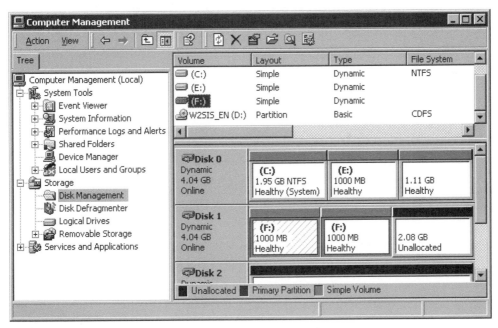

FIGURE 10.11 The extended volume is now displayed.

Creating Spanned Volumes

Spanned volumes, called volume sets in Windows NT, allow you to combine areas of unformatted free space on several disks in order to create one logical drive. For example, let's say that you have three hard drives, each containing 1 GB of unallocated space. You can combine those three 1 GB areas of unformatted space on each disk to create one drive that is 3 GB in size. This solution allows you to make use of "leftover" space, but it does not give you any fault tolerance. If one of your hard disks fails, all of the data on the spanned volume is lost. Also, you cannot delete a portion of the spanned volume without deleting the entire spanned volume. However, spanned volumes are an effective way to use small pieces of unallocated space on different disks. You can combine space on 2 dynamic disks up to 32 disks, and the space you use from each can vary. In order words, one disk may have 1 GB of unallocated space while another only has 500 MB of free space—it doesn't matter—and after you combine these pieces of space, Windows 2000 handles the rest of the task and treats all of the pieces as one drive.

Once you create a spanned volume, you can later extend it by including another portion of available disk space, but again, you cannot delete any portion of the spanned volume without losing the entire volume. You cannot extend spanned volumes that are formatted with FAT.

 Windows 2000 offers fault-tolerant solutions that protect your data against the failure of a single hard disk. These solutions are implemented using multiple hard disks installed on your system. Although a spanned volume uses two or more hard disks, a spanned volume is a storage solution and not a fault-tolerant solution. Data on a spanned volume is not protected against a hard disk failure and all data on the spanned volume is lost if one disk fails.

To create a spanned volume, follow these steps:

1. Select an area of unformatted free space on a desired disk, click the Action menu, point to All Tasks, then click Create Volume.

2. Click Next on the Welcome screen.

3. In the Select Volume Type window, click the Spanned Volume radio button, then click Next.

4. On the Select Disks window, select the desired disks you wish to include in the spanned volume, then click Add to move them into the selected window, shown in Figure 10.12. Use the Size dialog box to specify the size (in megabytes) of the free space you want to use for the spanned volume. Make your adjustments, then click Next.

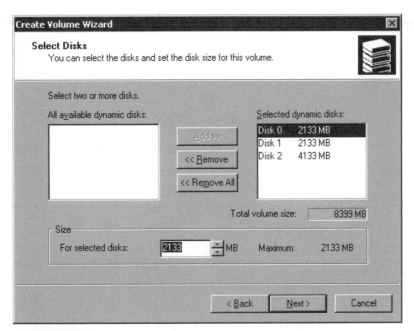

FIGURE 10.12   Select desired disks and click the Add button.

5. In the Assign Drive Letter or Path, assign a drive letter or mount the spanned volume to an NTFS folder, then click Next.

6. On the Format volume window, choose to either format the volume at this time or not. If you choose to format the volume, choose the desired file system, allocation unit size, and volume label. As with a simple volume, you can perform a quick format and you can enable compression if desired. Click Next.

7. Click Finish to complete the wizard. The spanned volume is created and appears on each disk as one drive letter with a purple title bar, shown in Figure 10.13.

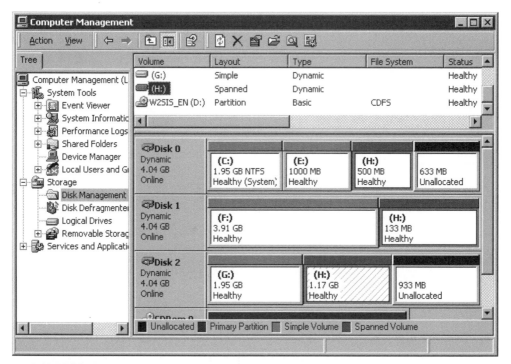

FIGURE 10.13 The spanned volume now appears in the Disk Management console.

Creating Striped Volumes

Another storage solution that uses multiple hard disks, much like a spanned volume, is the striped volume, called a stripe set in Windows NT. As in a spanned volume, a striped volume combines areas of free disk space on 2 to 32 physical hard disks and treats the pieces of space as one drive. However, in a striped volume, data is written in organized blocks across the stripe so that data is written to all physical disks at the same rate. Because of this, the free space on each disk must be the same size. The Add Volume wizard helps you configure this and will not allow you to stripe unequal amounts of free space. For example, let's say you have three hard disks. One disk you have 500 MB of free space and on the other two, you have 1000 MB each. The most space you can use on each disk is 500 MB, creating a striped set of 1.5 GB. You can, however, use a smaller amount of space if desired.

Like spanned volumes, striped volumes are storage solutions that do not offer any fault tolerance. If one disk in the stripe fails, all data on the stripe is lost. The advantage of using striped volumes over spanned volumes is performance. Striped volumes provide the best read and write performance of all disk management solutions in Windows 2000. Because of the way data is written to a striped volume, it cannot be extended.

To create a striped volume, follow these steps:

1. Select an area of free space on a desired hard disk, click the Action menu, point to All Tasks, then click Create Volume.

2. Click Next on the Create New Volume welcome screen.

3. In the Select Volume Type window, click the Striped Volume radio button, then click Next.

4. On the Select Disks window, select the desired hard disks to be included in the striped volume and move them into the Selected window using the Add button, shown in Figure 10.14. Adjust the amount of free space you want to use for the striped volume for each disk by selecting it and adjusting the Size entry as desired. Notice you can only use the maximum amount of free space that is available on the smallest unallocated area. Click Next.

5. In the Assign Drive Letter or Path window, select a drive letter for the striped volume or assign a mounted path as desired. Click Next.

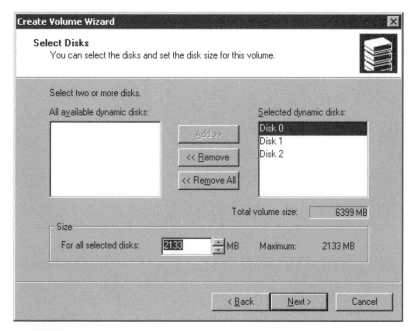

FIGURE 10.14 Select the desired disks and click the Add button.

6. On the Format Volume window, choose to either format the volume or not. If you choose to format the volume, select a file system, allocation unit size, and volume label. You can also choose to perform a quick format and use compression if desired. Click Next.

7. Click Finish. The striped volume is created and now appears in the Disk Management window as one volume, shown in Figure 10.15.

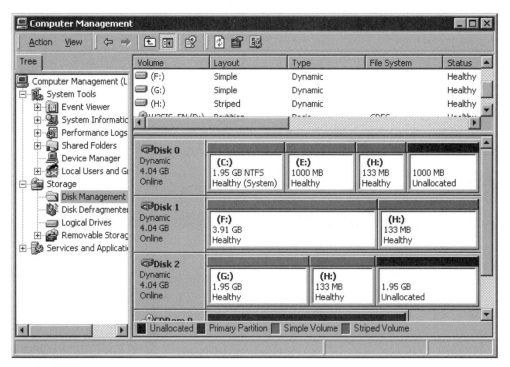

FIGURE 10.15 The striped volume now appears as one drive.

Common Volume Tasks

One of the great advantages of Windows 2000, both in the Professional and Server software, is that it tends to be very forgiving. For most major configurations you make, you can easily make changes without causing too many problems. Volume configuration is no exception to this rule. Once you create volumes, whether they be simple, spanned, or striped, you can select the volume in the Disk Management console, click the Action menu, point to All Tasks, and perform several operations, explained in the following list:

- Open—This option opens the volume and allows you to browse through your folders and files.
- Explore—This option also opens the volume, but it presents it in an Explorer window so you can easily navigate through your folder structure.
- Extend Volume—For simple and spanned volumes, use this option to extend the volume with the help of the wizard (see the Extending a Volume section earlier in this chapter).
- Change Drive Letter and Path—For volumes that already have a drive letter and path (or ones which you did not initially configure with a drive letter or path), you can access this option to change or create the drive letter, or mount the volume to an NTFS folder.
- Format—If you created a volume that is not formatted, or if you want to reformat a volume, you can use this option which allows you to select the volume label, file system, allocation unit size, and whether or not to perform a quick format or enable compression. Of course, if data is stored on the volume, it will be destroyed if you choose to reformat it.
- Reactivate Volume—Use this option to attempt to bring an offline volume back online (see Chapter 10).
- Delete Volume—This action deletes the volume and all data contained on the volume.
- Properties—Use this option to access the properties sheets for the volume, which are explored in the following section.

Dynamic Volume States

As with online and offline hard disks, each volume can also be in a particular state. In the Disk Management console, you can view a volume list. In the top part of the right pane, the volume label is displayed with additional information about the disk: layout, type, file system, status, capacity, and free space. The status label gives you information about the disk and may be displayed as follows, depending on the condition of the disk:

- Healthy: The volume is accessible and has no known problems.
- Healthy (At Risk): The volume is accessible, but I/O errors have been detected on the disk. In this case, all volumes on the disk are displayed as Healthy (At Risk). The underlying disk is displayed as Online (Errors). Normally, you can return the disk to Online status by reactivating the disk. This can be done by right-clicking on the disk and choosing Reactivate disk.
- Initializing: The volume is being initialized and will be displayed as Healthy once the initialization is complete. This status does not require any action.
- Resynching: This status indicator occurs on mirror volumes when resynchronization between the two disks is occurring. When the resynchronization is complete, the status returns to Healthy, and no action is required. See Chapter 12 to learn more about mirror volumes.
- Regenerating: In the case of RAID-5 volumes, this status indicator occurs when data is being regenerated from the parity bit. This status does not require any action. See Chapter 11 to learn more about RAID-5 volumes.
- Failed Redundancy: This status indicator appears when the underlying disk is no longer online. In this case, the data is no longer fault-tolerant in either the mirror volume or RAID-5 volume. In order to avoid potential data loss, the volume should be repaired (see the Fault Tolerance section later in this chapter). See Chapter 11 to learn more about RAID-5 volumes.
- Failed Redundancy (At Risk): This status is the same as Failed Redundancy, but the underlying disk status is usually Online (Errors). To correct the At Risk problem, Reactivate the disk so that its status returns to Online. See Chapter 11 to learn more about RAID-5 volumes.
- Failed: The volume cannot be automatically started and the volume needs to be repaired.

Configuring Volume Properties

You can access a volume's properties sheet by right-clicking the volume in Disk Management and selecting properties. The properties sheets, shown in Figure 10.16, gives you several tabs where can configure various volume options. These are explained in the following list.

- General—The General tab gives you information about the volume, such as the amount of free and used space, the file system, and total capacity. You can change the volume label, launch the disk cleanup tool, and choose to compress the drive on this tab.
- Tools—The Tools tab allows you to launch the error checking, backup, and defragmentation tools, all of which you can learn more about in Chapter 13.

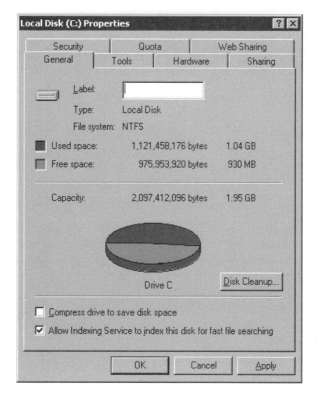

FIGURE 10.16

Volume Properties sheets

- Hardware—The Hardware tab gives you a list of hardware devices, such as hard disks, floppy drives, CD-ROM drives, and other removable media applicable to Disk Management and volumes. You can launch the Windows troubleshooter from this tab, or access the individual properties of each device.
- Sharing/Security—The Sharing and Security tabs allow you to share the volume and configure permissions and security for the volume.
- Quota—The Quota tab allows you to configure disk quotas for the volume, which you can learn about in Chapter 17.
- Web Sharing—The Web Sharing tab allows you to share the volume to a web site, such as an intranet site through which users on a network can access the volume on your computer.

■ Summary

Dynamic volumes in Windows 2000 offer you a number of solutions for disk management. You can configure any number of volumes per physical disk, and even assign those volumes to an NTFS folder instead of assigning a drive letter. You can format volumes with NTFS, FAT, or FAT32, with NTFS being the preferred choice. Dynamic volumes also include the option to create spanned volumes and striped volumes on systems that have multiple hard disks for additional shortage management possibilities.

Q&A

Review these questions and answers to resolve problems or check your knowledge of this chapter's content.

Q: *On a hard disk on my Windows 2000 computer, I cannot seem to create any volumes. Why?*

A: Your disk has not been upgraded to a dynamic disk. Volumes are only available on dynamic disks, so perform the disk upgrade from basic to dynamic first, then you can create and manage dynamic volumes.

Q: *What file systems are available for volumes?*

A: Windows 2000 supports NTFS, FAT, and FAT32. Of course, your best choice is NTFS, so consider your reasons carefully before formatting a volume with FAT or FAT32.

Q: *Should I use the quick format option when formatting a volume?*

A: A quick format erases all of the data on a volume, but it does not scan the disk for bad sectors. Typically, you should not use the quick format option unless the disk is new. Although a normal format takes more time than a quick format, it is best to allow Windows to check the disk for bad sectors and make repairs while you are performing the format option.

Q: *What is the purpose of mounting a volume to an empty folder?*

A: The option to mount a volume to an empty NTFS folder allows you to have disk volumes with names instead of drive letters. This feature removes the 26 alphabet letter limit for volume labels and enables you to configure a number of potentially helpful options that give volumes and drives "real" names instead of drive letters.

Q: *When creating a spanned volume, do you have to use free areas of space that are the same size?*

A: No. When you create spanned volumes, you can use any pieces of free, unallocated space available on 2 to 32 disks. Spanned volumes are written to in order—in other words, the first disk is filled, then the second, and so on. Due to the way data is written, the sizes of the free, unallocated space do not matter. For striped volumes, the free, unallocated spaces on the disks must be the same size because data is written across the disk in a stripe fashion.

Q: *Can you remove one disk from a spanned volume or striped volume without damaging the data?*

A: No. If one disk is removed, or if it fails, all of the data in the spanned volume or striped volume is lost.

Configuring Windows 2000 Fault Tolerance

Windows NT offered two kinds of fault tolerance, mirror sets and striped sets with parity. These two solutions are available in Windows 2000 Professional and Server, now called mirror volumes and RAID-5 volumes. If you are new to the idea of fault tolerance, this chapter will teach you all you need to know and show you how to configure fault-tolerant solutions on a Windows 2000 computer that contains multiple hard drives.

What is Fault Tolerance?

Fault tolerance simply means that a computer system can "tolerate" a failure of some kind. In terms of disk management, fault tolerance is the ability of the computer to continue functioning and not lose data due to a hard disk failure. There are other means of fault tolerance that can exist on your system, such as Uninterrupted Power Supplies (UPS) that allow your system to keep functioning during a power failure. Systems that have more than one hard disk can use the fault-tolerant solutions provided with Windows 2000, and you may also be able to gain additional fault tolerance solutions through the use of third party software and additional hardware.

Windows 2000 defines fault tolerance according to the Redundant Array of Independent Disks (RAID) standard. RAID categorizes different levels of disk arrays, or a combination of multiple disk solutions that provide both performance and fault tolerance. The following list explains each category of RAID:

- RAID 0: Disk Striping—Disk striping, which you learned about in Chapter 11, is a performance solution that writes data in blocks across 2 to 32 hard drives. There is no fault tolerance at RAID 0, but disk striping is an effective storage and performance solution.

- RAID 1: Disk Mirroring—Disk mirroring, called mirrored volumes in Windows 2000, copies data from one volume to another on different physical disks. The mirror volume provides an exact copy of another volume so that if the first volume fails, the system can continue operating with the mirror volume. Disk mirroring is the best way to protect a single volume against failure. You can also use Disk Duplexing with RAID 1, which uses a separate disk controller on each disk. This option provides better performance and also provides fault tolerance for disk controllers.

- RAID 2: Disk Striping with ECC—This method of fault tolerance, which is not supported in Windows 2000, uses the striping method to write data, but an error-checking procedure is used to provide fault tolerance in case of a single disk failure. Disk Striping with ECC does not perform as well as RAID 5.

- RAID 3: ECC Stored as Parity—RAID 3 is similar to RAID 2, but the ECC data is stored as "parity." Parity is an error-checking procedure that reviews the stored data and creates parity information about that stored data. In the event of disk failure, the parity is read and can be used to recreate the data on the lost disk. RAID 3, which is not supported in Windows 2000, still does not perform as well as RAID 5 and consumes about fifteen percent of your disk space for the parity information.

- RAID 4: Disk Striping with Large Blocks—This fault-tolerant solution writes data across the disk in complete blocks of data rather than in a stripe fashion. A separate disk is used to store the parity information that can be used to regenerate data should a hard disk fail. RAID 4 is not supported in Windows 2000 and is typically not used because of the high overhead.

- RAID 5: Striping with Parity—Striping with parity, called RAID-5 volumes in Windows 2000, provides superior fault tolerance. Data is written in a stripe across all of the disks, and the parity information is written on each disk as well. The data and the parity information for that data is arranged so they are always stored on different disks. If a single disk fails, the parity information (which is stored on a different disk) can be used to regenerate the data. You can create a RAID-5 volume on 3 to 32 hard drives, and this is the most popular form of fault tolerance.

As you read in the bullet list, Windows 2000 natively offers two hard disk fault tolerance solutions, mirror volumes and RAID-5 volumes, which you learn about in the next two sections.

Fault tolerant solutions should not be used to replace a backup plan. You should still regularly back up your data on a removable media drive. You can learn about using Windows 2000's backup utility in Chapter 13.

Configuring Mirrored Volumes

A mirrored volume duplicates data from one volume onto another volume on a different physical disk. If one disk fails, the system can continue to operate using the mirror. Mirrored volumes are an effective way to provide fault tolerance for a single disk volume; however, it does have a high overhead. Since you are copying everything on one volume to another volume, your storage space usage doubles. For example, if you have data on a volume that consumes 500 MB of storage space, the data is mirrored on another disk volume, so now that data consumes 1 GB of your total storage space. However, any volume can be mirrored, and mirrors are most often used for system and boot volumes. Also, there is no loss of performance when a mirror fails—your system can use the mirror without interrupting operations. When a volume fails in a mirrored volume, you break the mirror so that the good volume has its own drive letter. You can then recreate the mirror using another disk. The following sections show you how to create and configure a mirrored volume.

Creating a Mirrored Volume

To create a mirrored volume, you need two physical disks with enough free space on one disk to create the mirror. To create the mirrored volume, follow these steps:

1. Open Disk Management in your Administrative Tools folder.
2. Select an area of free space on a disk where you want to create the mirror. For example, in Figure 11.1, I want to mirror the C volume on Disk 0, so I have selected the free space on Disk 1 where I will create the mirror of C.
3. Click the Action menu, point to All Tasks, then click Create Volume.
4. The Create Volume wizard begins. Click Next on the welcome screen.

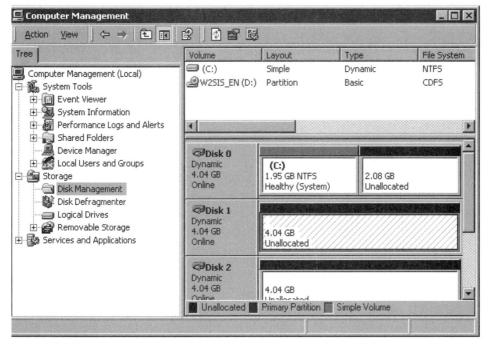

FIGURE 11.1 Select an area of free space on the disk where you want to create the mirror.

5. On the Select Volume Type window, click the Mirrored volume radio button, then click Next.

6. On the Select Disks window, shown in Figure 11.2, select the disk that will be mirrored in the right window, then click the Add button to move it to the selected window. The size for the mirror is selected for you, but you can change it if necessary. Click Next.

7. On the Assign Drive Letter or Path window, assign a desired drive letter for the mirrored volume, or mount the volume to an empty NTFS folder if desired (see Chapter 11 for details about mounting volumes). Click Next.

8. In the Format Volume window, shown in Figure 11.3, choose to format the volume, preferably with NTFS, select an allocation unit size if desired (you can use Default) and enter a desired label. You can also choose to use the quick format option and enable compression, both of which you can learn about in Chapter 17. Click Next.

9. Click Finish to complete the wizard. The mirror is created and now appears in the Disk Management Console. Notice that both sides of the mirror have the same drive letter, shown in Figure 11.4.

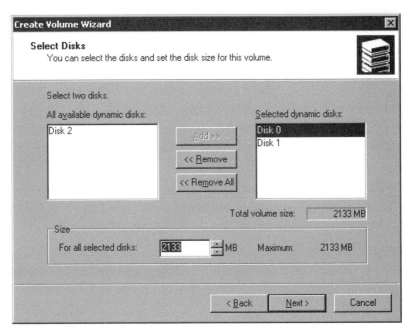

FIGURE 11.2 Select the desired disks and use the Add button.

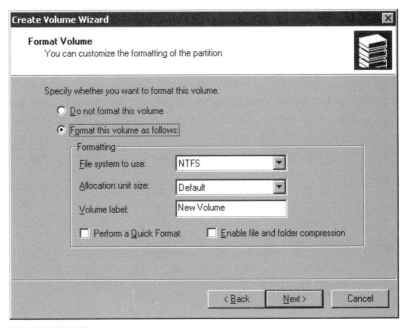

FIGURE 11.3 Format Volume Option

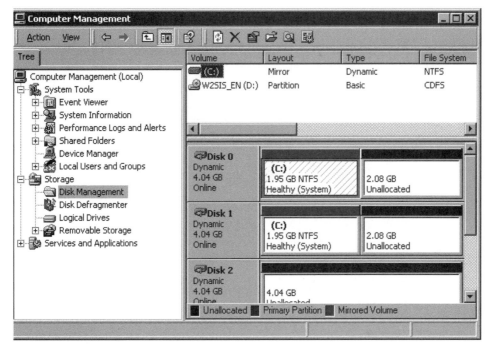

FIGURE 11.4   The mirrored volume now appears in the Disk Management console.

Aside from using the wizard steps to create a mirrored volume, you can also right-click on the volume you want to mirror and click Add Mirror. This action opens a single window, shown in Figure 11.5, that allows you to select a disk with free space where the mirror can be created. Select the desired disk, then click the Add Mirror button to create the mirrored volume.

Resynchronizing the Mirrored Volume

In most cases, you do not need to perform any actions to make certain the data on both the volume and mirrored volume are synchronized. Windows 2000 performs this task automatically on dynamic disks. However, if there has been a problem with a mirrored disk, such as its being offline or disconnected, then the data on the mirror becomes stale. This occurs because changes are still written to the primary volume, but they have not been written to the mirror. In this case, the data on the mirror is old and does not accurately reflect the data on the primary volume. You can easily resolve this problem by right-clicking on the mirrored volume in the Disk Management console and clicking Resynchronize Mirror. But as mentioned previously, this is normally not a task you need to perform on dynamic disks.

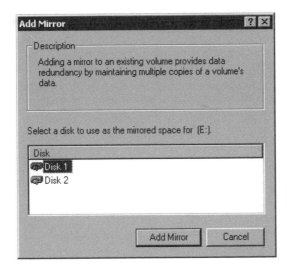

FIGURE 11.5

Select the desired disk on which you want to create the mirror.

Breaking a Mirror

There may come a time when you no longer want to use the mirrored volume you have created. In this case, you can choose to break the mirror so that the two volumes in the mirrored set simply become two independent volumes. This action, of course, removes any fault tolerance that exists. To break a mirror, right-click on the mirrored volume and click Break Mirror. Once the mirror is broken, you have two volumes with the same data, but as changes are made, the volumes are no longer synchronized and you cannot recover from one volume failure. A new drive letter is assigned to the mirrored volume and it is now an independent volume.

Removing a Mirror

When you break a mirror, the mirrored volume still exists and contains the files that were mirrored at the time the mirror was broken. You can also choose to remove a mirrored volume, which deletes the mirror and returns the mirrored disk to free space. Of course, you lose your mirror and the fault tolerance provided by it. To remove a mirror, right-click on the mirrored volume and click Remove Mirror.

Repairing a Mirrored Volume

Of course, the purpose of a mirrored volume is to copy data to a second drive so it can be used in the case of a disk failure. In Disk Management, when a mirrored volume's status is Failed Redundancy, the volume is no longer fault-tolerant. To avoid data loss, you must repair the volume and create a new mirrored volume. In this case, you can attempt to repair the disk that has failed by right-clicking on the missing or offline disk and clicking Reactivate Disk. If this does not work, you will probably need to replace the physical disk and reestablish the mirrored volume on the new disk or on another disk attached to your system. To perform this action, right-click on the existing mirrored volume and click Remove Mirror, then right-click on the volume you want to re-mirror and click Add Mirror. You can then recreate the mirrored volume.

Booting From a Mirror

Windows 2000 dynamic disk support allows you to repair and regenerate failed mirrored volumes without rebooting your system. However, if you need to reboot your system while your computer is running on a mirrored system and boot volume, then you will need to manually edit a file called `Boot.ini`. `Boot.ini` contains information your system uses to boot your computer. If your original system and boot volumes were located on your first hard disk (0), then when your system boots, it will look for the system and boot volumes on Disk 0. However, in the case of a failed volume, you are now using a mirror which exists on a different disk, such as Disk 1 or Disk 2, Disk 3, and so forth. In order for your system to know to look for the system and boot volumes on a different disk than Disk 0, you must edit `Boot.ini` so that it points to the correct hard disk.

`Boot.ini` is located in the root of the volume for the first hard disk, and is the file the computer reads to find the system and boot files. In order to boot from your mirror, you need to create a set of boot disks using the MAKEBOOT utility found on your Windows 2000 installation CD-ROM. Then, edit `boot.ini` so that it points to the correct disk number to locate the system and boot files. You can then open it with Notepad and edit and save the file. You should however, be cautious as incorrect entries can leave your system unbootable using the boot disks.

Configuring RAID-5 Volumes

RAID-5 volumes provide exceptional fault-tolerant performance with a lower cost than mirrored volumes, however, you cannot use RAID 5 on your system or boot volumes. Also, you cannot mirror or extend a RAID-5 volume. RAID-5 volumes require at least 3 physical disks and support up to 32 physical disks. As mentioned at the beginning of the chapter, RAID 5 writes data in a stripe while writing the parity information across the stripe. Data and its corresponding parity information are not stored on the same physical disk, so that in the event of a single disk failure, the data that existed on that disk can be regenerated using the parity information. Regenerating a failed RAID-5 disk does take more time than a mirrored volume, but that is a small price to pay to retrieve your data. The following sections show you how to configure and manage a RAID-5 volume.

Creating a RAID-5 Volume

To create a RAID-5 volume, you need at least 3 physical disks with equal amounts of free space on each. In other words, if you want to create a RAID-5 volume beginning with 500 MB of free space on one disk, then the other disks must have this amount of free space also. You can use up to 32 hard disks. To create the RAID-5 volume, follow these steps:

1. Open Disk Management within the Computer Management console located in your Administrative Tools folder.
2. Select the desired free space on one of the disks, click the Action menu, point to All Tasks, then click Create Volume.
3. Click Next on the Welcome screen.
4. In the Select Volume Type window, click the RAID-5 volume radio button, then click Next.
5. In the Select Disks window, select the desired disks in the left window, then use the Add button to move them to the selected disks window, as shown in Figure 11.6. You must use three disks. Adjust the size as desired using the Size dialog box, but remember that RAID-5 volumes must contain volumes of the same size. Click Next.

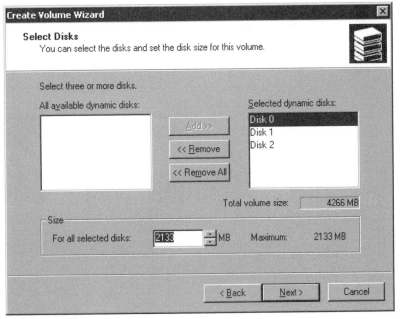

FIGURE 11.6   Use the Select Disks window to choose the disks for the RAID-5 volume.

6. In the Assign Drive Letter or Path, select a desired letter or mount the volume to an empty NTFS folder (see Chapter 11). Click Next.

7. Format the volume with the desired file system on the Format Volume window. Click Next.

8. Click Finish. The RAID-5 volume is created and now appears in the Disk Management console, shown in Figure 11.7.

Repairing a RAID-5 Volume

RAID 5 protects from a single hard disk failure. In the case of a hard disk failure, the data that was contained on the failed disk can be regenerated on a new disk with the parity bit. When a disk failure occurs, its status will read Failed Redundancy. You can attempt to reactivate the volume by right-clicking it and clicking Reactivate Volume. If you have to replace the disk, you can repair the volume (or use another existing disk) by right-clicking on the RAID-5 volume and clicking Repair volume. You will need another disk (or the new disk you have replaced) that has an appropriate amount of free space for regeneration to occur. Windows 2000 reads the parity information and regenerates the data on the new RAID-5 volume member. This process may take some time, depending on the size of the volume and the amount of data that must be regenerated.

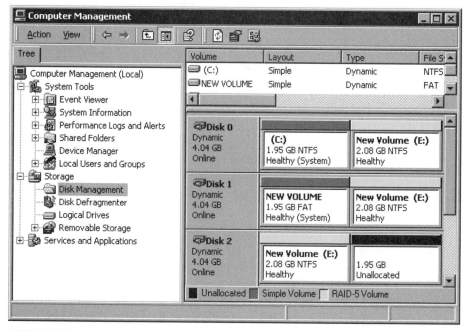

FIGURE 11.7   RAID-5 volume now appears in the console.

■ Summary

Windows 2000 supports mirrored volumes and RAID-5 volumes for fault tolerance. Mirrored volumes allow you to create a mirror of an existing volume which can be used in the case of a disk failure. Mirrored volumes can be used to mirror the system and boot volumes. RAID-5 volumes require at least 3 physical disks and provide fault tolerance for data by writing data in a stripe using parity information to achieve the fault tolerance. In the case of a single disk failure, the lost data can be regenerated with the parity bit. Both of these fault-tolerant solutions are an effective way to prevent data loss due to a failed hard disk.

Q&A

Review these questions and answers to resolve problems or check your knowledge of this chapter's content.

Q: *What is the difference between RAID 2 and RAID 3?*

A: RAID 2 and RAID 3 are fault-tolerant solutions that use an error checking (ECC) procedure to provide fault tolerance. Data is written in a stripe and the ECC is used to regenerate the data should a single disk failure occur. The difference between the two is that RAID 3 stores the ECC data as parity. Neither RAID 2 or 3 are supported in Windows 2000 because they do not provide the performance of RAID 5, which is supported.

Q: *What is the greatest disadvantage of disk mirroring?*

A: Disk mirroring provides an exceptional means of fault tolerance because an entire copy of a hard disk is mirrored, or maintained at all times. Should the primary disk fail, the mirror can take over. The disadvantage of mirrored volumes is the cost per megabyte of the mirror. Since an exact copy is maintained, you have a fifty percent cost. In other words, you are storing the exact same data on two different physical disks. Because of the mirror, you can only use half of your total disk space.

Q: *What are the disk requirements for a RAID-5 volume?*

A: In order to create a RAID-5 volume, you must have three physical disks (and you can have up to 32). Because data is written in a stripe, the free, unallocated space you use to create the RAID-5 volume must be equal size on each disk. In the case of a failure, the parity bit is used to reconstruct the data on the failed disk.

Windows 2000 Backup

A regular backup plan stores your data in a remote location, such as on tape or even Zip or CD-ROM drives. Backup is one of those things you may have a tendency to ignore until it is too late. With an effective back-up plan, you can restore data in the case of a system or disk failure. Depending on how critical your data is, your backup plan should be carefully thought out and implemented. Windows 2000 provides a Backup utility to help you configure backup jobs and make certain your data is protected. In this chapter, I examine how to backup data using the utility and explore the options available both in Windows 2000 Professional and Server.

Backup Options in Windows 2000

The purpose of backing up data and system information, such as the registry, is to restore that data should a system failure or data loss of some kind occur. If data is properly backed up on a regular basis, that data can be restored in its entirety regardless if the data is a single file or an entire disk. To make backup operations easy, Windows 2000 Server includes a backup tool called Windows Backup that is accessible from Start ➤ Programs ➤ Accessories ➤ System Tools ➤ Backup.

There is no one correct way to backup data. The goal is to be able to restore critical data at any given moment, so the type of backup you choose to use and the frequency of backup depends on your needs. You don't need to backup files that rarely change on a regular basis, but daily backup of constantly changing data is of utmost importance in order to restore the most current version of that data.

Windows 2000 allows you to choose your backup media such as tape backup and removable media such as Zip drives, CD-ROMs, or hard drives on remote computers.

Backup Types

Windows Backup provides five types of backup that enable you to manage and plan your backup sessions. If you have used backup in Windows NT, you will recognize these. The following list describes the five backup types:

- Normal—In a normal backup, all files and folders that you select are backed up. A normal backup does not use markers to determine which files have been backed up, and any existing markers are removed and the file is marked as having been backed up. This type of backup is the fastest to restore, but backup time can be slow depending on the amount of data.
- Copy—A copy backup is similar to a normal backup in that all files and folders selected are backed up. A copy backup does not look at markers and it does not clear existing markers. You can use the copy backup if you do not want the markers cleared, which may affect other backup types.
- Differential—In a differential backup, only selected files and folders that contain a marker are backed up. A differential backup does not clear the existing markers.
- Incremental—An incremental backup is like a differential backup in that it backs up selected files and folders with a marker, but an incremental backup clears the existing markers.
- Daily—In a daily backup, all selected files and folders that have changed during the day are backed up. A daily backup does not look at or clear markers, but this is an effective way to backup files and folders that have changed during the day.

Determining how to backup your files is an important planning step. The most effective solutions normally use a combination of backup types, and each design has its advantages and disadvantages. For example, you can use a normal and differential backup together. A normal backup can be performed on Monday and a differential backup performed on the following week days. If there is a failure on Saturday, only Monday's backup and Friday's backup are needed to reconstruct the data. This combination takes more time to backup but less time to restore. Or, you could use a normal and incremental backup in the same manner. In the case of a failure, each incremental backup would have to be restored since it clears the markers. This solution takes less time to backup, but more time to restore the data. The key question is to determine the speed of restoration you need should a failure occur. Typically, faster restoration solutions take more backup time on a daily basis.

Using Windows Backup

You can access Windows Backup by clicking Start ➤ Programs ➤ Accessories ➤ System Tools ➤ Backup. Windows Backup appears, as shown in Figure 12.1. As you may imagine, backup operations are dependent on user rights. If you are an administrator or a backup operator in a local group, you can backup any file or folder on the local server to which the group applies. If you are an administrator or backup operator on a domain controller, you can backup any file or folder in the domain if there is a two-way trust relationship, with the exception of System State data which can only be backed up on the local machine. For Windows 2000 Professional, you need to have an account with administrative rights for your machine.

System state data is a collection of system specific data on Windows 2000 computers. For all Windows 2000 operating systems, system state data includes the registry, COM+ class registration database, and the system boot files. For Windows 2000 Servers, system state also includes the certificate services database, if the server is a certificate server. For Windows 2000 domain controllers, system state also includes the Active Directory database and the SYSVOL folder.

The Welcome tab, as shown in Figure 12.1, gives you three button options; Backup Wizard, Restore Wizard, and Emergency Repair Disk. The following sections examine each of these options.

BACKUP WIZARD

You can use the Backup wizard to create a backup plan for your files and programs to protect them against a catastrophic failure. To use the Backup wizard, click the Backup Wizard button to begin the process and follow these steps:

1. After clicking the Backup Wizard button, the wizard begins. Click Next.
2. The second screen asks you what you want to backup. You have the following options, as shown in Figure 12.2.
   - Backup everything on my computer—This option backs up all files on the local machine except certain power management files that are not backed up by default.

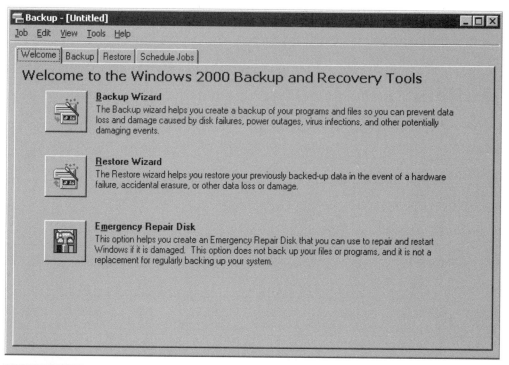

FIGURE 12.1 Windows Backup

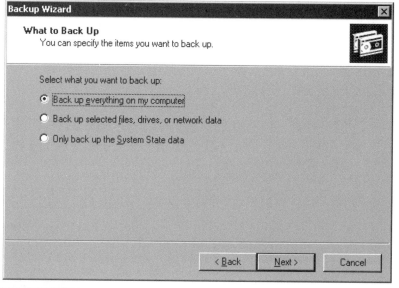

FIGURE 12.2 What to Backup Window

- Backup selected files, drives, or network data—This option backs up the files and programs you select. You can use this option to also backup any network shares or disks.

- Only backup the System State data—This option backs up the registry, COM+ class registration components, system boot files, and certificate server on the local computer (if the server is a certificate server). If the server is a domain controller, the Active Directory and the SYSVOL directory are also backed up. If you choose the system state data option, all of the data relevant is backed up—in other words, you cannot choose which components to backup. If are using certificate server, note that the certificate server service cannot be running or the backup operation will fail.

If you choose to backup everything on your computer or only backup system state data on your domain controller, you are taken to the Where to Store the Backup window, shown in Figure 12.3. If you choose to backup selected files, drives, and network data, you are taken to the Items to Back Up window, as shown in Figure 12.4. This Explorer-based window allows you to backup selected files or disks or even network data by using the checkboxes provided. By expanding My Network Places, you can choose any network drive or individual files as desired. Make your selections and click Next.

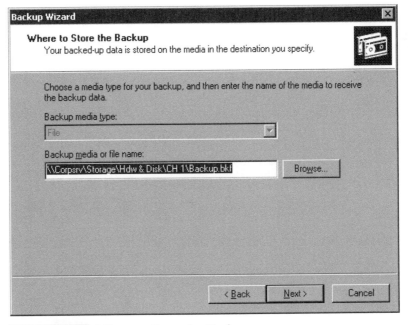

FIGURE 12.3 Where to Store the Backup

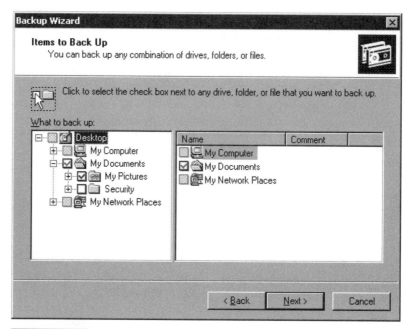

FIGURE 12.4 Items to Backup

3. In the Where to Store the Backup, as shown in Figure 12.3, use the Browse button to select your backup media, then click Next. You can backup your job to tape drives, removable media drives (such as Zip and CD-ROM), or to a network location.

4. The next window gives you a summary of the selections you made. If you click the Advanced button before clicking Finish, you can specify additional backup options, as shown in Figure 12.5.

5. In the Type of Backup window, you can select the type of backup you would like to perform. If you use the drop-down menu, you can select either normal, copy, incremental, differential, or daily backup. Make your selection and click Next.

6. The Next window presents you with two check boxes, one to verify data after backup and one to use hardware compression if available. Make your selections and click Next.

7. The next window, Media Options, allows you to select two radio buttons that tell Windows to append the backup to an existing backup on the media, or overwrite the old backup file with a new one. Make your selection and click Next.

8. The Backup Label window appears. On this page, you can accept the default labels or create your own. The default media name is media created on *date* at *time*. Click Next.

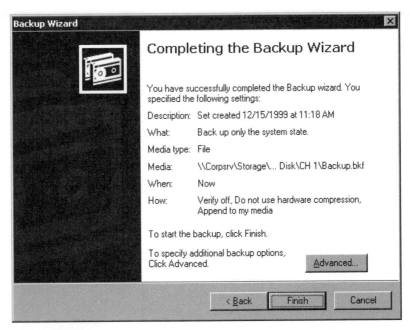

FIGURE 12.5   Click the Advanced button on the summary window.

9. The When to Backup window asks you when you want to run the backup. You can select the Now radio button or the Later button and specify a start date for the job. Click Next.

10. You return to the final summary page of the wizard. Review your selections and click Finish.

11. The Backup wizard estimates the size of the backup job and begins the backup job to the selected backup media. When the backup is complete, Windows Backup creates a summary file and directory information in a backup set catalog, which is stored on the backup media.

In addition to using the Backup wizard, you can also click the Backup tab in Windows Backup. This presents you with a selection screen where you can select drives, files, folders, and even network drives or files and start the backup process immediately without the wizard, as shown in Figure 12.6.

From this view, when you click the Start Backup button, you are given a condensed window of several options available in the wizard, as shown in Figure 12.7.

On the Information window, you can specify the label and append or replace the previous backup jobs. You can also click the Advanced button

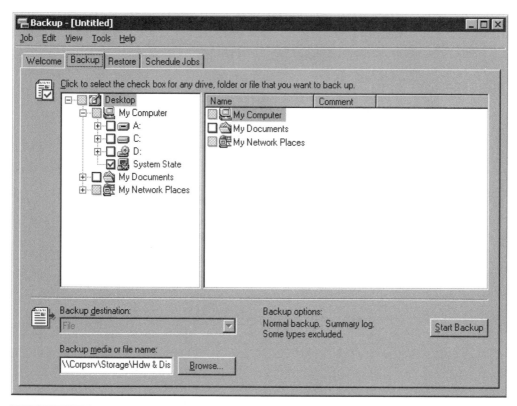

FIGURE 12.6   Backup tab

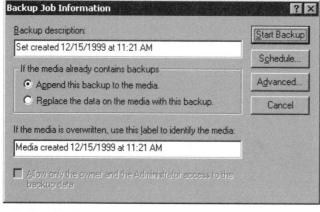

FIGURE 12.7   Backup Job Information

to select the type of backup you want to perform. If you click the Schedule button, you will be asked to first save the backup job and provide your administrator password to complete the action. Once you do this, you are taken to the schedule job window shown in Figure 12.8 where you can select the time and date you wish to perform the backup.

RESTORE WIZARD

Once you have completed a backup job, you can restore the backup by using the Restore wizard. You can restore data on either FAT or NTFS volumes, but if you have data backed up on an NTFS volume, you should restore it to an NTFS volume. If you restore it to a FAT volume, you could lose some data and you will lose certain features, such as access permissions, encrypting file system settings, disk quota information, mounted drive information, and possibly other information that is specific to NTFS.

Begin the Restore wizard by clicking on the Restore Wizard button on the Welcome tab, then follow these steps:

1. After clicking the Restore Wizard button, the wizard begins; click Next.

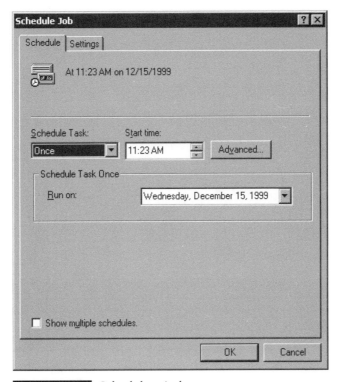

FIGURE 12.8 Schedule window

2. The What to Restore window appears, as shown in Figure 12.9. In the What to Restore pane, select the items you want to restore and click Next.

3. The summary window appears. If you click the Advanced button, you can specify additional actions for your restore operation. The first window asks you where you want to restore the files. By default, the original location is selected, but you can use the drop-down menu to select an alternative location or a single folder. Click Next.

4. The How to Restore window asks you if you would like to restore files that already exist. The default and recommended selection is to not replace the file from backup since the file still exists in the original location. This action prevents backup from replacing newer files with older files from the backup job. Click Next.

5. The Advanced Restore Options window appears. Here, you can choose to restore security, restore the Removable Storage Management database, or restore junction points instead of the folders and file data they represent. Make your selections and click Next.

6. You now return to the summary page. Review your selections and click Finish.

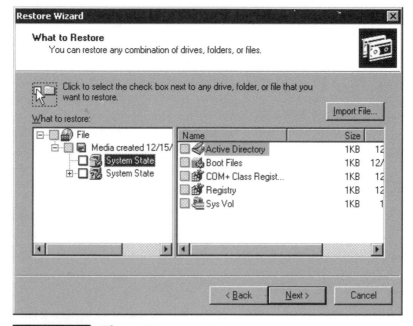

FIGURE 12.9   What to Restore option

7. You are asked to confirm the media path where the backup job resides, then click OK.

8. The restoration process begins.

As with the backup process, you can also access the Restore tab of Windows Backup. This is the same window as seen in the wizard so you can quickly select what job to restore. If you click the Start Restore button, you can access the Advanced options that are seen in the wizard, or you simply start the Restore process. Once you are comfortable with the restore process, you can use this tab instead of the wizard.

If you are restoring system state data on Windows 2000 domain controllers, you should be aware of a process called "authoritative restore." If you have more than one domain controller in your organization where your Active Directory is replicated to the other domain controllers, an authoritative restore ensures that your restored data is replicated to the other domain controllers. The authoritative restore updates the Active Directory sequence number so that the restored data does not appear as "old" to the other domain controllers. If this is the case, the data will not be replicated and the restored data will actually be updated with replicated data from other servers. The authoritative restore corrects this issue by updating the sequence number so the data is current. To use authoritative restore, you restore system state data in a usual restore operation, but you then need to run Ntdsutil available on the Windows 2000 Server CD-ROM so that the sequence numbers will be updated. You need to run this utility before you reboot your server.

EMERGENCY REPAIR DISK

You can also use the Windows Backup to create an Emergency Repair Disk (ERD). The ERD saves settings and files that can help you start Windows in the event of a failure. The ERD is not a replacement for a backup plan, and it does not protect your data in the event of a failure. You should keep a current ERD at all times—any time you make a system change, such as a new service pack, you should recreate the ERD so it is current. In order to create an ERD, you will need a one 1.44 MB floppy disk. To create the ERD, click the Emergency Repair Disk button on the Welcome tab. You are prompted to insert the blank floppy disk into your drive. After doing this, click OK. The ERD is created.

CHANGING DEFAULT BACKUP OPTIONS

Windows provides a number of default backup settings, which you can alter as needed using Windows Backup. If you access the Tools menu and select Options, you are given a window with several tabs, as shown in Figure 12.10. The following list tells you what options are available on each tab.

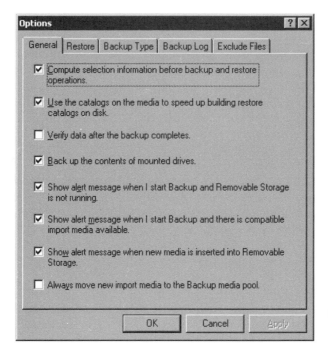

FIGURE 12.10

Backup Options

- General—On the General tab, you have several checkboxes which affect how Windows handles backup jobs and storage media:
    - Compute selection information before backup and restore operations—allows backup to determine the size of the backup operation.
    - Use the catalogs on the media to speed up building restore catalogs on disk.
    - Verify data after the backup completes.
    - Back up the contents of mounted drives.
    - Show alert message when I start Backup and Removable Storage is not running.
    - Show alert message when I start Backup and there is compatible import media available.
    - Show alert message when new media is inserted into Removable Storage.
    - Always move new import media to the Backup media pool.

- Restore—The Restore tab allows you to choose whether restoration should not replace a file that already exists on the computer, replace the file only if the file is older, or always replace the file.

- Backup Type—The Backup Type tab again allows you to choose either normal, copy, differential, incremental, or daily backup.
- Backup Log—The Backup Log tab allows you to select the type of backup log that is generated. By default, a Summary log is selected, but you can select a detailed log or no log at all.
- Exclude Files—The Exclude Files tab allows you to select files that are excluded from the backup process.

USING THE COMMAND LINE

You can use the command prompt to perform backup operations or you can use a batch file. This is accomplished using the ntbackup command. The ntbackup command syntax is listed below and an explanation of the parameters are listed in Table 12.1 for easy reference.

```
Ntbackup backup [systemstate] "bks file name" /J {job name}
/P {pool name} /G {GUID name} /T {tape name} /N {media
name} /F {file name} /D {set description} /DS {server name}
/IS {server name} /A /V {Yes or No} /R {yes or no}
/L:f|s|n /M {backup type} /RS {yes or no} /HC {on or off}
```

■ TABLE 12.1	NTBACKUP Command Line Parameters
Parameter	**Explanation**
systemstate	Specifies that you want to backup system state data.
bks file name	Specifies the name of the selection information file to be used.
/J	Job name. Specifies the name of the job to be used in the log file.
/P	Pool name. Specifies the media pool. You can learn more about media pools in Chapter 8.
/G	GUID name. Overwrites or appends to this tape. Do not use this with the /P parameter.
/T	Tape name. Overwrites or appends to this tape. Do not use this with the /P parameter.
/N	Media name. Specifies the new tape name. Do not use with the /A parameter.
/F	File name. The logical disk path and file name. Do not use with the /P, /G, or /T parameters.
/D	Set Description. Specifies a label for each backup set.
/DS	Server name. Backs up the Directory Service file for a specified exchange server.
/IS	Server Name. Backs up the Information Store file for a specified exchange server.
/A	Specifies an append operation which is used with either the /G or /T parameter. Do not use /A with /P.
/V	Yes or No. Verifies the data after the backup is complete.

/R	Yes or No. Restricts access to the tape to the owner or Administrators.
/L	f, s, or n. Specifies f for full, s for summary, or n for no log for the log file created.
/M	Backup type. Specifies the backup type (normal, copy, incremental, differential, or daily).
/RS	Yes or No. Backs up the removable storage database. You can learn more about removable storage in Chapter 8.
/HC	On or Off. Specifies whether or not to use hardware compression if it is available.

■ Summary

The Windows 2000 Backup utility provides you with an easy, flexible way to create and manage your backup jobs. With the Windows 2000 Backup utility, you can choose what data you want to backup, restore that data if necessary, and create an Emergency Repair Disk. An effective backup plan is very important to protect your data against catastrophic failure, and the backup utility allows you to easily configure and implement an effective plan.

Q&A

Review these questions and answers to resolve problems or check your knowledge of this chapter's content.

Q: *Which type of backup backs up selected files and folders with markers and clears the existing markers?*

A: An incremental backup backs up the selected files and folders with markers, and it clears the existing markers.

Q: *Which type of backup is the fastest to restore?*

A: A normal backup is the fastest backup to restore, but it takes the longest amount of time to backup.

Q: *What is the difference between system state data on member servers and domain controllers?*

A: System state data is a collection of system specific data on Windows 2000 computers. All Windows 2000 computers' system state data contains the registry, COM+ class registration database, and the system boot files. For Windows 2000 Servers, system state also includes the certificate services database, if the server is a certificate server. Finally, Windows 2000 domain controllers' system state data also includes the Active Directory database and the STSVOL folder.

Q: *Can a backup job be stored on a writeable CD?*

A: Yes. Windows 2000 allows you to use a number of media types, such as tape drives, CD drives, Zip drives, as well as other options.

Windows 2000 Disk Tools

If you have previously used Windows 98, the new tools available in Windows 2000 to help you manage your hard disk will not be anything new. If you have been using NT, you may think, "it's about time!" The disk tools included in Windows 2000 help you easily manage your system's hard disk(s), which in turn helps your disk(s) operate better. In this chapter, I show you what is available and how to use these tools.

Disk Cleanup

Over time, your hard disks can collect a lot of clutter. Disk Cleanup is a utility that scans your hard disks and looks for temporary files, Internet cached files, and old program files you can safely delete from your system. By occasionally running Disk Cleanup, you remove these old files so that more usable, free disk space exists on your system.

Cached files are temporary files held by your system. A common example is Internet files. As you browse the Internet, web pages and graphics are cached by your system so you can return to that Internet page and not have to completely download all of the page's content again. This speeds up your surfing, but does cause your disk to collect a lot of clutter. Disk Cleanup can remove these temporary files so you can use this disk space for other purposes.

You can access Disk Cleanup by clicking Start ➤ Programs ➤ Accessories ➤ System Tools ➤ Disk Cleanup, or you can access it on the General tab of any volume's properties sheets. When the Disk Cleanup utility opens, select the drive that you want to clean and click OK. Disk Cleanup scans your drive and calculates how much free space can be recovered by deleting old files, as shown in Figure 13.1.

Once the scanning is complete, a window appears showing you the different kinds of files that can be deleted and how much space can be regained after deleting those files, shown in Figure 13.2. Common categories include

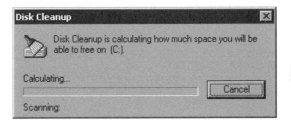

FIGURE 13.1

Disk Cleanup scans your disk or volume.

FIGURE 13.2

File Categories are displayed

downloaded program files, temporary internet files, files in your recycle bin, etc. You can click OK to remove the old files, or you can select a category and click the View Files button to see the files that will be removed.

You can also click the More Options tab, which allows you to scan your system for Windows components that are not in use and installed programs that you can remove in order to create more space. Once you determine which files or programs you want to delete, simply click OK and Disk Cleanup will remove those old files.

Error Checking

Error Checking is a tool that examines your hard disk for file system problems and bad sectors on your hard disk. When you run Error Checking, you have the option to automatically fix errors that are found. The Error Checking utility is a lot like Scandisk in Windows 98. You can access it from the Tools tab of a volume's properties sheets, shown in Figure 13.3.

Once you click the Check Now button, a Check Disk window appears with two check boxes so you can choose to automatically fix file system

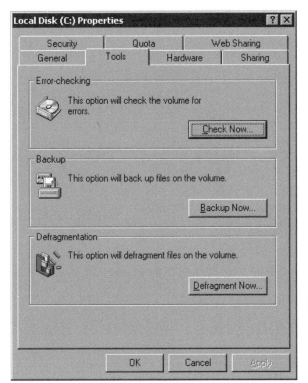

FIGURE 13.3

Access the error checking tool on the Tools tab of a volume's properties sheets.

FIGURE 13.4

Check Disk window

problems and to scan for and attempt recovery of bad sectors, shown in Figure 13.4. If you do not choose to automatically fix file system problems, you will be prompted to fix problems as Error Checking finds them. Also, if you do not choose to scan and attempt recovery of bad sectors, then only the file system on the volume is checked.

Error Checking needs exclusive access to the drive. If it cannot gain exclusive access to the drive, then a message appears asking if you want to schedule the task to run the next time you start your computer.

Disk Defragmenter

A Disk Defragmenter utility is included in Windows 2000, which is a utility you will need to run from time to time. Fragmentation on your drive occurs when data is saved to your disk in different locations. When data is saved, the disk is written in blocks of data. As your disk fills and you move, delete, and alter files, the files become fragmented. This means that pieces of the files are stored in different locations because there is not room to store them in one location. For example, let's say you write three Word documents. You save the first, then the second, then the third. The documents are saved to the disk one after another and in a contiguous format. Later, you edit the first document and resave it. The saved changes are now stored in a different location because there is no room to save the document in one place. When the system attempts to open the document, it has to read the data from these two locations. If your drive becomes severely fragmented, you may notice that your system is performing more slowly and files take longer to open.

The Disk Defragmenter utility rearranges data on your hard disk so that it is stored more contiguously so that performance is not hindered. Although some fragmentation is normal, you should run Disk Defragmenter on a regular basis, especially if a number of files have been moved, edited, or deleted. After I finish writing a book, I always run Disk Defragmenter on my computers to keep my hard disks in peak working order.

To run Disk Defragmenter, access it on the Tools tab of the volume's properties sheets for which you want to run the utility, or you can access by clicking Start ➤ Programs ➤ Accessories ➤ System Tools ➤ Disk Defragmenter. The utility provides a two-pane window where you can select the volume you want to defragment, and then choose to either analyze the volume or defragment the volume. You should always choose to first analyze the volume to see if it needs to be defragmented. Simply click the Analyze button so the utility can check your volume, as shown in Figure 13.5.

After the analysis is complete, the utility tells you whether or not you need to defragment your volume. You will notice that the analysis is displayed in different colors, with fragmented files appearing in red. This helps you visually examine the amount of fragmentation that exists on your hard disk. To defragment your drive, click the Defragment button. The utility then begins to rearrange data on your hard disks so that it is stored in a more contiguous format. Defragmentation can take some time, depending on the size of your volume and the amount of fragmentation.

Once the defragmentation is complete, you can view a report about the process by clicking View Report. The report gives you statistical infor-

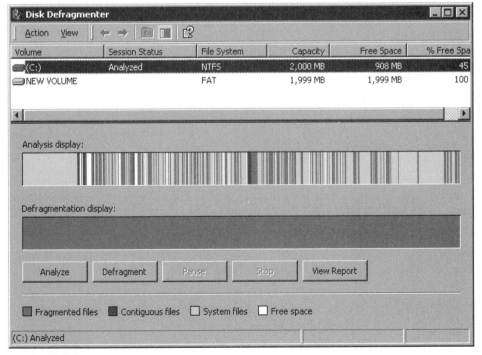

FIGURE 13.5 Disk Defragmenter allows you to select the desired volume and analyze it.

mation about the defragmentation job, the number of files that could not be defragmented and the overall usage and free space on your volume. An important aspect of the report you may want to examine is the average number of fragments per file, shown in Figure 13.6. This tells you how fragmented the files in the volume are. A reading of 1.0 is the best figure you can get, which tells you that nearly all files are contiguous. A reading of 1.10 tells you that about 10 percent of the files are fragmented, 1.20 is twenty percent, and so forth. A reading of 2.0 tells you that your files average two fragments each. Under normal circumstances, this reading is not something you have to worry about, but if you seem to be having excessive problems with fragmentation, this report can help you get information about your disk.

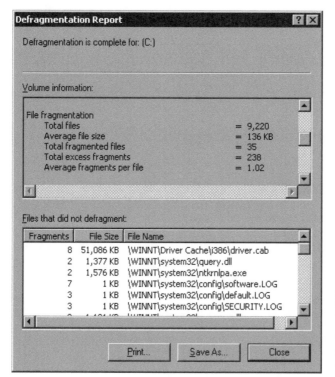

FIGURE 13.6

Use the report to examine the fragmentation on your volume.

Scheduled Tasks

Though not a disk utility per se, Scheduled Tasks is an effective way to schedule certain disk tools, such as Error Checking and Disk Defragmenter, to run automatically at certain times. This feature is particularly helpful for administrators that run Windows 2000 Servers. In order to keep disk mainte-nance utilities from interfering with the server's operation or performance, you can schedule the utilities to run at non-peak hours, such as late in the evening or at night. Also, by using Scheduled Tasks on either Professional or Server, you can set up the schedule one time, then never have to worry about manually running the utilities again.

You can access Scheduled Tasks by clicking Start ➤ Programs ➤ Accessories ➤ System Tools ➤ Scheduled Tasks. This action opens a folder, shown in Figure 13.7, which contains the Add Scheduled Task wizard.

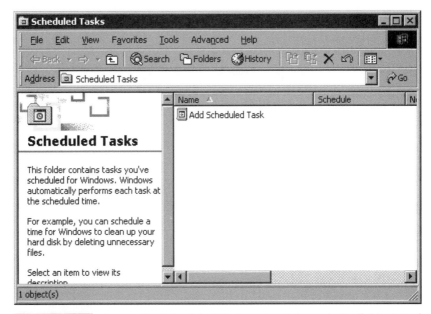

FIGURE 13.7 Access the Scheduled Tasks wizard through the folder interface.

Once you have created scheduled tasks, they will appear in this window as well. To create a scheduled task, follow these steps:

1. Double-click the Add Scheduled Tasks wizard, then click Next on the welcome screen.

2. In the provided window, select the tasks you would like to automatically run, shown in Figure 13.8. You can also use the Browse button to select another application if it does not appear in this window.

3. In the next window, enter a desired name for the task, then click the desired radio button to select when the tasks should run, such as daily, weekly, when your computer starts, etc. Make your selection and click Next.

4. Depending on your selection, a window appears where you can enter the starting time, day of the week, month etc. Make your selections, and click Next.

5. If you are connected to a network, enter your username, password, then confirm your password, then click Next.

6. Click Finish to complete the wizard. The task you have added now appears in the Scheduled Tasks folder.

FIGURE 13.8   Select desired tasks

Event Viewer

Event Viewer is a utility that records system events. Event Viewer records logs of different kinds of events that occur on your system so you can gather information about hardware, software, and system problems that occur. Event Viewer does not solve any problems; it simply reports the event to you so you can take further action. Event Viewer is particularly helpful when you are having some kind of system or hardware problem so you can examine events that are relevant to that problem. This will often help you solve problems that may be occurring. There are three basic kinds of logs that Windows 2000 records in Event Viewer:

- Application Log—The application log contains events logged by programs.
- Security Log—The security log contains valid and invalid logon attempts and other events that relate to the security of your system.
- System Log—The system log contains events logged by Windows 2000 System components. If a device driver fails to load, this kind of event would be recorded.

Concerning disk and hardware management, you can examine the system log to see if any problems are occurring, or if you suspect there is some kind of problem.

Event Viewer is available in your Administrative Tools folder in Control Panel, or you can access it directly from the Computer Management Console. Expand Event Viewer and select the log, such as System, that you want to view, as shown in Figure 13.9.

You can examine the types of events that have occurred, such as warning, error, or information, and you can see the source. For example, in Figure 13.9, there is an error generated by a disk. If you right-click on the desired error, warning, or information event and click Properties, you can read more about it. You are then presented with a Properties page listing the date and time of the event and a description of what happened. For example, in Figure 13.10, the device driver detected a controller error on Disk 2.

By using Event Viewer, you can gain helpful information about events occurring on your system, the causes of those events, and how to proceed with troubleshooting.

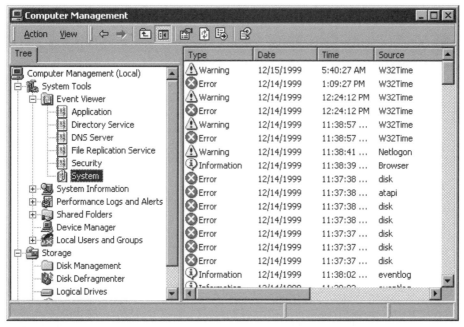

FIGURE 13.9   Access Event Viewer through Computer Management.

FIGURE 13.10

Error Properties

■ Summary

Windows 2000 provides several tools to help you manage your hard disks and keep them functioning in an appropriate manner. Disk Cleanup, Error Checking, and Disk Defragmenter are all used to resolve storage problems and file system errors. In addition to these tools, you can also schedule tasks to run by using the Task Scheduler, and Event Viewer provides a place where you can examine log files pertaining to events that occur on your system. All of these tools help you better manage your hard disks in Windows 2000.

Q&A

Q: *How do I know if my drive needs to be defragmented?*

A: Defragmentation is a good maintenance task you should perform from time to time. On heavily fragmented drives, you may notice that file reading takes longer than it should. In other words, the amount of time your system requires to read a file from the hard disk may be too long. This is a good indicator that your drive needs to be defragmented.

Q: *Does the removal of cached files help free up disk space?*

A: Yes. Cached files are temporary files, such as web page downloads, that your system collects over time. These cached files do take up hard disk space, and you can use Disk Cleanup to remove them from time to time.

Q: *I'm having problems with Error Checking not running or completing its operation. What is the problem?*

A: Error Checking needs exclusive access to the drive. Most likely, some other utility or application is using the drive as well. You can schedule Error Checking to run when you restart your computer in order to avoid this problem.

Q: *I would like to see events that are logged by certain applications. Where can I view this information?*

A: Check the Application log in Event Viewer—it logs events created by programs.

Q: *I want to see if there have been any invalid logon attempts to my computer. Where can I get this information?*

A: Check the Security log in Event Viewer. The Security log contains valid and invalid logon attempts and other events related to the security of your system.

Troubleshooting Disk Problems

As with any operating system component, you may experience some problems with your hard disks and hard disk configuration in Windows 2000.Typically, disk problems are either going to be caused by hardware problems or configuration problems. In this chapter, I explore troubleshooting information for the disk configuration options explored in Part 2 of the book.

Troubleshooting Specific Disk Problems

As with all hardware devices in Windows 2000, you can use Device Manager to access the properties sheets of the hardware device. You can access your hard disk's properties sheets, then use the Troubleshooter feature found on the General tab, shown in Figure 14.1.

The Troubleshooter button opens the Windows 2000 Help files that guide you through a series of questions to attempt to help you solve the problem you are experiencing with the hard disk. You can use the troubleshooter to walk through the steps, and the following sections also point out the problems and solutions you may encounter when using the troubleshooter to attempt to solve hard disk problems.

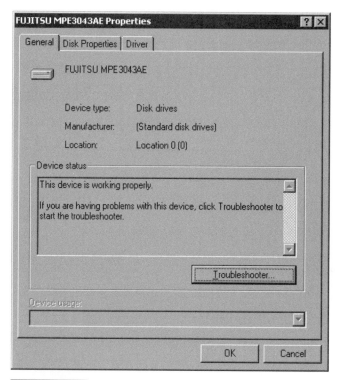

FIGURE 14.1 Click the Troubleshooter button to access Windows 2000 Help.

Problems with a SCSI Hard Disk

If you are using a SCSI hard disk with multiple devices connected to a single adapter in your computer, then there may be a problem with either the SCSI adapter or the chain of devices connected to the SCSI adapter. When several devices are in use, one device can conflict with another device in the SCSI chain. First, check to see if the SCSI chain is terminated. Each SCSI device has two connections—one that connects to the computer and one that allows you to connect to another device in the chain. The last device in the SCSI chain needs to have a terminator plugged into the second SCSI connection. Even if your hard disk is the only SCSI device, it still needs a terminator.

If the terminator is present, then check to see if there is a power problem with the SCSI adapter or chain. Some SCSI adapters and chains need power from an external source in order to communicate with the computer. If this is the case, make certain the adapter or chain is plugged in and has power. Check to see if other devices in the chain are working or not.

Next, check the SCSI ID number. Each device in a SCSI chain has a unique ID number between 0 and 7. Two devices cannot share the same ID, so check to make certain there are no SCSI ID conflicts between devices.

Check for Access to the Boot Partition

If you remove access for the Everyone group to your boot partition or volume, no one can log onto the computer. If this is happening, you will need to restore access to the boot partition.

Tape Devices and Floppy Disk Drive

Some tape backup devices use the same hardware resources as the floppy disk drive. If this is the case, you cannot use the floppy disk drive when the tape drive is running.

Using More than Two IDE or ESDI Devices

By default, PC computers can directly recognize only two IDE or ESDI devices. If you want to use more than two IDE or ESDI devices, you can possibly do so by editing the registry. This is a complicated procedure and should be performed only by a service center or authorized personnel.

Test the Drive on Another Computer

If you still cannot get the hard drive to work, test the drive on another computer to see if it works. If it doesn't, the problem is most likely with the drive itself. In that case, you should contact the manufacturer of the drive for assistance.

Check the Drivers

As with all hardware devices, problems with hard disks can occur due to problem drivers. If you are having a problem with a particular hard disk, access the properties sheets for the disk and click the Driver tab (Figure 14.2). You can update the driver from this tab or click Driver Details to learn more about the driver currently installed.

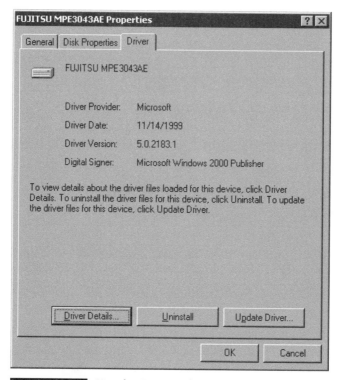

FIGURE 14.2 Use the Driver tab to update and examine driver information.

General Troubleshooting

Aside from specific problems with a hard drive failure, you may experience some problems with configuration. The following problems and solutions point out some of the most common problems and the solutions to those problems.

PROBLEM: Several disk management options are not available for a particular volume.

SOLUTION: The volume is probably formatted with FAT or FAT32. While Windows 2000 supports FAT and FAT32 volumes, you do not have as many management features as you do with NTFS. Consider converting your volumes to NTFS for the best performance, security, and management options in Windows 2000.

PROBLEM: Disk configuration from Windows NT cannot be managed in Windows 2000.

SOLUTION: When you upgrade a Windows NT computer with Windows 2000, you have limited management capabilities with the basic disks. You need to upgrade the disk(s) to dynamic in order to take advantage of the full range of management features in Windows 2000.

PROBLEM: Spanned volumes, striped volumes, mirrored volumes, or RAID-5 volumes cannot be created.

SOLUTION: There are two possible causes of this problem. First, your disks are not dynamic. You cannot create these disk solutions on basic disks. Upgrade your disks to dynamic, then establish the desired disk configuration. The second problem is that you do not have the proper number of hard disks to accomplish the desired configuration. For spanned volumes, striped volumes, and mirrored volumes, you must have at least two physical disks. For RAID-5 volumes, you must have at least three physical disks.

PROBLEM: A disk's status is online (errors).

SOLUTION: When a disk's status is online (errors), this tells you that the disk is available, but I/O errors have been detected. Use the Reactivate Disk command to fix the errors, and you may also want to run ScanDisk to make certain all errors have been corrected.

PROBLEM: A disk's status is offline or missing.

SOLUTION: An offline or missing status message tells you that the disk is not available. This can be caused by corruption or the disk has become disconnected from the computer. Check the disk and make certain it is available. Repair any controller or cable problems, then use the Reactivate Disk option to attempt to bring the disk back online.

PROBLEM: A disk's status is displayed as foreign.

SOLUTION: If a disk is displayed as foreign, the disk has been imported from a different Windows 2000 computer and is not set up to be used on your computer. Right-click the disk and click Import Foreign Disk so Windows 2000 can use the disk on your computer. Only dynamic disks are displayed as foreign.

PROBLEM: A disk's status is displayed as unreadable.

SOLUTION: If a disk is displayed as unreadable, the disk is not available or I/O errors have occurred. In this case, use the Rescan Disk command to attempt to bring the disk back online. Also, this problem can sometimes be corrected by simply rebooting your computer.

PROBLEM: A disk's status is displayed as unrecognized.

SOLUTION: If a disk's status is displayed as unrecognized, then the original equipment manufacturer's (OEM) signature and Disk Management will not allow you to use the disk. This problem occurs if a disk is used that is designed for another system, such as UNIX. You cannot use this disk with Windows 2000.

PROBLEM: A mirrored volume's status is failed redundancy.

SOLUTION: If a mirrored volume's status is failed redundancy, then one or both of the mirrored volume's members have failed and the volume is no longer fault-tolerant. In this case, you need to break the mirrored volume, replace or reactivate the failed disk, and reestablish the mirrored volume so that the volume is fault-tolerant.

PROBLEM: A RAID-5 volume's status is failed redundancy.

SOLUTION: One of the RAID-5 members in the RAID-5 volume has failed and the volume is no longer fault-tolerant. Replace the failed disk and regenerate the lost data using the Disk Management console.

■ Summary

Troubleshooting Windows 2000 hard disks and disk configuration does not have to be a painful experience. For most problems that you may encounter, begin by looking at the problem logically and try to determine the most likely causes. Also, you can use other tools, such as System Information and Windows 2000 Troubleshooters to help you resolve most problems you may encounter.

Windows 2000 Storage Features

In This Part

▶ **CHAPTER 15**
Remote Storage

▶ **CHAPTER 16**
Removable Storage

▶ **CHAPTER 17**
Additional Storage
Technologies

▶ **CHAPTER 18**
Distributed File
System

▶ **CHAPTER 19**
Troubleshooting
Windows 2000
Storage

Aside from the powerful features of Windows 2000 dynamic disks, Windows 2000 also provides a number of new features to help you manage data storage. The features explored in this section are all new to Windows operating systems, and as you read, you will find they are all beneficial. The following chapters are contained in this part:

Chapter 15: Remote Storage
Chapter 16: Removable Storage
Chapter 17: Additional Storage Technologies
Chapter 18: Distributed File System
Chapter 19: Troubleshooting Windows 2000 Storage

Remote Storage

The amount of data stored by network servers can seem overwhelming. Even with the large hard drives available today, many servers quickly become overloaded with files so that a limited amount of disk space is available. Windows 2000 Server introduces a new feature that allows your system to automatically move files from your local NTFS volumes to a remote tape library. These files are not only stored in the tape library, but are also still available to your system, as though the files were directly stored on the local volume. In this chapter, you learn about remote storage, which works in conjunction with removable storage, which you can learn about in Chapter 17.

Remote Storage Concepts

Remote storage, which is supported only in Windows 2000 Server, works by moving eligible files from the server's hard disk volumes to a remote storage location. When the space on your local, or managed, volume falls under the level you specify, Remote Storage automatically removes the content from the original file (which you select) and moves it to the remote storage location. The file still appears on the server's local drive, but the file size is zero since the file actually resides in a remote location. When the file is needed,

Remote Storage recalls the file and caches it locally so the file can be accessed. Since response time is slightly slower than if the file was actually stored on the local volume, you specify the files that should be stored remotely so the most commonly used files remain on the local volume. Remote Storage uses tape libraries only, and supports any 4mm, 8mm, or DLT tape library. In order to use Remote Storage, you must have a tape drive attached to your computer that supports 4mm, 8mm, or DLT tape. Microsoft does not recommend that you use Remote Storage with Exabyte 8200 tape libraries. Additionally, QIC tape libraries and optical disc libraries are not supported.

There are two levels of Remote Storage. The first is the upper level, which is called local storage. The local storage is the NTFS disk volumes on Windows 2000 Server that run Remote Storage. The second level, which is the lower level called remote storage, is the robotic tape library or stand-alone tape drive that is connected to the server computer.

Remote Storage works with Removable Storage, which you can learn about in Chapter 17. In addition to the ability to remotely store data, you can also use Remote Storage to generate multiple copies of data in remote storage locations, which extends Windows 2000 Server's fault-tolerance features.

Before you can use Remote Storage, you must install it and make certain that you have enough tapes in a "free media pool" using Removable Storage (see Chapter 17). Once this is accomplished, you then follow these steps:

1. Determine which local disk volumes you want Remote Storage to manage. You then define the amount of free space you want maintained on the volumes and determine the file selection criteria for copying files to remote storage as well as the kind of tape that will be used.

2. Remote Storage then copies files that meet the criteria you have specified to the tape. The original data is cached on the local volume.

3. Remote Storage then compares the amount of available space on the managed volume. If the actual free space is less than the desired amount, Remote Storage moves the data on the local volume into the tape library. The file still appears on your local volume, but its file size becomes zero. This process continues until the free space on the volume has been met.

4. When you access a file that has been placed into remote storage, the data is recalled from the remote storage location and copied back to your local volume.

It is important to keep in mind that you specify which volumes you want Remote Storage to manage, and that those volumes must be formatted with NTFS. Remote Storage cannot manage volumes formatted with FAT or FAT32.

How Remote Storage Works with Removable Storage

Remote Storage uses Removable Storage to access the tapes in a library. You can use Remote Storage to support multiple-drive robotic libraries if all of the drives within the library are identical. This feature allows Remote Storage to access two drives at the same time, which allows it to copy data to and read data from two drives at the same time on different tapes. All remote storage tapes exist in a single "application media pool," which is automatically created when you set up Remote Storage. You use Removable Storage to verify that you have a sufficient amount of media in a free media pool so that Removable Storage can use the tapes from that pool. Tapes used by Remote Storage contain only data that has been copied from managed volumes, which you specify. The tape library, however, can contain additional media, such as backup files, that has been created by other applications. Remote Storage does not support recalling data for a volume that has been managed at different times by two different Remote Storage installations.

Setting Up and Using Remote Storage

Remote Storage is not installed on your Windows 2000 Server by default, but you can specify that it be set up during installation. If this has not been done, you can install Remote Storage by completing the following steps. Before you perform the steps, you must be logged on as an administrator, there must be remote storage media available in a free media pool (see the Removable Storage section for more information), and you must format volumes managed by Remote Storage with the Windows 2000 version of NTFS.

1. Click Start ➤ Settings ➤ Control Panel. Double-click Add/Remove Programs.
2. In Add/Remove Programs, click Add/Remove Windows Components. The Windows Components wizard begins. Click Next.
3. Select the Remote Storage check box and click Next, as shown in Figure 15.1. Windows copies the files and installs Remote Storage. Click Finish and reboot your computer.
4. When your computer reboots, log on with an account that has administrative privileges, then click Start ➤ Programs ➤ Administrative Tools ➤ Remote Storage.
5. The Remote Storage Setup wizard begins, shown in Figure 15.2. Click Next.
6. Setup checks for logon security privileges and a supported media device.

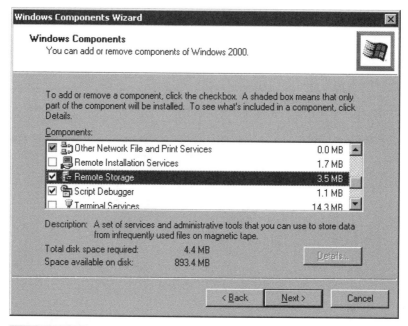

FIGURE 15.1 Select Remote Storage and click Next.

FIGURE 15.2 Click Next to begin Remote Storage Setup.

7. Select the device you want to use for remote storage, then complete the steps in the wizard.

Once you have set up Remote Storage, you can manage it within the Remote Storage snap-in, which includes both Remote and Removable Storage. As explained in the wizard, you cannot manage the System volume, but you did specify which volumes Remote Storage manages during setup. At this point, Remote Storage can manage these volumes by copying selected files to remote storage while leaving the original files cached on your local volumes. You can automatically copy files with the schedule you provide or you can do this manually as needed. In the following sections, I show you the tasks you can perform with Remote Storage and how to perform those tasks on your server.

Volume Management

In order to effectively use Remote Storage, you will have to make some decisions about how you want Remote Storage to function. The first thing you need to decide is the parameters you want Remote Storage to use when determining which files should be moved to remote storage and which should be left on the local volume. You can specify the following criteria so Remote storage can determine which files to store:

- Minimum file size.
- Elapsed time since the file was last accessed.
- Exclude or include files based on a specified folder and subfolders, file type, file name, or wildcard characters.

Remote Storage gives you a set list of file inclusion and exclusion rules which cannot be changed, but you can create, remove, or edit your own rules. In the following sections, I show you how to configure various file selection parameters.

BASIC FILE SELECTION

To change the file size and file time parameters, follow these steps:

1. Right-click on the volume you want to manage and click Settings.
2. On the Settings tab, under File Criteria in Larger Than, click the Up or Down arrow to adjust the file size value.
3. Under File Criteria in Not Accessed In, click the Up or Down arrow to change the time value.

ADDING A FILE RULE

You can add your own file rules by following these steps:

1. Right-click the appropriate volume and click Include/Exclude Rules.
2. On the Include/Exclude tab, click Add.
3. In Path box, type the full path to the file.
4. In File Type, type the file name extension.
5. To exclude files when the rule is applied, click Exclude Matching Files, or to include files when the rule is applied, click Include matching files.
6. You can also apply the rule to any files stored in subfolders by clicking the Apply Rule to Subfolders check box.

CHANGING OR DELETING A FILE RULE

You can easily change or delete a file rule by following these steps:

1. Right-click the appropriate volume and click Include/Exclude Rules.
2. To edit a rule, click the rule you want to edit and click Edit, then change the settings and click OK.
3. You can delete a rule, select the rule and click Remove, then click OK.

CHANGING THE PRIORITY OF FILE RULES

To change the priority of file rules, follow these steps:

1. Right-click the applicable volume, then click Include/Exclude Rules.
2. On the Include/Exclude tab, select the applicable rule.
3. Click the Up or Down arrow to adjust the rule priority.

ADDING OR REMOVING VOLUMES FOR MANAGEMENT

Aside from creating and editing rules and rule management, you may also need to add new volumes that you would like Remote Storage to manage from time to time. This is an easy task and one that you can perform at any time after you run the Remote Storage Setup wizard. Remember that you may need to adjust the file criteria and rules for that volume. To add the new volume, double-click Remote Storage in the console tree and right-click Managed Volumes. Point to New, then click Managed Volumes. Follow the instructions that appear in the Add Volume wizard.

You can also remove volumes from Remote Storage management as needed. In this case, you have the option of either keeping the remote files in storage or allowing Remote Storage to recall them as necessary. Remote Storage simply does not continue to manage the volume and remove files to remote storage any longer. Or, you can have all the volume's data in Remote Storage moved back to the volume. To perform this action, right-click the appropriate volume and click Remove. Follow the wizard's instructions to determine what Remote Storage should do with the stored volume files.

SETTING FREE SPACE

You determine how you want Remote Storage to respond to storage conditions of the volume. Once the volume drops below an amount of free space that you specify, Remote Storage automatically begins deleting cached data from files that have already been copied to remote storage. This way, Remote Storage can manage the volume by keeping the amount of free space desired available. You can adjust the free space setting on a volume by right-clicking the applicable volume and clicking Settings. Then, on the Settings tab in Desired Free Space, click the Up or Down arrow to increase or decrease the free space value. You can also create free space immediately if it is needed. This action tells Remote Storage to remove all cached data from the volume, which creates immediate free space. To perform this, right-click the applicable volume, click Tasks, then click Create Free Space.

SETTING THE RUNAWAY RECALL LIMIT

The runaway recall limit is the maximum number of successive file-recalls a user can make on a file during the same session. Once a user makes a file recall, if the user requests another recall within 10 seconds, the count is increased. This causes the file to be copied back to the managed volume and moved out of remote storage. The runaway recall limit stops this from occurring by limiting the number of successive recalls a user can make with less than 10 seconds between each recall. Therefore, the file remains in remote storage but is still accessible. To set the runaway recall limit, follow these steps:

1. Right-click Remote Storage in the console tree and click Properties.
2. On the Recall Limit tab, change the value in Maximum Number of Successive Recalls by clicking the Up or Down arrows.
3. To exclude users with administrative permissions from the limit, click the Exempt administrators from this limit check box.

SETTING VALIDATION

Validation in Remote Storage means that the data stored in the remote storage media correctly points to the correct file on the managed volume. Validation is automatically performed two hours after a backup program is used to restore a file, and validation can also detect if a file has moved from one volume to another. Validation should be performed on a regular basis, and one of the easiest ways to do this is to use validation with Windows 2000 Scheduled Tasks. To manually validate a volume, right-click the appropriate volume, point to All Tasks, and then click Validate Files.

CHANGING THE FILE COPY SCHEDULE

You can change Remote Storage's default schedule used to copy files which was initially created during setup. To change the schedule, follow these steps:

1. In the console tree, right-click Remote Storage and click Change Schedule.

2. In the Remote Storage File Copy Schedule dialog box, click the arrow in Schedule Task, and click an interval.

3. In Start time, set the start time using the Up or Down arrows.

4. In Schedule Tasks Daily change the value in Every by clicking the Up or Down arrow.

In a case where you need to copy files without waiting for the scheduled time, right-click the appropriate volume and click Copy Files to Remote Storage.

Managing Media

In addition to setting up and managing Remote Storage so it meets your needs, you may need to take a few actions concerning the management of the Remote Storage Media. Remote Storage supports all SCSI class 4mm, 8mm, and DLT tape libraries. All libraries used by Remote Storage exist in a single media application pool which is created during Remote Storage setup. This media is used for all storage procedures.

For fault tolerance, you should consider creating copies of the media so that your stored files can be recalled should there be a problem with the media master set. Remote Storage can automatically create copies of the media master set, called media copy sets, so you have redundant copies at all times. This process can only occur if there are two or more drives in the tape library—one functions as the media master while the other functions as the media copy. You can also use additional drives to create additional copies if desired. To adjust the number of media copies you would like to create, right-click Remote Storage and click Properties. On the Media Copies tab, adjust the Number of Media Copy Sets value by using the Up or Down arrow. In the case of a failure or corruption with the media master, the data can be recreated using a media copy. To recreate the media master, right-click on Remote Storage and click Media. In the details pane, right-click one of the media shown and click Properties. Click the Recovery tab and click Re-create Master. Follow the wizard that appears.

Finally, if you are using a media master and media copy sets, synchronization of the two should be performed regularly so the copy always accurately reflects the master. To synchronize the media copies, right-click Media in the console tree and click Synchronize Copies Now. Follow the wizard that appears.

■ Summary

Removable Storage is a powerful feature of Windows 2000 Server that allows you to manage your NTFS volumes so that selected files can be automatically moved to a tape library for storage, thus maintaining a desired level of free space on your local volumes. With remote storage, which functions with Removable storage, you can devise an effective plan to manage your data and maintain your local hard disks. You can learn more about removable storage in the next chapter.

Q&A

Review these questions and answers to resolve problems and to check your knowledge of this chapter's content.

Q: *Does Remote Storage support devices such as Zip or Jazz drives?*

A: Zip and Jazz drives, along with writeable CD-ROMs and other such devices are supported as a part of Removable Storage, but are not supported with Remote Storage. Remote Storage uses only tape libraries.

Q: *What kinds of tape drives are supported for use with Remote Storage?*

A: Remote storage can use any 4mm, 8mm, or DLT tape library. Microsoft does not recommend that you use Remote Storage with Exabyte 8200 tape libraries. Additionally, the use of QIC Tape libraries and optical disc libraries is not supported in Remote Storage.

Q: *I would like to manage a FAT volume with Remote Storage, but cannot seem to do so. What is the problem?*

A: Remote Storage can only be used with volumes formatted with Windows 2000 NTFS.

Q: *What permissions do I need to be able to configure and use Remote Storage?*

A: You must have administrative privileges to install and configure Remote Storage.

Removable Storage

With the use of Zip drives, writeable CD-ROM drives, and other types of removable media, Windows 2000 Server provides a way for the operating system to manage your removable media and drives. This system, known as Removable Storage, allows Windows 2000 to automatically track and label your removable media and the data contained on it. Removable Storage is used as an individual component, or in conjunction with Remote Storage or Windows 2000 Backup. In this chapter, you learn about Removable Storage and how to use it on your Windows 2000 system.

Understanding Removable Storage

Removable Storage allows you to extend your local volumes by using removable storage media to store information. Removable Storage Manager handles this process and keeps track of the location of data stored on removable media, such as CD-ROMs, digital audio tape (DAT), Zip disks, and DVD. Removable Storage is designed to work with other Windows 2000 features, such as Remote Storage and Windows Backup. With Removable Storage, the operating system can automatically label, catalog, and track media, and control library drives. Removable Storage also provides automatic drive-cleaning operations.

Removable Storage organizes data in libraries so it can track the storage location of individual files. There are two major types of libraries. The first is robotic libraries, often called changers or jukeboxes, that hold multiple tapes or disks and can automatically switch between tapes and disks as needed. For example, a ten-CD stereo player can automatically mount the various CDs loaded to the CD drive. The second type is stand-alone libraries, which are single drives that hold one tape or disk at a time and must be manually changed by the administrator. Removable Storage can also manage and track offline media that is not currently contained in a library. For example, you could store some of the disks or tapes in a file folder until they are needed. Even though the disks or tapes are not currently available, Removable Storage is aware of them and still considers them a part of the storage library.

Understanding Media Pools

A media pool is a collection of media, such as tapes or disks, that contain the same properties. For example, writeable CD-ROMs would belong to one media pool while DAT tapes would belong to another. This design allows you to configure properties that apply to a group of media. A media pool can span a number of libraries, and you can even create media pools that are designed to hold other media pools. This structure allows you to design your media pools as best fits your organization.

There are two major classes of media pools, system and application. System media pools include unrecognized media pools, or blank media; import media pools, which is media Remote Storage recognizes, but has not been used in the system; and free media pools, which contain media that is not currently used by applications. Application media pools contain media created by applications and are controlled by those applications (or an administrator). A typical example is Backup. Windows Backup may use one media pool for full backup storage and another for differential backup storage. Unrecognizable media must be moved into free media pools before it can be used, and Import media pools can be used once they are catalogued.

Removable Storage classifies media in one of two ways—either as physical media, which is an actual storage media such as a tape or a disk, or as logical media. Logical media refers to media that has more than one side, such as double-sided CD-ROM. Removable Storage sees each side as a separate medium, and each side can belong to a different media pool, as needed.

Understanding Media States

Media states define the status of each tape or disk within the Removable Storage system as to whether the media is working or not. Media states are broken into two categories, physical states and side states. The physical states show the operational condition of the media, such as idle, in-use, loaded, mounted, and unloaded. The side states show the usage of the tape or disk instead of its current physical state. For example, a side state can be listed as allocated, available, completed, imported, reserved, etc.

Using Removable Storage

As mentioned earlier in the chapter, Removable Storage allows you to store data on removable disks such as Zip disks and CD-ROMs. Removable Storage can use jukeboxes or individual media drives, which can be grouped together in media pools. Removable storage functions by configuring libraries to keep track of the location where data is stored. Even if, for example, a Zip disk is removed and put in another physical location, the library is still aware of that disk and data on it. When you install Remote Storage (see Chapter 15), Removable Storage is installed as well, and both Remote and Removable Storage are managed from the same MMC snap-in, Remote Storage, which is available in Administrative Tools and shown in Figure 16.1.

Configuring and Managing Libraries

Removable Storage automatically configures all libraries whenever you add or remove a library, but Removable Storage allows you complete control over library management. The following sections show you how to manage and configure these options.

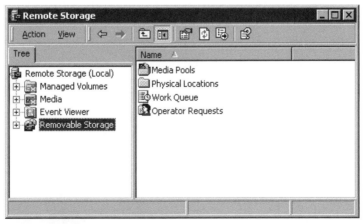

FIGURE 16.1   Remote and Removable Storage MMC snap-in.

ENABLING OR DISABLING A LIBRARY OR DRIVE

You can easily enable or disable a library by following these steps:

1. Expand Removable Storage in the Remote Storage Management Console.

2. In the Console Tree, double-click Physical Locations.

3. Right-click the library you want to enable or disable and click Properties.

4. On the General tab of the Properties sheet, click the Enable Library check box to enable it or clear the box to disable it, as shown in Figure 16.2.

To enable or disable a drive, follow these steps:

1. Expand Removable Storage, expand Physical Locations, expand the library you want to enable or disable, and select Drives.

2. In the details pane, right-click the drive and click Properties, as shown in Figure 16.3.

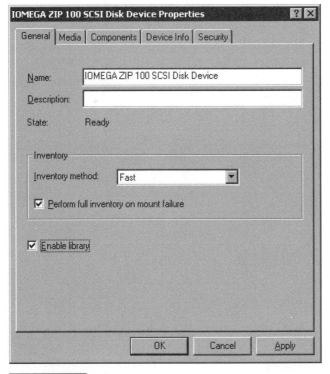

FIGURE 16.2 Library properties

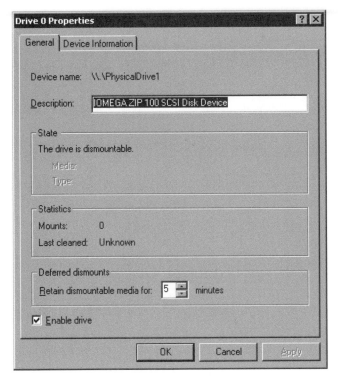

FIGURE 16.3

Drive properties

3. On the General tab, click the Enable Drive check box to enable the drive, or clear it to disable the drive.

CHANGING MEDIA TYPES

To change a media type, follow these steps:

1. Double-click Physical Locations.
2. Right-click the library you want to change and click Properties.
3. Click the Media tab and click Change.
4. In the Change Media Types dialog box, you can add a new media type by selecting the entry in Available types and clicking Add, or you can remove an existing media by clicking Remove in Selected types, as shown in Figure 16.4.

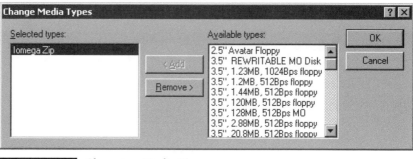

FIGURE 16.4   Changing Media Types

CREATING A LIBRARY INVENTORY

Removable Storage allows you to create either a fast inventory or a full inventory of all media in a library. A fast inventory is created by reading bar-codes if a bar-code reader is present, or by checking slots that have changed status from either occupied or unoccupied. A full inventory is performed when Removable Storage mounts each media in the library and reads the identifier. To create a library inventory, simply double-click Physical Locations and right-click the library you want to inventory, then click Inventory.

If you want to change the inventory method from fast to full or vice-versa, right-click the library and click Properties. On the General tab, select either None, Fast, or Full.

CLEANING LIBRARIES

Removable Storage can manage the cleaning of both stand-alone drives and robotic libraries. In this design, the robotic library can contain one cleaner cartridge, which Removable Storage can use to periodically clean the drive. The cleaner cartridge removes dust from the drive. If this is done, Removable Storage keeps a count of the number of times the cleaner cartridge is used and will generate an operator request when the cartridge needs to be replaced. For a stand-alone drive, you have to manually insert a cleaner cartridge, then click Drives and, in the results pane, right-click the drive and click Mark as Clean. This action tells Removable Storage the drive has been cleaned so it can keep a record of the cleaning. To clean a robotic library, right-click on the library you want to clean and click Cleaner Management, then follow the instructions in the Cleaner Management wizard. The wizard will prompt you to insert a cleaner cartridge, and you should always use the wizard to insert a cleaner cartridge.

Configuring Media Pools

Once you have configured your libraries, you need to configure your media pools so they function in an organized manner and are appropriate for the needs of your environment. The following sections show you how to perform various tasks in order to configure your media pools.

CREATING OR DELETING A NEW MEDIA POOL

To create a new media pool, follow these steps:

1. In the console tree, right-click Media Pools and click Create Media Pool. If you want to create another media pool within a media pool, right-click the media pool and click Create Media Pool.

2. Type a name and description on the General page.

3. Click the Contains Media of Type radio button, then select the media from the drop-down menu as shown in Figure 16.5.

4. In the Allocation/Deallocation policy, choose the Draw Media From Free Media Pool check box if desired, or choose Automatically Return Media to Free Media Pool when no longer needed by clicking appropriate check box, or choose both if desired.

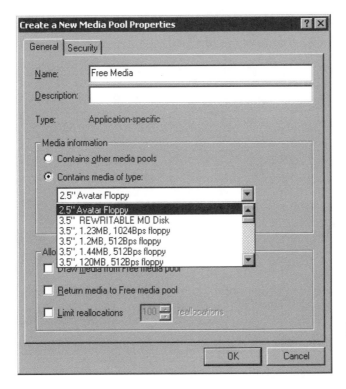

FIGURE 16.5

Media Pool properties

5. To set an allocation limit for the media in the media pool, click the Limit Reallocations check box and adjust the value as desired.

If you want to delete an application media pool, simply right-click it and choose delete. You cannot delete the free, import, or unrecognized media pools.

Configuring and Managing Physical Media

Removable Storage allows you to completely manage and control tapes and disks in your libraries. Once you create and configure various media pools as needed, you move media into a specific media pool, but you do need to leave enough media in the free media pool so it can be used by applications as needed.

A tape or a disk can be inserted or ejected from a robotic library using either a library door or an insert/eject port. A library door gives you unrestricted access to the media in the library while an insert/eject port allows you controlled access by inserting or ejecting the media through a port. The library then uses a transport to move the media to a storage slot. Additionally, you have full control in terms of disk mounting and dismounting and the same media can be mounted or dismounted many times before it is deallocated.

In the following sections, I show you the control options you have to manage your media.

INSERTING, EJECTING, OR MOUNTING A TAPE OR DISK

To insert a tape or disk into a robotic library, double-click on Physical Locations, then right-click the appropriate library, then click Inject. Follow the Media Inject wizard to insert the new tape or disk. To insert a tape into a stand-alone drive, manually insert the tape.

To eject a tape or disk from a stand-alone drive, right-click the appropriate library in Physical locations and click Eject. To eject a tape or disk from a robotic library, in the console tree, expand Physical Locations, expand the appropriate library, then select Media. In the right pane, right-click the tape or disk you want to eject and click Eject.

To mount a tape or disk, navigate once again to media, then in the right pane, right-click the tape or disk you want to mount and click Mount. To dismount from a stand-alone drive, perform the same steps but click Dismount. To dismount a tape or disk in a robotic library, navigate to Physical Storage, Physical Locations, the appropriate library, then Drives. In the right pane, right-click the drive you want to dismount the tape or disk from and click Dismount.

Configuring Queued Work and Operator Requests

In Removable Storage, the work queue provides a list of all requests made to the library from an application or remote storage. If you expand Removable Storage in the Console tree and click on Work Queue in the list, you will see a list of operations that have been performed, as shown in Figure 16.6.

The work queue can display five different states for the operation:

- Completed—The operation has been completed successfully.
- Failed—The operation request has failed.
- In Process—The operation is currently being completed.
- Queued—The operation has been requested and is waiting for Remote Storage to examine the request.
- Waiting—The operation is waiting for service by Remote Storage.

The Queued Work Properties sheet, which can be accessed by right-clicking Queued Work and selecting Properties, simply allows you to automatically delete completed requests and specify whether or not you want to keep or delete failed requests. By default, the requests are deleted after one hour, but you can change that by selecting the amount of time you want in the dialog box, as shown in Figure 16.7.

You can also right-click any operation in the list and click Properties to find out more information about the operation, when it was completed, or who initiated the request. Also, you can re-order the work queue item by right-clicking it and choosing Re-order Mounts. This allows you to move the

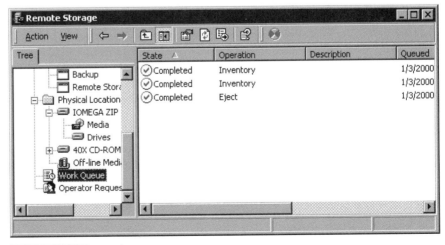

FIGURE 16.6 Work Queue

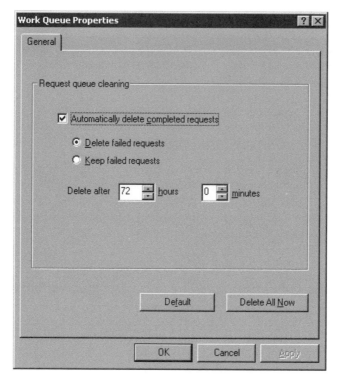

FIGURE 16.7

Work Queue
properties

item to the front or end of the work queue. You can also cancel an operation request by right-clicking the request and clicking Cancel Request.

A related topic to the work queue is Operator Requests. An operator
request is a message that requests that some task or action be completed.
Programs that are aware of removable storage or remote storage can generate operator requests when an application begins a mount request for a
medium that is offline, a library fails, there are no available media online,
and a drive needs cleaning but usable cleaner cartridges are not available.

You can complete or refuse an operator request as desired, and if you
refuse a request that was generated by a remote storage-aware application,
Remote Storage will notify the application that the request has been refused.
The Operator Requests icon appears in the Removable Storage console tree,
and the following sections show you how to manage operator requests.

RESPONDING TO AN OPERATOR REQUEST

To respond to an operator request, follow these steps:

1. In the console tree, double-click Operator Requests.
2. In the right pane, double-click the request you want to answer.

3. In the Operator Request dialog box, click Complete to complete the request, then perform the requested action, or to refuse, click Refuse. This cancels the request.

DELETING OPERATOR REQUESTS

You can delete an operator request by right-clicking on Operator Requests and clicking Properties. This gives you the same kind of Properties sheet as Queued Work. You can use the Properties Sheets to manage how operator requests are deleted.

CHANGING OPERATOR REQUESTS DISPLAY

You can change how operator requests are displayed with these steps:

1. Right-click Removable Storage in the console and click Properties.
2. On the General tab, you have two check boxes, as shown in Figure 16.8. You can choose to send the operator requests to the messenger service so they are displayed in a pop-up window, and you can choose the tray icon for pending operator requests, which displays an icon in the system tray for requests that are waiting to be serviced. Click the selections you want to use.

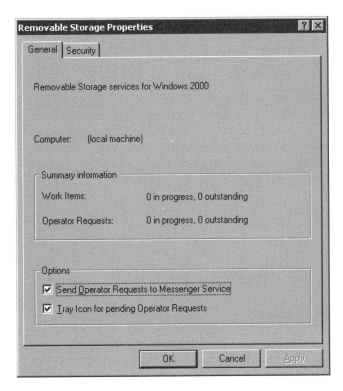

FIGURE 16.8

Removable Storage properties

Configuring Removable Storage Security

You can easily configure Removable Storage security by right-clicking Removable Storage in the console tree, clicking Properties, then clicking the Security tab, as shown in Figure 16.9.

You can further refine security by configuring this same interface for each library. Simply right-click on the library and choose Properties, then choose the Security tab. In this way, you can allow one user certain rights to one library and restrict rights to others.

By default, members of the system and administrators group have use, modify, and control permissions, backup operators have use and modify permissions, and users have use permission. You can change these default settings as needed, and you can click the Add button to specify individual user settings or add new groups. As with any user access permissions and security, careful consideration should be made before implementing a security plan for remote storage.

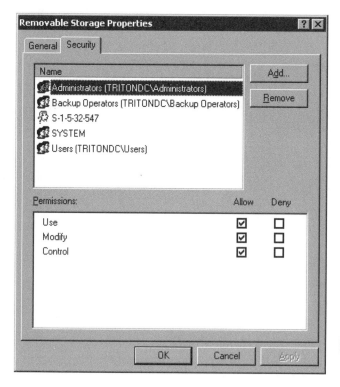

FIGURE 16.9

Security tab

Using Removable Storage Command Line

As with many Windows 2000 components, you have the option of administering Removable Storage at the command line. This feature allows you to write batch scripts for applications that do not support the Removable Storage API. The command line syntax is

```
rsm {allocate|deallocate|deletemedia|dismount|help|mount|view}
```

Each command has its own argument switches that can be used in conjunction with the command. You should keep in mind that no spaces are allowed after an argument switch or in the names or information following a switch. Also, all commands are case-sensitive and you can only use one command at a time. In the following sections, I explain the argument switches that can be used with each command.

ALLOCATE

The allocate command allows you to allocate media to a particular media pool. The argument switches for the allocate command are as follows:

- /m—Media pool name
- /n—Logical media name (optional)
- /p—Media side to allocate (optional)
- /t—Time-out value (optional)

The syntax for the allocate command is:

```
rsm allocate /mmediapoolname [/ppartid /nlogicalmedianame /ttimeout]
```

DEALLOCATE

You can use the deallocate command to deallocate media from a media pool. The deallocate command has the following argument switches:

- /l—Logical media ID (if the /n switch was used when the media was allocated, it can be reused here in place of the logical media ID).
- /n—Logical media name

The syntax for the deallocate command is:

```
rsm deallocate /llogicalmediaid /nlogicalmedianame
```

DELETEMEDIA

The deletemedia command allows you to delete data on the tape or disk from the Removable Storage Database. The deletemedia command has the following argument switches:

- /p—Physical media ID
- /n—Physical media name

The syntax for the deletemedia command is:

```
rsm deletemedia /pphysicalnameid /nphysicalmedianame
```

DISMOUNT

The dismount command is used to dismount a drive. The logical media name can be used to specify the logical medium if it was assigned during the allocate command using the /n switch. If not, then the logical media ID must be used. The /l and /n argument switches are used with the dismount command, and the syntax is as follows:

```
rsm dismount /llogicalmediaid /nphysicalmedianame
```

MOUNT

The mount command allows you to mount a drive and that is specified by the /l or /n switch. The mount command also contains the following optional switches:

- /d—Drive ID (if you do not assign this, Removable Storage assigns a drive).
- /p—Priority from 1 to 100, which specifies the drive-mount priority.
- /t—Time-out value

The syntax for the mount command is:

```
rsm mount /llogicalmediaid /nlogicalmedianame [/ddriveid /ppriority
/ttimeout]
```

HELP

The help command allows you to get argument switch and syntax information for each command. The syntax for the help command is:

```
Rsm help {allocate | deallocate | dismount | mount | view |rsm}
```

VIEW

The view command displays a list of media pools or a list of logical media. The view command contains the following argument switches:

- /c—Object type, such as media pool
- /I—Object ID

The syntax for the view command is:

```
rsm view /cobjecttype /iobjectid
```

■ Summary

Removable Storage allows Windows 2000 to manage removable storage devices and the media for those storage devices. With Removable Storage (and in conjunction with Remote Storage), you can store data in removable media, such as tape drives, Zip drives, and CD-ROM drives. This feature allows your system to continue to manage your data, even though the data is not stored locally on the computer's hard disks. With removable storage, you can devise a storage plan that optimizes the use of removable storage media while allowing your system to track and control your stored data.

Q&A

Review these questions and answers to resolve problems and to check your knowledge of this chapter's content.

Q: *What is the advantage of using Removable Storage?*

A: You can use removable storage devices, such as Zip drives and CD-ROM drives, on your computer and manually control them, but Removable Storage is a Windows 2000 feature that allows your operating system to manage the devices and the media. Removable Storage can label and catalog, as well as track media. It can also control library drives, slots, and doors, and even automatically clean some devices. The best feature of Removable Storage is that it can keep track of your media and the information stored on that media, even if the media is not always present.

Q: *What is the best way to use Removable Storage?*

A: You can use Removable Storage as an individual component, but it is best used with other application devices, such as Remote Storage or Windows 2000 Backup. This feature allows Removable Storage to manage your remotely stored data or backup files.

Q: *What are libraries?*

A: Libraries are composed of data storage media devices that read and write data to the media. In removable storage, there are two types of libraries— robotic and stand-alone. Robotic libraries (often called changers or jukeboxes) can robotically switch to and from different media, such as a multiple CD-ROM drive that can automatically change disks. A stand-alone library contains a single drive that holds a single tape or disk that must be manually changed.

Q: *What is a media pool?*

A: A media pool is a logical collection of removable media that have the same management policies. Media pools are used by applications to control access to tapes or discs within libraries that are managed by removable storage. Each media pool can hold either media or other media pools, and there are four types: unrecognized, import, free, and application-specific.

Additional Storage Technologies

In the previous chapters, you learned about different data storage features available in Windows 2000 and how those different storage features can give you a number of management options. This chapter continues to explore storage management technologies by examining compression, the encrypting file system, and disk quotas. As you work with either Windows 2000 Server or Windows 2000 Professional, you may find these easy-to-implement technologies useful to you in many ways.

Using Compression

You can compress NTFS drives, volumes, folders, and files in Windows 2000. Compression is not available on FAT or FAT32 volumes or for file and folders stored on FAT or FAT32 volumes. Compression helps save disk storage space by reducing the size of folders and files so they do not take up as much room. Compression functions by taking a block of data and looking for redundant information that can be removed. This redundant information is then replaced by a marker that Windows can use to replace the information when the data is needed. By removing redundant portions of the data, the disk space needed to store the data is reduced. For a basic example, consider the sentence, "Help me please." This example sentence can be reduced by removing redundant ele-

217

ments and replacing them with markers, such as the letter "e" that appears in each word. The "e" is replaced with markers, such as "H*lp m* pl*as*," which can be used to reconstruct the data when it is needed. Of course, this is just an example, and compression actually works on a lower level of data storage.

You can easily compress entire drives, volumes, folders, and files by accessing their properties sheets. For drives or volumes, click the Compress drive to save disk space check box on the General tab, shown in Figure 17.1.

When you choose this option and click Apply, a confirmation window appears, shown in Figure 17.2, that allows you compress the volume or all files and folders within the volume. Under most circumstances, you should choose to compress the folders and files residing on the volume to make the best use of compression. Make your choice, then click OK.

Once you make your selection, the system compresses the volume. This may take some time, depending on the size of the volume and the amount of data stored on the volume.

For folders or files, click the Advanced button on the General tab of the folder or file's properties sheets, then click the Compress contents to save disk space check box found on the Advanced Attributes window, shown in Figure 17.3.

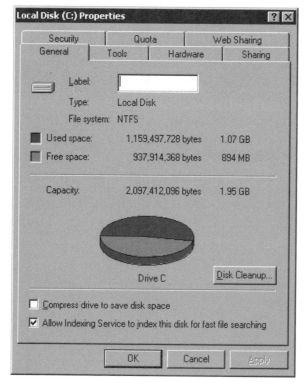

FIGURE 17.1

Click the compress drive to save disk space check box.

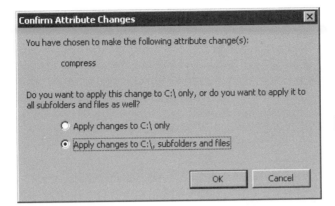

FIGURE 17.2

Choose to compress the volume only or all subfolders and files.

FIGURE 17.3

Click the Compress contents to save disk space check box to compress the folder or file.

Once files and folders, or volumes, are compressed, you continue to use them just as you would any other file, folder, or volume. From a user's perspective, you are not aware of the compression. If you add or copy a file into a compressed folder, the added or copied file is compressed automatically. If you move a file from a different NTFS volume into a compressed folder, it is also compressed. However, if you move a file on the same NTFS drive into a compressed folder, the file retains its original state, either compressed or uncompressed.

To allow you to easily view which files and folders are compressed on your system, you can choose to display compressed files and folders in a different color. To configure this option, open Folder Options in Control Panel, click the View tab, then click the Display compressed files and folders with alternate color check box, then click Apply, as shown in Figure 17.4.

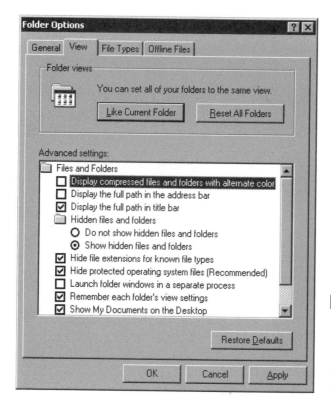

FIGURE 17.4

Use Folder Options to display compressed files or folders in an alternate color.

Aside from using your Windows interface to compress and decompress drives, files, and folders, you can also use the compact command at the command line. The syntax for the compact command is shown below, along with an explanation of switches that are available to you.

```
Compact {/c|/u} [/s[:dir]] [/a] [/q] [/I] [/f] [filename[...]]
```

- /c   Compresses the specified folder or file.
- /u   Uncompresses the specified folder or file.
- /s:dir   Specifies that a compress or uncompress command be applied to all sudirectories.
- /a   Displays hidden or system files.
- /I   Ignores errors.
- /f   Forces compression or decompression of a certain folder or directory. This option can be used if an original compression command was interrupted.
- Filename Specifies the folder or file to be compressed or decompressed.

Using Encrypting File System (EFS)

Encrypting File System (EFS) is a powerful new security feature in Windows 2000 that allows you to encrypt files or folders on your computer so they cannot be read by other users. EFS is a feature of NTFS volumes and does not work on FAT or FAT32 volumes. In addition, you cannot encrypt files or folders that are compressed. In order to use EFS on a folder or file, you must decompress it first.

tech check

Encryption scrambles data so that it cannot be read without an encryption key. The key is used to decipher the data, and in the case of EFS, the encryption key is attached to your username. This feature allows you to use encrypted data that is readable by you and you alone.

When you encrypt data on your computer, you continue to use the data just as you normally would. You can open and close files, move them, rename them, and other related actions without being aware of the encryption. In other words, once you set encryption on files and folders, the encryption is invisible to you. However, if you encrypt a file or folder and another user attempts to access it, they receive an error message.

As mentioned, you can only encrypt files and folders on NTFS volumes. If you move data to FAT or FAT32 volumes, the encryption is lost. Also, system files cannot be encrypted, and encryption does not protect files and folders against deletion. Anyone with delete permission can delete an encrypted file or folder.

If you choose to implement EFS, Microsoft recommends that you encrypt your Temp folder so that folders remain encrypted while they are in use or being edited. This action keeps temporary files created by some programs encrypted while they are in use. It is also a good practice to encrypt the My Documents folder. Also, an important note to remember is that you cannot drag and drop files into an encrypted folder for encryption to take effect on those files. If you want encryption to take effect on those files, use the copy and paste method so they will be encrypted when they are pasted into the encrypted folder.

To encrypt a file or folder, access the file or folder's properties sheets, then on the General tab, click the Advanced button. Click the Encrypt contents to secure data check box and click OK, as shown in Figure 17.5.

As with compression, you can use the command line interface to manage encryption through the cipher command. The syntax for the cipher command is shown below, along with an explanation of the switches you can use.

FIGURE 17.5

Click the Encrypt contents check box to encrypt the file or folder.

Cipher [/e| /d] [/s:*dir*] [/a] [/I] [/f] [/q] [/h] [*pathname* [...]]

- /e   Encrypts the specified folders. Folders are marked so that files added to the folder later will be encrypted.
- /d   Decrypts the specified folders. Folders are marked so that files added to the folder later will be decrypted.
- /s:*dir*   Either encrypts or decrypts selected folders and subfolders.
- /I   Continues performing the encryption process, even if errors occur. By default, cipher stops if an error occurs.
- /f   Forces encryption or decryption of all specified objects.
- /q   Reports only the most essential information.
- /h   Displays files with hidden or system attributes. By default, these files are not encrypted or decrypted.
- *Pathname*   Specifies a file or folder.

Although EFS management is valuable and very easy to configure, problems can arise in some circumstances where data needs to be deencrypted by a person other than the one who encrypted the data. In the case of an employee leaving the company, or even in the case where a user loses the file encryption certificate and private key due to a disk failure, the data can still be recovered through the use of a recovery agent.

By default, an administrator is the default recovery agent when he or she logs onto the system for the first time. Recovery can then begin by using the Import and Export command in the Certificates MMC snap-in, which allows you to backup the recovery certificate and associated private key to a secure location. The default recovery policy is configured locally for standalone computers. For networked computers, the recovery policy can be configured at either the domain, organizational unit, or individual computer level and applies to all Windows 2000 computers within the scope.

You can also specify a recovery agent for a local computer by opening the Group Policy MMC snap-in in Local Computer Mode. Click Public Key Policies, found under Computer Configuration, Windows settings, Security settings, and shown in Figure 17.6, then right-click Encrypted Data Recovery agents and click Add.

A wizard appears that helps you specify a recovery agent for the local computer. The wizard allows you to select a user from the Active Directory if certificates are published in the directory, or you need the certificate files (.cer) for the user you want to designate if certificates are not published in the Active Directory.

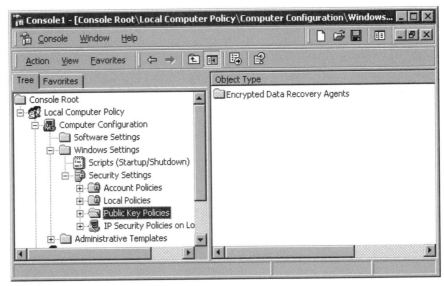

FIGURE 17.6   Navigate to Public Key Policies.

Using Disk Quotas

Disk quotas are a new feature of Windows 2000 and are only available on NTFS volumes on Windows 2000 computers—NTFS partitions on Windows NT computers do not support disk quotas. Disk quotas allow you to track and control disk storage usage by users. You can use disk quotas to limit the amount of storage space available to a user or simply track how much space has been used. Disk quotas are effective for computers that are used by several users or for servers that store user files and documents. Through disk quotas, you control the amount of space each user can fill with data, which helps you manage the overall system and encourage users to only store important data.

When you configure disk quotas on a Windows 2000 computer, you establish a disk usage limit and a warning level. For example, you could assign a user a limit of 100 MB of storage space and a warning level of 90 MB. When the user reaches 90 MB of consumed storage space, the user receives a warning message that disk space is running low. You can allow a user to exceed the disk space storage limit if desired. This feature is effective if you want to track disk space storage usage, but not actually restrict users from storing data.

Also, compression does not affect disk quotas. If a user only has 100 MB of storage space, compression does not allow the user to store more than 100 MB of data. Disk quotas also do not affect users as a group. If each user has 50 MB of storage space on a disk, one user's consumption of his or her disk space does not affect the other user. This feature is useful for network volumes where users store data. You can assign different storage limits for different users, and users are not aware of the storage limits of other network users.

Disk quotas apply to the volume (and can be used on spanned volumes), not to the underlying file and folder structure. In other words, each user has a set limit of space—it doesn't matter how many files and folders are stored, as long as the space limitation is not exceeded. Disk quotas are figured based on file ownership, so if one user becomes the owner of a file previously owned by a different user, that file counts toward the new user's quota limit.

To enable disk quotas for a particular volume, access the volume's properties sheets through either My Computer or Disk Management, then click the Quota tab, shown in Figure 17.7.

Click the Enable quota management check box to enable quotas on the volume. If you want users to be denied disk space once they exceed their quota, then click the Deny disk space to users exceeding quota limit check box. Then, use the dialog boxes in the window to set a disk space limit and a warning level limit. Finally, you can choose log events when a user exceeds the quota limit or warning limit, or both.

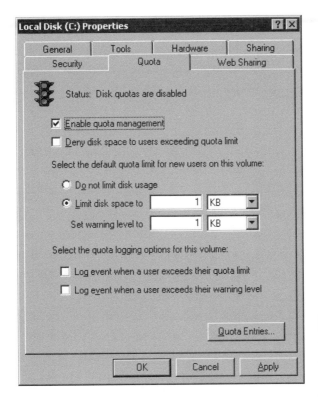

FIGURE 17.7

Use the Quota tab to configure volume disk quotas.

You can configure individual quota limits for various users by creating quota entries. Click the Quota Entries button on the Quota tab. This action opens the Quota Entries window, shown in Figure 17.8.

To Add quote entries, click the Quota menu, then click New Quota Entry. This action opens the Users windows where you can select the desired user from the list. The Add New Quota entry window, shown in Figure 17.9, appears and you can then enter a disk space and warning level limit for that particular user.

Once quota entries are configured, you can easily edit them by selecting the user in the Quota Entries window and clicking the Properties button on the taskbar. The properties sheet allows you to change the storage and warning levels and see how much disk space has been used.

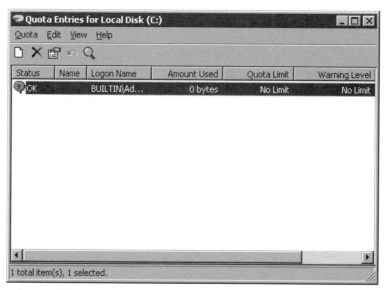

FIGURE 17.8 Use the Quota Entries window to configure individual quota entries.

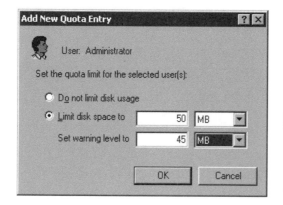

FIGURE 17.9

Enter the desired quota limits for the user in this window.

■ Summary

Windows 2000 includes compression, EFS, and disk quota technologies to enable you to carefully manage your data as well as protect it. Through compression and the implementation of disk quotas, you can more easily manage the disk storage space consumed both on the local machine and on network volumes. EFS allows you to protect your data by encrypting it so that it cannot be read by other users. All of these technologies are effective ways to manage disk storage in Windows 2000.

Q&A

Review these questions and answers to resolve problems and to check your knowledge of this chapter's content.

Q: *I want to enable compression on a particular folder's, but there is no advanced button on the General properties tab. Why?*

A: If there is no Advanced button on the folder's (or file's) General tab, then the folder is stored on a FAT or FAT32 volume. Compression is only available on NTFS volumes and folders and files must be stored on NTFS volumes for compression to be available. Likewise, if you attempt to compress a volume that is not formatted with NTFS, the compression option will not appear on the General tab of the volume's properties sheets.

Q: *What happens if I copy a file into a compressed folder?*

A: If you copy a file into a compressed folder, the file is compressed automatically. This same principle is true if you create a new file in a compressed folder. The file is automatically compressed.

Q: *What happens if I move a file residing in an NTFS folder that is not compressed to a compressed folder on the same NTFS volume?*

A: If you move a file residing on the same NTFS volume from an uncompressed to a compressed folder, the file retains its state. In this instance, the file would be uncompressed, even though it resides in a compressed NTFS folder. If you were to move a file from a different NTFS volume to a compressed folder on an NTFS volume, then the file would be compressed. The key point to remember is that files moved on the same NTFS folder retain their state in terms of compression.

Q: *I moved an encrypted folder to a different volume on my computer, but the encryption has been lost. Why?*

A: You have moved the folder to a FAT or FAT32 volume. Encryption is only available on NTFS volumes, and when you move any encrypted data to a FAT or FAT32 volume, the encryption will be lost.

Q: *Can encrypted folders be shared?*

A: No. Encryption does not allow another user to access your data, so there would be no point to sharing encrypted data.

Q: *I want to protect a collection of Word documents by using EFS. I have encrypted the files I want to protect; I also want them to be protected by encryption when I am working on them. How can I do this?*

A: You can protect files that are being edited by encrypting your Temp folder. Some applications create temporary files when you are editing a file. These temporary files are kept in the Temp folder, so you can encrypt this folder to protect your documents while you are editing them.

Q: *I moved several files into an encrypted folder, but the files are not encrypted. Why?*

A: You moved the files by dragging and dropping them in the folder. To make certain that files moved into a folder are encrypted, use the copy and paste method instead.

Q: *I would like to compress and encrypt a file, but I cannot select both check boxes on the Advanced Attributes window. Why?*

A: Windows 2000 does not support compression and encryption of the same data. In order to encrypt a file, you must remove the compression. Therefore, Windows will not allow you to select both check boxes on the Advanced Attributes window.

Q: *I want to setup disk quotas on a Windows 2000 Server so that users are denied disk space once their quota limit is met. How can I enforce this?*

A: On the Quota tab of the volume's properties sheets, select the Deny disk space to users exceeding quota limit check box. Likewise, if you do not want users denied disk space even if their quota limit has been exceeded, then make certain this check box is not selected.

Q: *I want to use disk quotas on an NTFS volume on a Windows NT server but can't seem to do so. Why?*

A: Disk quotas are only available on NTFS volumes on Windows 2000 computers.

Distributed File System

One of the major networking goals of Windows 2000 is to make life easier for the end user. With the Active Directory and other technologies, such as Intellimirror and Group Policy, network users can more easily find the information they need in a timely and organized manner. One way this can be accomplished is through the Distributed File System (Dfs). Dfs allows you to set up the many network shares offered by many servers to appear as one hierarchical tree. Users no longer need to browse multiple servers looking for resources—Dfs makes them appear as if they reside in one place. Dfs is configured on Windows 2000 Servers and is included in this book because it is an important storage solution available in Windows 2000, but since it is a server function, the rest of this chapter focuses only on Windows 2000 Server, not Windows 2000 Professional.

Understanding Dfs

In a networking environment, different servers hold different resources. Some servers may contain shared applications that users can access while others contain documents and databases. In the past, to locate a resource, you had to know which server held that resource, then either map to that server or browse the network. If you didn't know which server held which resource, you had to look for it on your own. In large networks with many servers, this process can be difficult and frustrating. Along with the Active Directory, Dfs provides a way for you to logically organize your shared network folders so that they appear in a single location to the users. This approach removes the network structure from the end user. The user does not need to know which server holds which resource, they only have to find it in a Dfs tree, which makes all of the shared resources appear in one location.

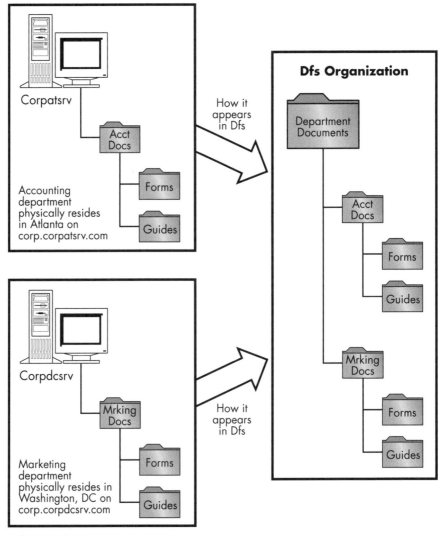

FIGURE 18.1 Dfs makes shared folders appear as though they reside in one location.

To users, Dfs appears as a tree-like structure. Users can browse the structure to find the shared folder they want to use. In reality, different servers still hold various resources within the tree-like structure, but this aspect of the network is hidden from the user. In Figure 18.1, you can see that several network servers hold different resources, and you can see how Dfs makes all of these resources appear in one location. This approach makes shared folders much easier to find.

There are two kinds of Dfs—stand-alone and domain-based, or fault-tolerant. A stand-alone Dfs is stored on a single server, which is accessed by network users. Users access the server, which then presents the network resources in a tree-structure so that users can access all resources from that one server. However, if the server fails, then Dfs is not available to the users—in other words, there is no fault tolerance. A domain-based Dfs stores the Dfs topology in the Active Directory. If one Dfs server fails, other Dfs servers are still available to network users, so this solution provides fault protection.

As you can already see, Dfs can be a powerful feature, but clients have to support it to be able to use it. Clients running Windows 2000, Windows NT, and Windows 98 have built-in support for Dfs. Windows 98 clients can support stand-alone Dfs, but you will need to download the Dfs client 5.0 for domain-based Dfs support. Clients running Windows 95 can download the Dfs client from microsoft.com.

Dfs is available on your Windows 2000 Server after the initial server installation. It does not appear in your administrative tools, but it is an MMC snap-in that you manually add to the MMC console. You can then save the console as desired. To open the snap-in, click Start ➤ Run, then type MMC and click OK. Click the Console menu, then click Add/Remove snap-in. Click the Add button. Select Distributed File System in the list and click OK, shown in Figure 18.2.

Click Close on the snap-in window, then click OK. Dfs now appears in the MMC, shown in Figure 18.3. You can save the console to the desired location on your system for future use.

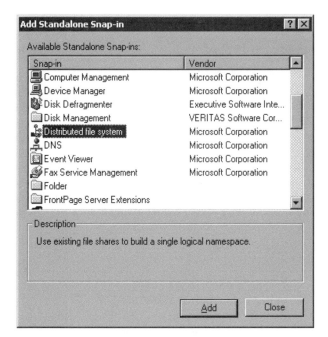

FIGURE 18.2

Select Dfs from the snap-in list.

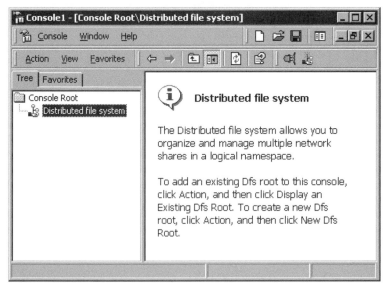

FIGURE 18.3   Dfs now appears in the console.

Configuring a Stand-Alone Dfs

Once you open the Dfs snap-in, you can either choose to display an existing Dfs root structure that resides on another server, or you can create a new Dfs root. This section examines creating a new Dfs root on a stand-alone Dfs. Keep in mind that a stand-alone Dfs is an effective solution, but it does not provide any fault tolerance. If the server should fail, Dfs will not be available to network clients. Also, with a stand-alone Dfs, you have a few other limitations. First, a stand-alone Dfs root cannot have root-level Dfs shared folders. This means that one root exists and all shared folders must fall under the hierarchy of the root folder and you have a limited hierarchy available. Also, a stand-alone Dfs can have only one single level of Dfs links. Dfs links are connections to different shared folders on a network. With a stand-alone Dfs, all links must reside directly under the root folder—in other words, you can not have a link within a link. Your best option is to use a domain-based Dfs, but you may see certain advantages of using a stand-alone Dfs, depending on your needs.

To create a new Dfs root, follow these steps:

1. In the Dfs console, click the Action menu, then click New Dfs Root. The Dfs Root wizard begins. Click Next on the Welcome screen.
2. In the Select the Dfs Root Type window, click the Create a stand-alone Dfs root radio button, then click Next, as shown in Figure 18.4.

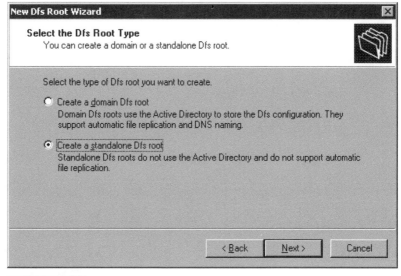

FIGURE 18.4   Choose the type of Dfs root.

3. Enter the name of the server that will host the Dfs root, or use the Browse button, then click Next, as shown in Figure 18.5.

4. In the Specify the Dfs Root Share window, you can choose to use an existing share or create a new one. The Dfs share holds the Dfs information, so you can use a share that already exists, or you may want to create a new one strictly for the Dfs root. To avoid confusion, this is usually the best option. Make your selections, as shown in Figure 18.6, then click Next.

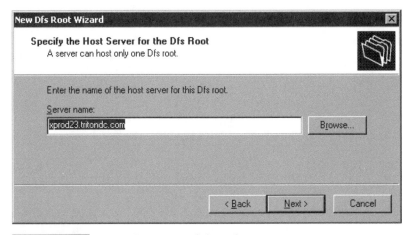

FIGURE 18.5   Enter the name of the Dfs server.

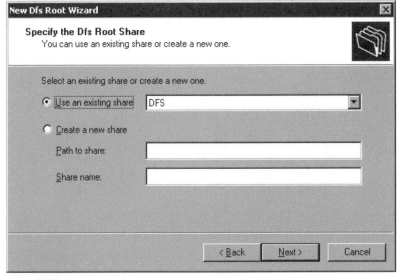

FIGURE 18.6   Specify the Dfs root share.

5. The Name the Dfs Root window appears. You can rename the Dfs root if desired and enter a comment. Click Next.

6. The completion window appears, shown in Figure 18.7, listing the Host server, root share, and Dfs root name. Click Finish to complete the wizard.

Once you complete the wizard, the Dfs root now appears in the console. From the Dfs root, shown in Figure 18.8, all Dfs folders can be built and reside under the Dfs hierarchy.

Creating Dfs Links

Once the Dfs root is established, your next task is to create Dfs links. The Dfs links provide the shared folder names in the hierarchy and contain information about the server that actually holds the shared folder. You can think of the Dfs as an Internet web page that contains links to different resources. By clicking on the hyperlinks, you are redirected to different web pages. You don't have to know each page's name, you just have to click on the hyperlink to get there. The same is true of Dfs. Users click on the folder in the hierarchy they want to use and are transparently redirected to the server that actually holds the shared resource.

To create a Dfs link, select the Dfs root in the console, click the Action menu, then click New Dfs link, or you can select the Dfs root in the console

FIGURE 18.7 Review your selections and click Finish.

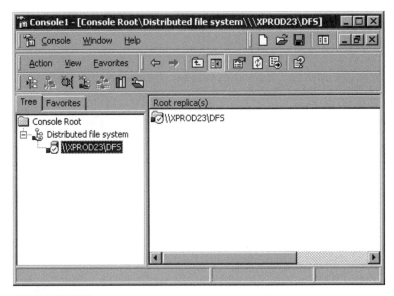

FIGURE 18.8 The Dfs root now appears in the console.

and click the Create a New Dfs Link button on the taskbar. This action opens a window where you enter the link name and the path to the shared folder. You can enter a comment if desired and adjust the cache referral time. The cache referral is the amount of time that clients can cache the link information on their systems. The default is 30 minutes (1800 seconds). If a link seldom changes, you can extend this time if desired, but under most circumstances, the default time is fine.

Once you enter the desired information in the New Dfs Link window, shown in Figure 18.9, click OK.

Continue this process to add the desired links to your Dfs. As you can see in Figure 18.10, the links appear as a hierarchical folder structure within the Dfs.

When clients access the Dfs shared root on the Dfs server, the contents of the folder hierarchy appear to the client as though they all reside in one location, shown in Figure 18.11. The client only needs to open the desired folder to be redirected to the server that actually holds the data.

Once links are created under the Dfs root, you can also create replicas for those links. A replica is an alternate location of a shared folder. For example, the Dfs link Standard Docs may reside in several locations. By definition, a replica participates in replication, so there may be two or more shared folders that hold the same information and replicate with each other as that information changes. The replica set keeps track of the possible locations that can be used to service clients. The alternate must be stored

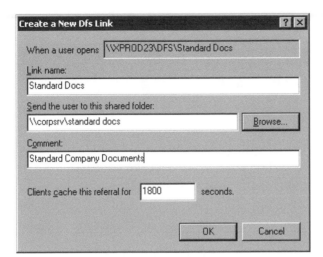

FIGURE 18.9

Enter the link information in this window and click OK.

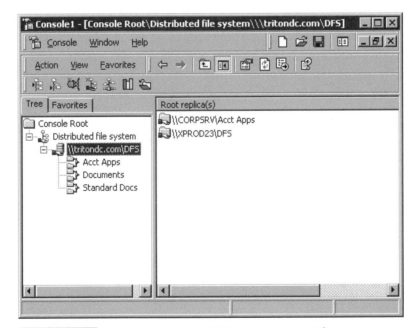

FIGURE 18.10 Links appear as a folder structure in Dfs.

on a Windows 2000 server running NTFS and the Dfs service. To create a replica, select the desired link, click the Action menu, then click New Replica. A window appears where you enter the location of the replica.

You can use the Action menu to perform other tasks, such as adding more links and removing links as necessary. Keep in mind that the link is

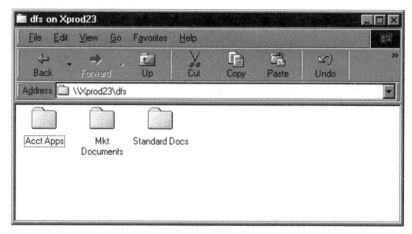

FIGURE 18.11 Client's view of the Dfs root.

simply that—a pointer to a shared folder on the network. If you remove a link, you are simply removing the pointer and are not deleting any information actually contained in the shared folder. Likewise, the Dfs console does not provide any security for the shared folders per se—security is configured on the server that actually holds the shared folder. A user can access a link in the Dfs, but if the user does not have permission to access the shared folder, access is denied.

Configuring a Domain-Based Dfs

The domain-based Dfs is your best choice for a Dfs implementation. In a domain-based Dfs, the Dfs topology, which is the roots and links, are stored in the Active Directory. Since the Active Directory database is stored on all domain controllers, fault tolerance is built-in. If one Dfs host server fails, clients can still access Dfs on other host servers. Also, with a domain-based Dfs, you can have root level-shared folders and there is no Dfs hierarchy limit—you can have multiple levels of Dfs links.

You create the domain-based Dfs root in the same manner you create the stand-alone Dfs root, by using the Create New Dfs Root wizard. The wizard is the same as explained in the previous section. The only difference is that you choose to create a domain-based Dfs instead of a stand-alone Dfs and you select the domain that the Dfs will serve. See the previous section specific steps.

Also, you add links to the domain-based Dfs in the same way as for the stand-alone Dfs, so refer to the previous section for specific instructions.

For domain-based Dfs, an important issue to understand is Dfs replication. Since one of the major purposes of the domain-based Dfs is fault tolerance, replication must occur between Dfs roots and shared folders to ensure that replicas hold an exact copy. In a stand-alone Dfs, you can create folder replicas, but replication must be performed manually. In a domain-based Dfs, replication can occur automatically. However, automatic replication cannot be used on FAT volumes on Windows 2000 Servers, so you should only use NTFS volumes on a domain-based Dfs.

When you create a root replica in the Dfs console, the Dfs Root wizard appears so you can specify the server where the replica will reside. Dfs shared folders can be replicated automatically on the domain-based Dfs. When you create a replica for a shared folder, select the Automatic replication radio button so that automatic folder replication can occur, shown in Figure 18.12.

Dfs uses the File Replication Service (FRS) to automatically perform replication. FRS manages updates across shared folders configured for replication, and by default, synchronization occurs at fifteen-minute intervals. When you set up automatic replication, a window appears, shown in Figure 18.13, where you can specify one share as the initial master (primary) so that one share replicates its contents to the other Dfs shared folders in the set.

Of course, you can choose to manually replicate changes for shared folders if desired, and even on a domain-based Dfs, you may want to use manual replication for some folders. If you have folders in which the content does not often change, you can use manual replication to reduce the amount of unnecessary synchronization traffic that would be created by automatic replication. However, within a set of Dfs folders, do not mix automatic and manual replication. Use one or the other to ensure that replication occurs properly.

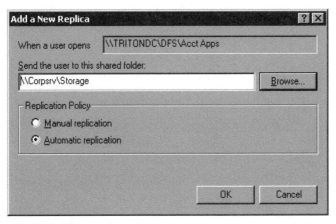

FIGURE 18.12 Select the Automatic replication radio button.

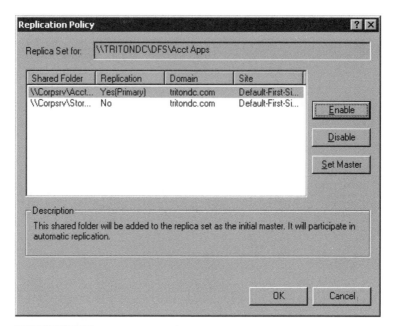

FIGURE 18.13 Use this interface to set the primary replication policy.

■ Summary

Windows 2000 Distributed File System is a storage solution that enables network clients to easily locate and use shared network resources. With Dfs, shared folders on servers throughout the domain appear as though they reside in one location. This occurs through the use of links, which transparently redirect the user to the appropriate server that holds the shared information. Dfs can be implemented as either stand-alone or domain-based, with domain-based being your best choice for fault tolerance. A domain-based Dfs can also provide automatic replication between roots and folders, providing fault tolerance and the assurance of correct information among replicas.

Q&A

Review these questions and answers to resolve problems and to check your knowledge of this chapter's content.

Q: *Can Dfs be used on FAT volumes?*

A: Yes. Dfs can be used on FAT volumes, but in a domain-based Dfs, automatic replication cannot be used if the Dfs root is stored on a FAT volume. Your best choice is to use Dfs on NTFS volumes.

Q: *What is the major difference between a stand-alone Dfs and a domain-based Dfs?*

A: A domain-based Dfs stores the Dfs topology (roots and links) in the Active Directory, which provides fault tolerance. A stand-alone Dfs stores the topology on the host server. If the host server fails, the Dfs becomes unavailable to network clients.

Q: *Which Windows platforms can use Dfs?*

A: Dfs is configured on Windows 2000 Servers, but there is a client component that allows clients to use the Dfs. Windows 2000 and NT 4.0 computers with Service Pack 3 can natively use Dfs. Windows 98 can use Dfs on a stand-alone server, but you need to download the 5.0 client from microsoft.com for a domain-based Dfs. Windows 95 clients can download the Dfs client from microsoft.com. DOS, Windows 3.x, and Windows for Workgroups do not support Dfs.

Q: *What is FRS?*

A: FRS is File Replication Service. FRS provides multi-master file replication for directory trees between Windows 2000 Servers. It is used both with Dfs and the Active Directory.

Q: *How can I configure Dfs security?*

A: Dfs does not provide any security for shared folders. Rather, shared folder security is configured on the server where the share actually resides. Keep in mind that Dfs contains links to the shared folders. Clients can access the links, but the security placed on the shared folder itself determines if clients can access the shared folder's contents. Dfs does not restrict clients from accessing links.

Q: *Is the shared folder affected if I delete a Dfs link for it?*

A: No. If you delete a Dfs link for a shared folder, you are simply deleting the link from the Dfs hierarchy. Clients will no longer be able to access the shared folder through Dfs, but the actual folder itself is not affected by a deletion of the link within Dfs.

Q: *How should I configure the client cache timeout period for shared folders?*

A: The client cache timeout period is the amount of time that link information is stored on the client computer. Dfs clients automatically cache this information. By default, the timeout period is 30 minutes. For folders that seldom change, you can extend the timeout period for a longer time; for folders that change frequently, you can reduce the cache timeout period so that is has to be refreshed more often.

Troubleshooting Windows 2000 Storage

....

As with any operating system component, you may experience some problems with the storage features of Windows 2000. Often, the problems you may experience are either hardware or configuration related. In the following sections, I explore the major problems you can encounter with the storage features and technologies explored in Part 3 of this book. Use this chapter as a handy reference to resolve the most common storage problems in Windows 2000.

Remote Storage

The following problems are most often encountered when configuring remote storage. For each problem presented, the possible solution(s) are presented.

PROBLEM: The Remote Storage snap-in is not available on your system.

SOLUTION: Remote Storage is not installed on your system by default. Use Add/Remove Programs to install it. This action installs the Remote Storage console as well as Removable Storage.

PROBLEM: You try to install Remote Storage, but are unable to do so.

SOLUTION: You must have administrative permissions to install and configure Remote Storage. Log off the server and log on with an account that has administrative permissions, then try to install Remote Storage again.

PROBLEM: Remote Storage cannot manage a particular volume.

SOLUTION: Remote Storage only manages nonremovable, local, NTFS volumes. Volumes formatted with FAT or FAT32 cannot be managed by Remote Storage. When you run the Remote Storage setup wizard, if no volumes appear for Remote Storage management, then your hard disk volumes are not formatted with the Windows 2000 version of NTFS. Format those volumes with NTFS then run the Remote Storage setup wizard again.

PROBLEM: Remote Storage cannot find a valid media type.

SOLUTION: When you launch the Remote Storage setup wizard, a message may appear telling you that Remote Storage cannot find a valid media type. Remember that Remote Storage only supports the use of tape libraries, specifically all SCSI class 4mm, 8mm, and DLT libraries. This message tells you that a tape library cannot be found. Verify that a tape drive is attached to your computer, installed, and functioning before continuing. Also, keep in mind that QIC or optical disc libraries are not supported with Remote Storage.

PROBLEM: Remote Storage file recalls are very slow.

SOLUTION: Depending on your hardware, file recall may be slow (in some cases, up to five minutes). Since the system has to locate the file on the tape drive and load it, your hardware certainly makes a big difference. If file recalls seem to be too slow, you can work around this problem by setting the desired free space value on your volumes lower so that data in cached files is not removed as often. By using the cache, you can keep data on your local disk for a longer period of time before it is removed. Also, make certain you are not sending files to remote storage that you use on a regular basis.

PROBLEM: You can not recall files from Remote Storage.

SOLUTION: Remote Storage uses a runaway recall limit to stop a user or an application from recalling files from remote storage more than a certain number of times in succession. Certain programs, such as virus protection software and indexing read all files on your computer and can cause the runaway recall limit to be reached. You can stop this behavior by increasing the runaway recall limit or closing the application that is causing the runaway recall limit to be met.

PROBLEM: Too many file recalls are occurring.

SOLUTION: Certain programs, such as virus software, backup, indexing, and several others read all files on your system. Remember that files in remote storage are still considered "local" files, so these programs can cause too many file recalls. Also, the Find function in Microsoft Office 95 or later will also recall remotely stored files. Take these factors into consideration and determine which programs are most likely causing the file recalls. You can then limit or stop the activity of those applications.

PROBLEM: You cannot perform a media copy using two libraries.

SOLUTION: Remote Storage may try to use a tape for a media copy from the same library as the media master. This happens if there is no media or no media that has enough capacity in the Remote Storage media pool. Use Removable Storage to move tapes in the second library from the free media pool to the Remote Storage media pool so that Remote Storage can use those tapes for the media copy.

PROBLEM: No files are copied to remote storage, even though you have a schedule established.

SOLUTION: More than likely, if Remote Storage is set up and you have established a schedule, yet no files are copied to remote storage, then there are no files that meet the criteria you have set. Re-examine your file rules and file-copy criteria and change if necessary.

Removable Storage

The following problems are most often encountered when configuring removable storage. For each problem presented, the possible solution(s) are presented.

PROBLEM: Removable Storage cannot automatically configure a robotic library.

SOLUTION: The most likely cause of Removable Storage not being able to configure a robotic library is that the library does not support drive-element address reporting. Check your library's documentation to see if it supports drive-element addressing and only use robotic libraries that support this feature.

PROBLEM: A particular library is configured, but is not working or is malfunctioning.

SOLUTION: This condition is normally caused by hardware problems. You can use Windows 2000's system event log to see if there are hardware problems, and you can also examine Event Viewer to look for both the device and specific Removable Storage error messages.

PROBLEM: Removable Storage has stopped configuring a robotic library.

SOLUTION: On some occasions, Windows 2000 will configure a drive inside a robotic library before the actual library has been configured. When this happens, Removable Storage will complete the configuration once Windows 2000 has configured the actual library. Make certain that Windows 2000 has recognized the library and the associated drives.

PROBLEM: Windows 2000 cannot detect an installed library.

SOLUTION: If Windows 2000 cannot detect an installed library, the library is most likely not supported in Windows 2000. Check the HCL to make certain. Also, make certain the library is properly connected to your computer. In the case of a robotic library being attached to a SCSI host adapter through a SCSI cable, make certain there are no SCSI ID conflicts with other SCSI devices.

PROBLEM: Removable Storage cannot detect the media type when configuring a new media pool.

SOLUTION: In this case, the library may not contain any tapes or discs. Before creating a new media pool, insert media into each robotic library so that Removable Storage can detect the media type.

PROBLEM: You cannot set or change security for Removable Storage.

SOLUTION: You must have administrative permissions to complete this task. Make certain you are logged on with an account that has administrative permissions.

Disk Quotas

The following problems are most often encountered when configuring disk quotas. For each problem presented, the possible solution(s) are presented.

PROBLEM: For a particular volume, the Quota tab does not appear in the volume's properties sheets.

SOLUTION: If the Quota tab does not appear in the volume's properties sheets, then the volume is most likely formatted with either FAT or FAT32. Disk Quotas are only supported on dynamic volumes formatted with Windows 2000's version NTFS. Format the volume with NTFS using the Disk Management console. Once the format is complete, the Quota tab will appear in the volume's properties sheets.

PROBLEM: On a computer dual-booting Windows NT and Windows 2000, users can exceed their quota limits, even though the quota is configured to deny users disk access once the quota is met.

SOLUTION: Disk quotas function on Windows 2000 computers only. When the computer is booted into Windows NT, users will be able to exceed their quota limit. The next time the computer is booted into Windows 2000, users who have exceeded their quota limit will not be able to add files. You work around this problem by changing permissions so that users do not have write permission while the computer is booted into Windows NT. However, even if users have not exceeded their quota limit, this will prevent them from saving files while the computer is booted in Windows NT.

PROBLEM: A quota entry cannot be deleted.

SOLUTION: You cannot delete a quota entry until all files the user owns have been deleted or until ownership of those files is assumed by another user. Once all of the user's files have been removed or ownership for the files has been transferred, the quota entry can then be deleted.

PROBLEM: A user receives a warning message just before exceeding the user's disk quote limit, but the user can still exceed the quota limit anyway.

SOLUTION: The disk quota is not configured to deny access to the user once the quota limit has been met. To configure this, access the Quota tab and click the Deny disk space to users exceeding quota limit check box, as shown in Figure 19.1.

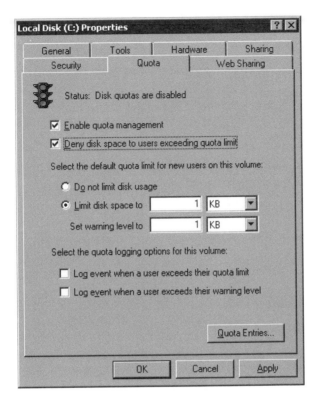

FIGURE 19.1

Click the Deny access check box to deny users access to storage space once the quota limit has been met.

Encrypting File System and Compression

The following problems are most often encountered when configuring encrypting file system and compression. For each problem presented, the possible solution(s) are presented.

PROBLEM: A file cannot be encrypted.
SOLUTION: EFS only works on files and folders on NTFS volumes. If a file cannot be encrypted, it is most likely on a FAT volume, or it is compressed.

PROBLEM: Compressed files cannot be encrypted.
SOLTUION: EFS does not work with compression. In order to encrypt compressed files, remove compression first.

PROBLEM: Files moved from an NTFS volume to a FAT volume lose their encryption.
SOLUTION: FAT and FAT32 volumes do not support encryption. When encrypted files or folders are moved from an NTFS volume to a FAT volume, all encryption protection will be lost.

PROBLEM: An encrypted folder cannot be shared.

SOLUTION: You cannot share encrypted folders. Since encryption only allows the owner to use the files in an encrypted folder, sharing is not an option.

PROBLEM: You cannot seem to encrypt system files.

SOLUTION: System files cannot be encrypted.

PROBLEM: Files placed in an encrypted folder are not encrypted.

SOLUTION: In order for files placed in an encrypted folder to be encrypted, use the copy and paste method. If you drag and drop files into an encrypted folder, those files will not be encrypted.

Distributed File System

The following problems are most often encountered when configuring Distributed File System. For each problem presented, the possible solution(s) are presented.

PROBLEM: Users cannot access a Dfs folder.

SOLUTION: The server that holds the folder is unavailable. If users can access Dfs, but cannot access a particular folder, then the server where the folder actually resides is not available. Keep in mind that Dfs contains links for shared folders. When a user accesses a folder through Dfs, the user is redirected to the server that actually holds the folder. If that server is not available, then the folder is not available, even though the folder appears in Dfs.

PROBLEM: Dfs is not available on the network.

SOLUTION: If Dfs is not available on the network, then you have configured a stand-alone Dfs and the Dfs server is not available. To avoid this situation, implement a domain-based Dfs, which stores the Dfs topology in the Active Directory. This way, if one Dfs server is down, Dfs is still available on other servers.

PROBLEM: A Windows 95 computer cannot access Dfs.

SOLUTION: Dfs contains both a server and client component. Windows 2000 and Windows NT 4.0 with Service Pack 3 can natively use both stand-alone and domain-based Dfs. Windows 98 computers can natively access a stand-alone Dfs and a domain-based Dfs with the 5.0 client download. Windows 95 computers must download the Dfs 4.x and 5.0 client. DOS, Windows 3.x, and Windows for Workgroups cannot use Dfs.

PROBLEM: Dfs security on folders cannot be set.

SOLUTION: Dfs does not offer any inherent security. Security for folders and files must be set on the server that holds the actual share. Keep in mind that Dfs simply provides a link to the shared folder. Whether or not a user can access the folder's contents is dependent on permissions configured on the server where the shared folder resides.

■ Summary

As with any Windows 2000 component, you may possibly have problems with storage features and technologies. Your first plan of attack is to always examine your configuration. Look for problems that can be resolved due to misconfiguration, then begin to examine hardware and other possible causes of the problem. Remember that effective troubleshooting is accomplished in a logical, step-by-step manner, and by logically exploring the problem, you can normally resolve Windows 2000 storage difficulties.

Windows 2000 File Management

In This Part

▶ **CHAPTER 20**
File and Folder
Management and
Security

▶ **CHAPTER 21**
Indexing Service

The final part of the book takes a look at file management in Windows 2000. Once your disks are configured as desired and you have implemented the desired storage features, you can manage your files and folders in a number of ways in Windows 2000. This section looks at file and folder management, security, and Windows 2000's indexing service, all of which are contained in these chapters:

Chapter 20: File and Folder Management and Security
Chapter 21: Indexing Service

File and Folder Management and Security

....

Once your hard disks, file systems, and storage decisions are in place, your final step to managing data is configuring file and folder options as well as security. This chapter assumes you are using NTFS, which provides you with rich security features. In this chapter, you learn about the file and folder security features offered in NTFS as well as a new feature in Windows 2000, offline files.

NTFS Permissions

NTFS permissions allow you to control what resources the network users can access and what they can do with those resources once they access them. You can control a folder with NTFS permissions and you can also control each file within a folder with NTFS permissions. In this manner, a user may be able to access a folder and some files within the folder, but not necessarily all of the files. NTFS permissions are available only on volumes that are formatted with NTFS—FAT and FAT32 volumes do not maintain any of the NTFS permissions, and this is why NTFS is the file system of choice.

NTFS Permissions

NTFS permissions in Windows 2000 work the same as in Windows NT. For individual files, you can assign the following permissions:

- Read—the user can read the file, view its attributes, permissions, and owner.
- Write—the user can perform any read function, but can also edit the file and change its attributes.
- Read and Execute—the user can perform all actions of the read function, but can also run applications.
- Modify—the user can perform all the actions of both read and read-and-execute, and the user can modify or delete the file.
- Full Control—the user can perform any action permitted by all other permissions, and the user can change permissions and take ownership.

For folders, you can assign the following permissions:

- Read—the user can view the files and subfolders within the folder and view the folder ownership, attributes, and permissions.
- Write—the user can create new files and subfolders within the folder and make changes to the folder attributes. The user can also view the folder ownership and permissions.
- List Folder Contents—the user can see the names of files and subfolders in the folder.
- Read and Execute—the user can perform all actions of the read and list folder contents permissions, and the user can move through the folders to other files and folders without permission for each folder.
- Modify—the user can perform all actions of the write and read-and-execute permissions, and the user can delete the folder.
- Full Control—the user can perform all action provided by the other permissions, and the user can change the folder permissions, take ownership, and delete any subfolders and files.

In addition to all of these permissions, you can also deny a user access to a file or folder.

For each file and folder, NTFS maintains an access control list (ACL) that contains a list of user and group accounts that have been granted access rights to the file or folder. When a user wants to access a file or folder, the ACL is checked to see if the user has access rights, and if so, what access rights the user has.

You can assign permissions to each user and to each group the user belongs to as well. Once this is done, the user will have what is called "effective permissions" for each resource, based on the combined NTFS permissions. NTFS permissions are cumulative—if a user has read permission assigned for a resource, but also has group membership in a group that has modify permission for the resource, then the user's effective permissions are read and modify. The only exception to this rule is deny. If a user has read access to a file but is a member of a group that is denied access to the same file, then the user has no access—deny overrides any other permissions. Also, file permissions override folder permissions. If a user has read access to a folder, but full control over a file in that folder, that user will retain the full control permission for the file and will not be reduced to read because the file is contained in the folder.

Another issue with NTFS permissions you should keep in mind is "inheritance." By default, subfolder and files inherit the NTFS permissions of the parent folder. You can prevent inheritance on subfolders if desired. When you perform this action, the subfolder becomes the new parent folder for all other folders and files contained in that folder. For example, if a folder has write permission, but there is a subfolder you want to have read only permission, then you block inheritance and assign read permission to that subfolder. This subfolder then becomes a new parent folder and everything within this folder will have read permission.

Finally, you should have firm understanding about moving and copying files and folders and the effect these actions have on NTFS permissions. When you copy a file or folder to a different NTFS volume, the file or folder receives the permissions of the destination folder. For example, if you have a file called "Companydocs" that has read permission, and the file is copied to a folder that has modify permission, the file will receive the modify permission. Windows 2000 considers the copied file a "new" file and therefore it inherits the permissions of the destination folder. In order to copy a file to another NTFS volume, you must have write permission for the destination folder and you will become the creator/owner of that file. Of course, if you copy a file or folder to a FAT or FAT32 volume, all NTFS permissions are lost. If you move a file or folder within the same NTFS volume, the file or folder retains its NTFS permissions. You must have write permission for the destination folder to move a file or folder into it, and you must have modify permission for either the file or folder you are moving. If you move a file or folder to a different NTFS volume, the file or folder will inherit the permissions of the destination folder. You must have write permission for the destination folder to move the file or folder to it, and you must have modify permission for the file or folder you are moving. As with copying files, any file or folder that is moved to a FAT or FAT32 volume loses all of its NTFS permissions.

Assigning NTFS Permissions

By default, when a volume is formatted with NTFS, the Everyone group has full control permission. You should change this setting so that you can control what resources are accessed by what users or groups and what rights those users and groups have to that resource. As with most administrative tasks, organization is of key importance. Group users so that you can assign access rights to groups instead of individual users. Also, it is usually best to assign NTFS permissions to a folder, then add appropriate documents to that folder. This action will make your job much easier. To set the NTFS permissions for a shared file or folder, right-click on the shared folder and click Properties. Click on the Sharing tab, as shown in Figure 20.1.

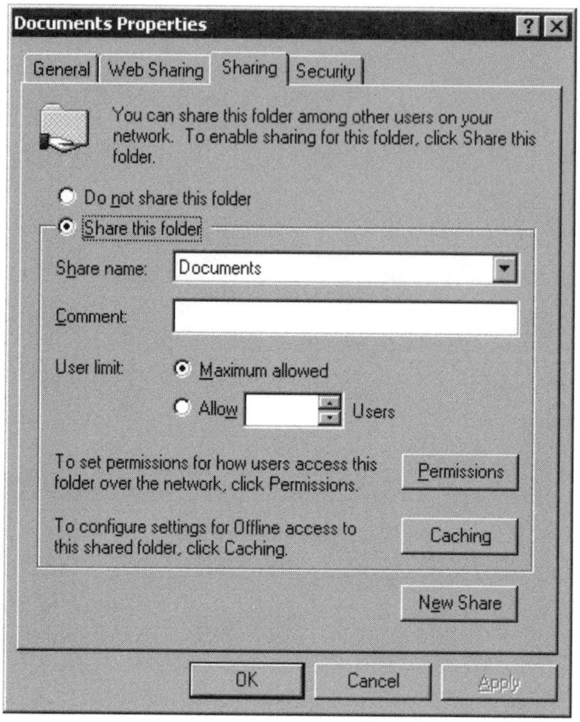

FIGURE 20.1

Sharing tab

On this page, you can see the shared folder's name and the user limit (if one has been configured). To set permissions for the folder, click the Permissions button. This action opens a Share Permissions page, as shown in Figure 20.2.

This window shows what permissions are given to the Everyone group. If you want to deny all permissions, click the Deny Full Control check box, which denies all NTFS permission for this group. Click the Add button to add other groups. A window from the Active Directory Users and Computers appears which allows you to select which groups you want to add permissions for. Select the group, click the Add button, and repeat the process until you have all groups that you want to include. Click OK when you are done. The new group(s) now appear on the Share Permissions page. Click the check boxes to assign what permissions you want to give, then click OK when you are done.

If you click the Security tab for the folder's properties, you can further define access rights for the folder, as shown in Figure 20.3.

Administrator and System groups are included by default with Full Control. You can add other groups and assign access rights as needed. This feature allows you to fine tune the rights you want to assign to individual groups. Also, at the bottom of the window, you can clear the Allow inheritable permissions from parent to propagate to this object check box to block inheritance. If you clear the check box, a security box appears asking what action you want to complete, as shown in Figure 20.4.

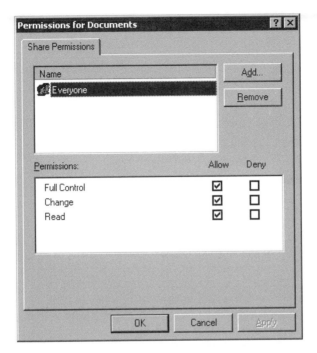

FIGURE 20.2

Share Permissions

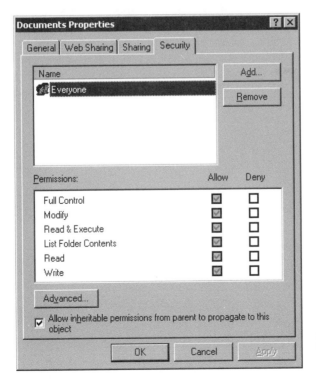

FIGURE 20.3

Security tab

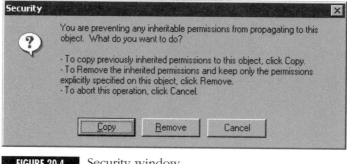

FIGURE 20.4 Security window

Advanced Access Permissions

Generally, the NTFS permissions you assign to users or groups for resource access is all you need to effectively manage a share. However, Windows 2000 provides additional access permissions if a specific type of access permission is needed. These advanced access permissions are available by clicking the Advanced button on the Security tab of the shared resource's properties, as shown in Figure 20.5.

You can click the Add button to add another user or group that you want to define additional rights for. For example, if I wanted to define advanced rights for a user, Karen Smith, I would click the Add button, select her user account, and click OK. Then, a permissions list will appear so I can select what rights I want to assign to Karen Smith, as shown in Figure 20.6.

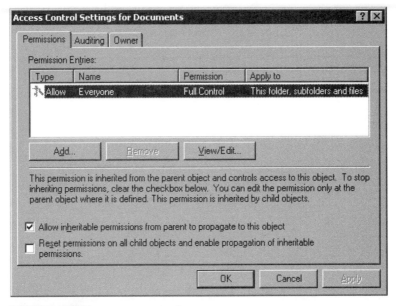

FIGURE 20.5 Access Control Settings

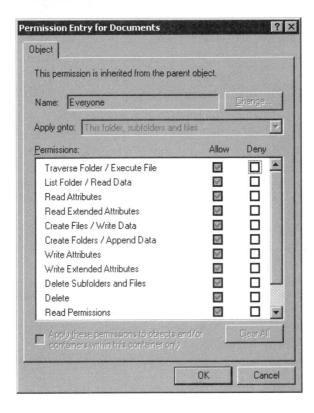

FIGURE 20.6

Permission Entry

Table 20.1 explains the thirteen entries that are available.

| **TABLE 20.1** | Advanced Permission Entries |

Parameter	**Explanation**
Traverse Folder / Execute File	Allows you to move through subfolders and execute files within those folders.
List Folder / Read Data	Allows you to list folder contents and read folder data.
Read Attributes	Allows you to read attributes.
Read Extended Attributes	Allows you to read all folder attributes.
Create Files / Write Data	Allows you to create files within the folder and write data to existing files.
Create Folders / Append Data	Allows you to create additional subfolders and append information to existing data.
Write Attributes	Allows you to write attributes for the folder.
Write Extended Attributes	Allows you to write extended attributes for the folder.
Delete Subfolders and Files	Allows you to delete any files and subfolders within the parent folder.
Delete	Allows you to delete any information within the folder and the folder itself.
Read Permissions	Allows you to read data within the folder and subfolders.
Change Permissions	Allows you to change ownership of the folder.
Take Ownership	Allows you to take ownership of the folder.

You can grant or deny any of these permissions to the selected user or group. Two particularly useful ones are Change Permissions and Take Ownership. You can give users or other administrators the ability to change the permissions of a shared folder without giving the person full control permission. This action allows the user to assign permissions for the folder without having the power to delete the folder or write to it. Another useful permission is take ownership. You can assign this permission to someone who can take ownership of the folder if the current owner either becomes unavailable or leaves the company—yet, you can still restrict the new owner from deleting the folder.

Additionally, you can select the check box at the bottom of the window to allow these permissions to become effective for all files and subfolders within that particular folder. Once the advanced permissions are configured, the Security tab of the folder's properties sheets displays the user, but provides a note telling you that additional permissions are present for the user but are only viewable by pressing the Advanced button, as shown in Figure 20.7.

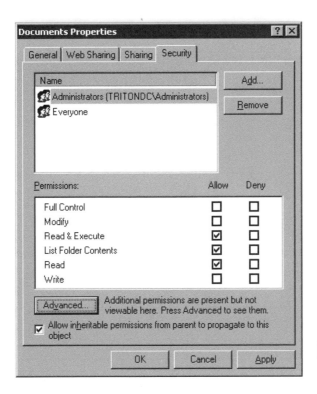

FIGURE 20.7

Security tab

Managing Shared Folders

NTFS permissions work with shares to give you a full plate of security options. By combining shared folder permissions and NTFS permissions, you have a great deal of control over what users and groups can do with the information in shared folders. NTFS permissions, however, do not work on FAT or FAT32 volumes, but shared folders do. You can place a shared folder on a FAT or FAT32 volume and still control which users can access the share. The default shared folder permission is full control assigned to the Everyone group, which is a setting you should change. A problem with shared folder permissions, however, is that the permissions apply only to the folder—not the files and subfolders within the folder. Obviously, shared folder permissions provide less security than NTFS permissions.

The shared folder permissions are read, change, and full control. You can allow or deny these permissions, just as you do in NTFS permissions. As with NTFS permissions, folder permissions are cumulative—if a user has read permission but is a member of a group that has full control permission, the user has full control. The deny permissions feature overrides all other permissions. If you copy or move a shared folder between FAT or FAT32 volumes, the folder is no longer shared in the new location.

You can easily share any folder by right-clicking on the folder and clicking Sharing. The folder's properties sheet will open to the Sharing tab, and you can click the Share this Folder radio button to share the folder. Shared folders appear on your drive with a hand icon under them. Click the permissions button to assign folder permissions. Generally, a good idea is to use the Security tab to assign permissions as desired, then remove the folder permissions, which you can access by clicking Permissions on the General tab. You can also click the Caching button to configure offline caching, as shown in Figure 20.8.

To allow offline caching of shared folder information, click the Allow caching of files in this shared folder check box. In the Setting drop down menu, you have three choices; Automatic Caching for Documents, Automatic Caching for Programs, and Manual Caching for Documents. Automatic caching for both documents and programs automatically downloads files and programs to the user so the user can access the documents and programs should the shared folder become unavailable. The cached version is automatically updated with newer versions as they become available. The manual caching feature forces users to manually cache the specific files they want when working offline or if the shared folder becomes available. This feature requires more work on the part of the user, but less work on the part of the server.

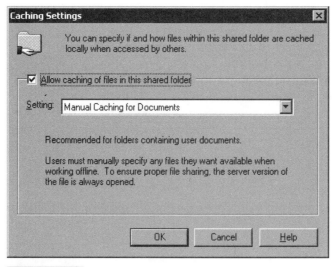

FIGURE 20.8 Caching Settings

Synchronization Manager

The Synchronization Manager is also a part of the Intellimirror technologies, and it allows you to use files offline. The Synchronization Manager is used to make certain that a user's offline files are synchronized with the server copy when changes have been made while working offline. This ensures that the cached copy and the server copy are exactly the same. Synchronization Manager can be set to synchronize files at the following times:

- Every time a user logs on or logs off the computer—or both.
- At specific intervals during computer idle time.
- At scheduled times.
- And combinations of the above three.

You can use Synchronization Manager to have certain files synchronized at one time and other files synchronized at another. For example, files that change on a daily basis can be synchronized every two hours while files that rarely change can be synchronized on a daily basis. Synchronization Manager can synchronize offline files, folders, and even Web pages.

Setting Up Your Computer to Use Offline Files

Before using Synchronization Manager, your computer must be configured to use offline files. To configure your computer to use offline files, follow these steps:

1. Open My Computer.
2. Click the Tools menu, then click Folder Options.
3. On the Offline Files tab, click the Enable Offline Files check box, as shown in Figure 20.9.

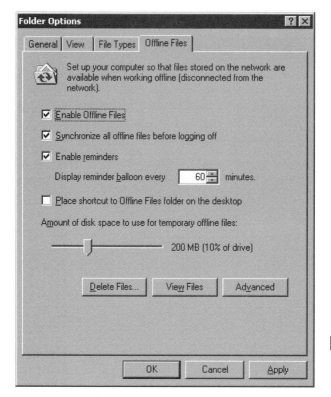

FIGURE 20.9

Offline Files
properties

Making a File or Folder Available Offline

To make a file or folder available offline, follow these steps:

1. In My Computer or My Network Places, click the file or folder you want to make available offline.

2. On the File Menu, click Make Available Offline.

Setting Up Synchronization Manager

To setup Synchronization Manager, click Start ➤ Programs ➤ Accessories ➤ Synchronize. The Items to Synchronize window opens, as shown in Figure 20.10. Click the Setup button.

   After clicking the Setup button, the Synchronization Settings properties pages appear. On the Logon/Logoff page, shown in Figure 20.11, use the drop-down menu to select the manner in which the computer is connected. In the Synchronize the Following Checked Items, select items that you want to synchronize by clicking the check box next to the item. At the bottom of

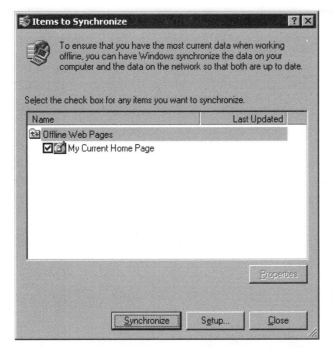

FIGURE 20.10

Items to Synchronize

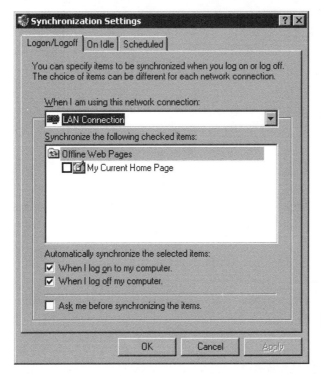

FIGURE 20.11

Logon/Logoff properties

the window, you can select whether to synchronize when you log on or log off your computer (or both) and you can click the Ask me before synchronizing the items check box, if desired.

On the On Idle property page, as shown in Figure 20.12, you can configure which files or folder you want synchronized when your computer is idle. Select the items by clicking the check boxes next to them, then click the Synchronize the selected items while my computer is idle check box.

If you click the Advanced button on this page, as shown in Figure 20.13, you can configure how many minutes of idle time should pass before synchronization occurs. You can also configure the amount of time to pass while your computer is idle for resynchronization to occur (such as every 60 minutes). Also you can use the Prevent synchronization when my computer is running on battery power check box if necessary.

On the Scheduled property page, as shown in Figure 20.14, you can add or remove synchronization tasks from your schedule.

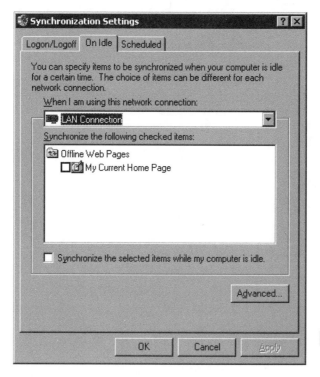

FIGURE 20.12

On Idle properties

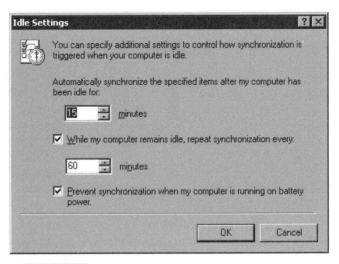

FIGURE 20.13 Idle Settings

FIGURE 20.14

Scheduled properties

If you click the Add button, the Scheduled Synchronization wizard begins. To complete the wizard, follow these steps:

1. Click Next on the Welcome screen.

2. In the next window, as shown in Figure 20.15, select the items for which you want to schedule synchronization by clicking the boxes beside the items. You can also select the If my computer is not connected when this scheduled synchronization begins, automatically connect for me check box if desired. Make your selections and click Next.

3. On the synchronization schedule window, adjust the start time and start date, and select either the every day, weekdays, or click the Every button and adjust the number of days desired. Make your selection and click Next.

4. Type a name for the schedule and click Next.

Once the wizard is completed, the synchronization tasks you selected are now scheduled.

FIGURE 20.15   Scheduled Item Selection

■ Summary

Windows 2000 NTFS provides advanced file and folder security. With NTFS, you can manage permissions not only for shared folders, but also for those files within the folder. With NTFS, you can finely control what users can do with the shares they access, and you can even further define permissions through the advanced permission entries. Along with NTFS, Windows 2000 also offers offline files, which allows you to work with network files while you are not connected to the network. When you reconnect, your offline (or cached) files are synchronized with the copies of the files that reside on the server.

Q&A

Review these questions and answers to resolve problems or review your knowledge of this chapter's content.

Q: *What is the difference between the NTFS permissions in Windows NT and Windows 2000?*

A: Windows 2000 provides an advanced version of NTFS that works with the new security features of Windows 2000. However, NTFS permissions in Windows 2000 work the same way they did in Windows NT.

Q: *If you move a folder that has NTFS permissions to a FAT volume, what happens to the permissions?*

A: FAT does not support the file and folder permissions available in NTFS. If you move an NTFS folder to a FAT volume, all NTFS permissions are lost.

Q: *How does effective permissions work with No Access?*

A: No access overrides all other permissions. When a user has no access permission for a folder, but also another permission, such as might occur in the case of multiple groups, then the user has no access to the folder.

Q: *How do offline files remain on my computer?*

A: Offline files work by using a copy of the file that is cached by your computer. When you are not connected to the network, the computer uses the cached copy. When you reconnect to the network, the file is synchronized with the server's copy.

Indexing Service

Windows 2000 Server provides an indexing service that enables users to perform a quick and easy search function to locate information stored on that server. The indexing service can be used through the Windows 2000 search function, an index service query form, or through a web browser. Indexing service is a powerful feature you can implement on your network that enables users to more easily locate documents by a particular author, on a particular subject, or containing key words. In this chapter, I show you how to set up the indexing service on your Windows 2000 Server.

Indexing Service

The Microsoft Indexing Service provided with Windows 2000 Server provides full text searching capabilities for text files, Microsoft Office 95 and later documents, HTML documents, and Internet mail and news documents (with Internet Information Services installed). The indexing service takes information from the documents and organizes it so that keyword queries can be performed through the Windows 2000 search function, an indexing service query, or from a web browser. The indexing service takes information from both a document's contents, or the actual words in a document, as well as the document's properties, such as the author's name. This feature allows you to search on a particular word or phrase and find all documents that contain that word or phrase, or you search for all documents by a particular author. The indexing service requires an initial setup and configuration, but after that, its services are automatic and it can even recover from a system crash or power failure.

The indexing service works by scanning documents. This process, which creates an inventory, determines what documents should be indexed. After you install the indexing service, a full scan will be run the first time, which means the service takes a full inventory of the document in cataloged folders and adds them to the list of documents that will be indexed. The indexing service will also run a full scan if a new folder is added to the index catalog or if a serious error has occurred. The index service can also run an incremental scan. An incremental scan looks for changes in documents and updates the catalog as needed. Whenever a document is changed, it sends a notification to the indexing service so it can be re-indexed. If the change notifications are lost, or if the service is shut down, the service performs the incremental scan to determine which documents have changed and need to be re-indexed.

Installing the Indexing Service

You install the Indexing Service just as you do any other service in Windows 2000, through the Add/Remove Programs option in Control Panel. Double-click the icon, then click Add/Remove Windows components. Select Microsoft Index Service from the list and click OK. The service will be installed on your machine. As with many Windows 2000 components, Internet Information Service (IIS) must be installed as well. IIS is automatically installed on your server by default.

Configuring the Indexing Service

Once installation is complete, you can configure the indexing service. Click Start ➤ Programs ➤ Administrative Tools ➤ Computer Management. Expand Server Applications and Services to reach the Indexing Service, as shown in Figure 21.1.

To begin the service configuration, right-click on the Indexing Service object and click Properties. The Properties sheets contain two tabs, Generation and Tracking.

On the Generation tab, shown in Figure 21.2, you have two options. First, you can choose to index documents with unknown extensions. In this case, the indexing service does not have filters for these types of documents, but the service will attempt to extract whatever information it can and index it. Click the check box if you want to use this option. Next, you have the option to generate abstracts. An abstract is a summary of the information

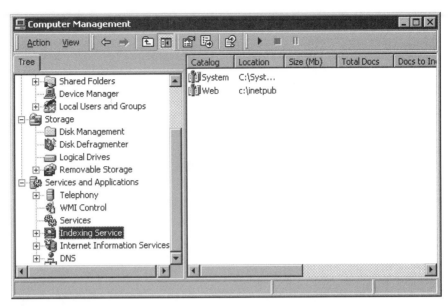

FIGURE 21.1 Indexing Service in Computer Management

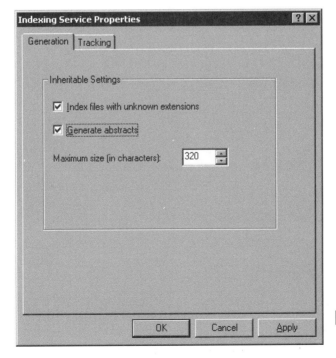

FIGURE 21.2

Generation tab

found in the document. The indexing service can generate an abstract that can be displayed with search requests so that readers can learn more about the document. If you choose this option, you can adjust the maximum abstract size permitted (in characters). The default setting is 320 characters.

On the Tracking tab, as shown in Figure 21.3, you can select the Add Network Share Alias Automatically check box. This feature tells the indexing service that you want to use the share name of any shared directory as the alias for that directory.

Creating a New Catalog

By default, a System catalog is created when you install the indexing service. The catalog stores all indexing information. The catalog(s) appear in the console tree under the indexing service object. You can create a new catalog by right-clicking the indexing service object in the console, pointing to New, then clicking Catalog. A dialog box appears asking you to enter a name for the catalog and a storage location for the catalog. Enter this information and click OK to create the new catalog. Once the catalog is added, the indexing service will have to be stopped and restarted. You can both stop and restart the service by right-clicking on the indexing service object in the console and clicking either Stop or Start.

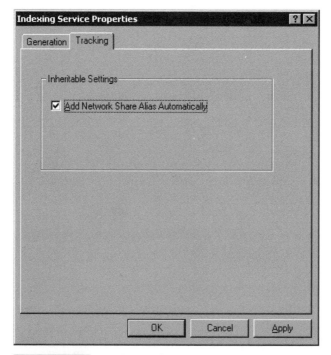

FIGURE 21.3 Tracking tab

Performing Manual Catalog Scans

You can manually perform a full or incremental catalog scan as desired. This action is useful when there has been some problem with the server or service being down and allows you to make certain the index is up-to-date. In the console tree, expand Indexing Service, then expand the catalog you want to scan. Click the Directories folder. Select the directory in the details pane you want to scan. Click the Action Menu, point to All Tasks, then click either Rescan (Full) or Rescan (Incremental), shown in Figure 21.4.

Checking Indexing Service Performance

You can run an indexing service performance check and make some adjustments if desired. In the console, right-click Indexing Service and click Stop. Then, point to All Tasks and click Tune Performance. The Indexing Service Usage window appears, as shown in Figure 21.5.

Click the radio button that best describes how the indexing service is used on this server and click OK. If you click the Customize radio button, click the Customize button to configure the desired setting. A Desired Performance window appears, as shown in Figure 21.6. Use the sliders to adjust the level of indexing performance you want, from Lazy to Instant for

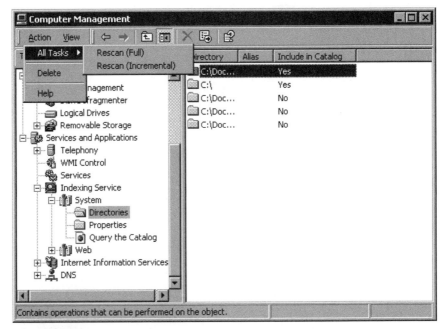

FIGURE 21.4   Use the Action menu to rescan a directory.

both indexing and querying, then click OK. Keep in mind that excessive indexing and querying may cause performance problems.

Click OK on the main window, then restart the indexing service.

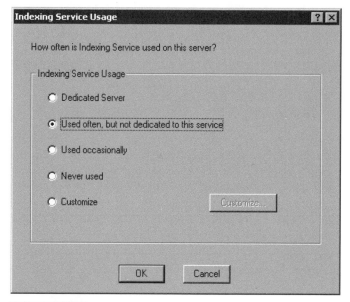

FIGURE 21.5   Indexing Service Usage

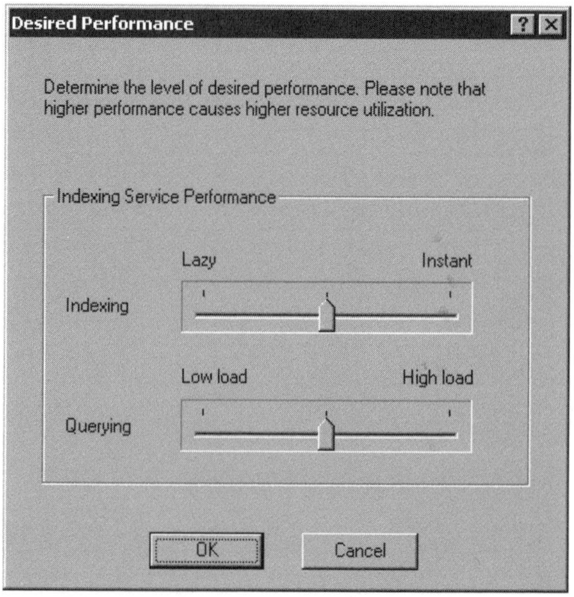

FIGURE 21.6

Desired Performance

Retrieving a List of Unindexed Documents

As an administrator, you will find it helpful to know which documents the indexing service could not index. You can easily retrieve a list of unindexed documents by expanding the Indexing Service object in the console and clicking Query the Catalog. In query line, type @Unfiltered=True, then click the Start button, as shown in Figure 21.7. An unindexed documents listing will appear.

Preventing an NTFS Directory or Document from Being Indexed

To prevent an NTFS directory or document from being indexed, access Windows Explorer in Start ➤ Programs ➤ Accessories ➤ Windows Explorer. Select the folder or document you do not want indexed, then click File ➤ Properties. On the General tab, click the Advanced button, then clear the For fast searching, allow Index Service to index to this folder check box, shown in Figure 21.8. Click OK, then OK again.

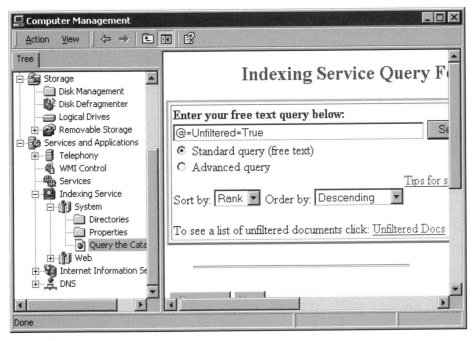

FIGURE 21.7   Indexing Service Query Form

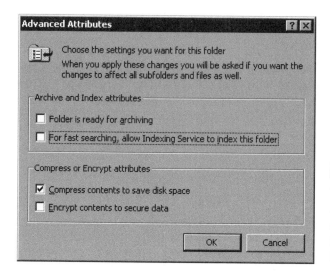

FIGURE 21.8

Use Advanced Attributes to stop an NTFS folder from being indexed.

■ Summary

Windows 2000 Indexing Service provides powerful search capabilities to network clients. With the indexing service installed on a server or web server, clients can search for desired documents by key words, document type, or even the author's name. The indexing service is just another feature of Windows 2000 Server that seeks to make network communications and data availability easier.

Q&A

Review these questions and answers to resolve problems or check your knowledge of this chapter's content.

Q: Can indexing service be run on a Windows 2000 Professional computer?

A: No. Indexing service is a server service that is only available on Windows 2000 Servers.

Q: *What kind of documents can the indexing service index?*

A: The indexing service in Windows 2000 provides full text searching capabilities for text files, Microsoft Office 95 and later documents, HTML documents, and Internet mail and news documents (with IIS installed).

Q: *What is the difference between a full scan and an incremental scan?*

A: A full scan completely rescans all documents. An incremental scan only scans for changes that have been made, then looks to see if any indexing information needs to be updated.

Using the Microsoft Management Console

As you play around with Windows 2000, you may notice that many of your tools and components seem to appear the same. They have the same explorer type of window and you use the Action menu for all kinds of tasks. This is due to the full integration of the Microsoft Management Console (MMC). The MMC is a powerful tool, and if you are unfamiliar with its use, this appendix gives you a tutorial so you can make the most of it. You use the MMC for all kinds of tasks both in Windows 2000 Server and Professional, so if it's new to you, this appendix is just what you need.

What is the MMC?

The MMC is a stripped-down GUI interface that looks very similar to an explorer window. The MMC itself is simply a shell. On its own, the MMC does not have any functionality, but it provides a place where various tools in Windows 2000 can be used. The tools you have worked with in this book, such as Device Manager, Computer Management, Disk Defragmenter, and so forth all use the MMC, and these tools are called "snap-ins." Snap-ins are loaded into the MMC so they can be used. A snap-in cannot function without the MMC, and the MMC alone doesn't do anything.

The tools you have used in this book are MMC consoles. They have been created by Microsoft for your use, but you can create your own consoles by loading any snap-ins that you desire. For example, you can create a console that only contains Disk Management and Device Manager, then you can save that console and use it instead of Computer Management. You can combine any number of snap-ins you wish and create as many consoles as you wish. This feature gives you more control over the OS and the tools you use.

The MMC first came onto the scene with BackOffice products, such as Internet Information Server (IIS), Systems Management Server (SMS), and Proxy Server. It is now fully integrated with Windows 2000. Although the MMC may give you a slight learning curve, you will find it is a great product that makes your work much easier. Instead of each tool or process having its own interface that you have to learn, the MMC provides one interface for all tools. In the end, this feature makes managing the many tasks available in Windows 2000 much easier.

When you open tools found in Administrative Tools, such as Computer Management, the snap-ins are automatically loaded into an MMC, but if you open your own MMC, you can decide what snap-ins you would like. Simply click Start ➤ Run, type MMC, then click OK. Figure A.1 shows you how the empty MMC looks.

As you can see, there is nothing you can do with this empty console without adding snap-ins. The next section shows you how to add snap-ins to the MMC.

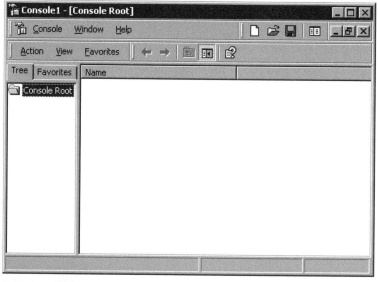

FIGURE A.1   Empty MMC console

Adding Snap-ins

Once you open an MMC, you then add snap-ins to the MMC by clicking the Console menu and clicking Add/Remove Snap-in. An Add/Remove Snap-in window appears. Click the Add button. A list of available snap-ins appears, shown in Figure A.2.

You can scroll through the snap-in list, select the one you want to load, then click the Add button. You can repeat this process to add other snap-ins as desired. Keep in mind that you can load more than one snap-in in a console. Once you have added the desired snap-ins, click the Close button. The snap-ins you have decided to load appear in the snap-in window. You can review your decision from this window, add others by clicking the Add button, remove one or more by clicking the remove button, and you can select a snap-in and click the About button to learn more about it. The Snap-in window appears in Figure A.3 and the About option appears in Figure A.4.

Click OK, and the snap-ins are loaded into the MMC. Expand the snap-in by clicking the plus sign next to it to see the snap-ins categories. As you can see in Figure A.5, I have loaded the Computer Management Console, which gives you the same interface if you had opened Computer

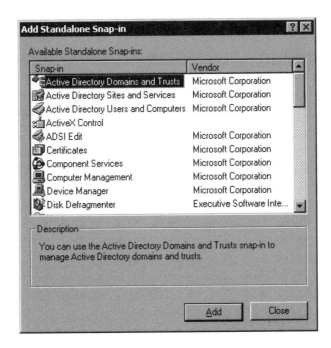

FIGURE A.2

Snap-in list

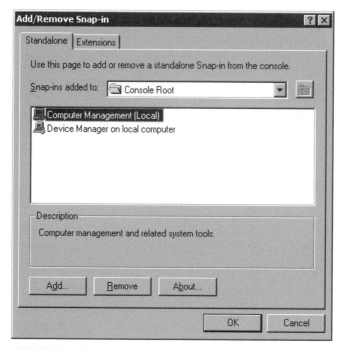

FIGURE A.3   Snap-in window listing snap-ins you selected

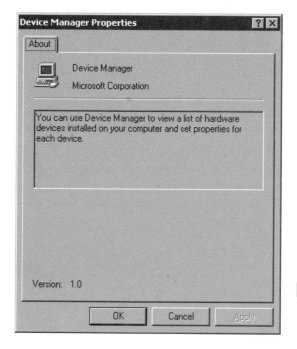

FIGURE A.4

Information about
the snap-in

Management in your Administrative Tools folder. In Figure A.6, you see that I have loaded several snap-ins. I can then click the Console menu, click Save As, and save the console to a desired location so I can use it at a later time. This feature allows me to combine several tools in one handy location.

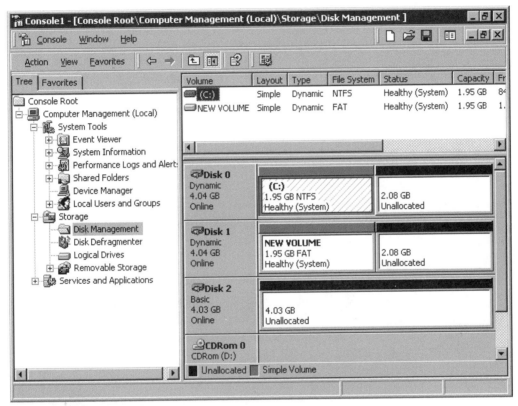

FIGURE A.5   Computer Management snap-in loaded into the MMC

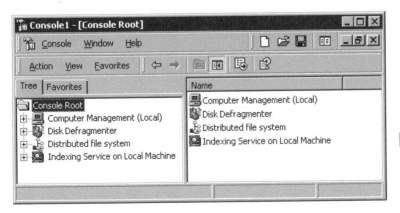

FIGURE A.6

Several snap-ins loaded into the MMC

Once the desired snap-ins are loaded, you perform tasks appropriate for each snap-in by selecting the snap-in, or a component of the snap-in, and clicking the Action menu. The Action menu presents you with the tasks that you can perform for that snap-in or the snap-in's components. What appears on the Action menu is determined by the snap-in you are using. For example, in Figure A.7, Disk Defragmenter is loaded into the MMC. The Action menu allows me to analzye or defragment the selected drive. If I select a different snap-in, different options appear on the Action menu. Aside from using the Action menu, you can also right-click on any snap-in or component within the MMC and see the same options that appear on the Action menu.

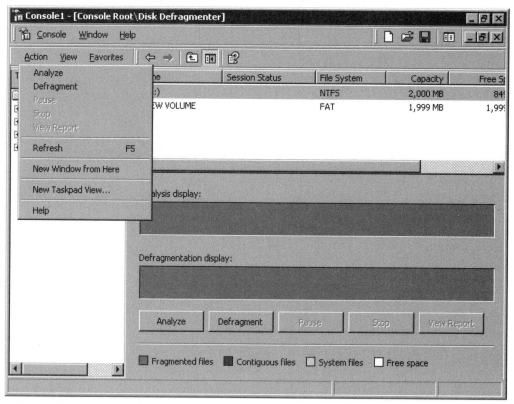

FIGURE A.7 Use the Action menu to complete various tasks.

Choosing an MMC Mode

Once you have created a desired console by loading the necessary snap-ins, and you have saved that console, you can also select a mode for the console. Modes allow you to choose what rights and functions other users can perform with the console. For example, in the case of a network server, several people may use the server. However, you can use the mode function to determine what other people using the server can do with the console you created. You configure the mode by clicking the Console menu and clicking Options, shown in Figure A.8.

As you can see in Figure A.8, you have a Console Mode drop-down menu. The following list tells you which options you can select:

- Author Mode—This mode grants full access to all MMC functionality, including the ability to add and remove snap-ins. You can also create new windows, create different views, and examine all portions of the console tree. Basically, you can do anything with the MMC in author mode.

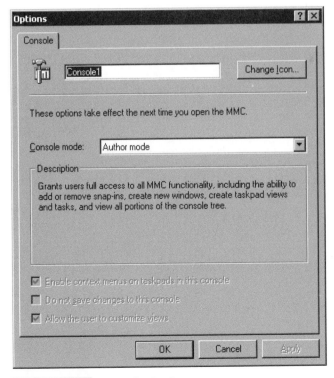

FIGURE A.8   Console Options

- User Mode—Full access. This mode grants full access to all management commands and to the console tree. However, users cannot add or remove snap-ins or change console properties.
- User Mode—Limited access, multiple window. This mode grants users access only to the areas of the console tree that were visible when the console was saved. Users can create new windows, but cannot close existing windows.
- User Mode—Limited Access, single window. This mode grants users access only to the areas of the console tree that were visible when the console was saved. This mode prevents users from opening any new windows.

As you can see, you can use one of these selected modes so that other users cannot make excessive changes to the console. Depending on your needs, the mode use can be very beneficial.

Using Multiple Windows

Some people like to load several snap-ins and have them all visible in one window while others like to load several snap-ins in one console, but have each snap-in appear in its own window. You can perform this action by selecting the snap-in, then clicking the Action menu and clicking New Window from here. This opens an additional window for the snap-in. You can then navigate through the different windows to use the snap-in you need. There is no right or wrong way to manage your snap-ins using either single or multiple windows; you simply have to decide which option works best for you. Figure A.9 shows you a console that has the snap-ins loaded in multiple windows.

When you use multiple windows, you can click the Window menu to adjust the way they appear. Aside from the cascade option, shown in Figure A.9, you can also choose to tile horizontally, shown in Figure A.10, which you may find easier in terms of working with each window.

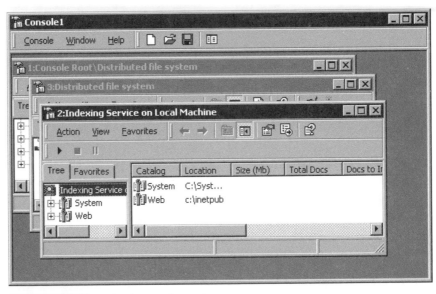

FIGURE A.9 Multiple window view

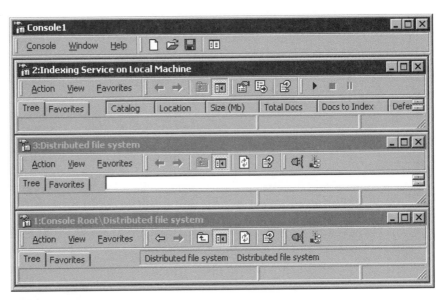

FIGURE A.10 Tile horizontally view

■ Summary

The Microsoft Management Console is your tool to effective management of your Windows 2000 operating system. All Windows 2000 tools function as MMC snap-ins, and you can create your own custom consoles by loading the desired snap-ins and saving them. You can also manage what other users can do with the console and adjust the appearance of the console as desired. The MMC is an effective tool and one you will grow to appreciate as you continue to work with Windows 2000.

INDEX

Active Directory, and printer information, 53, 56-58, 64
Administrative Tools
    Computer Management/Disk Management, 102-106
    Event Viewer, 179-180
    Remote Storage snap-in, 203
    Systems Information, 20-21
    see also Device Manager
Advanced Configuration and Power Interface (ACPI), 4
Allocation unit size, 126

Backup/restore
    Backup wizard, 157-161
    command line parameters (NTBACKUP), 167-168
    default settings, 165
        General tab, 166
        Restore tab, 166-167
    fault tolerances, 145
    media type, 156, 169, 215
    plan, 155, 156-157
    Restore wizard, 163-165
    Windows Backup in 2000 Server, 155-156, 157, 161-163, 165
        Copy type, 156
        Daily type, 156
        Differential type, 156
        Emergency Repair Disk (ERD) creation, 165
        Incremental type, 156, 168
        Normal type, 156, 168
Bandwidth usage, 48

Cached files, 172, 181
    client timeout periods for shared folders, 242
Cameras *see* Scanners and Cameras
CDFS, 100, 107
Certificates MMC snap-in *see* Security/EFS recovery

Cipher command *see* Security/EFS
Communication, analog vs. digital, 25, 39
Compression, 217
    common problems, 247-248
    and disk quotas, 224
    NTFS files, 217, 227
    volumes/folders/files via command line, 220
    volumes/folders/files via Windows interface, 218-219
Connection devices, 26

DCE rate, 26
Device Manager, 11
    Action menu
        disable device, 13
        Scan for Hardware Changes, 13
        uninstall device, 13
    Device Status window, 14
        Driver tab, 14-15
        Resource Tab, 15-17
    and NIC configuration, 42-43
    properties sheets, 71, 77
        troubleshooter feature, 183-184
Digital signature (signer), 15, 17
    for dynamic disks, 115
Disk management *see* Hard disk management
Disk tools
    Disk Cleanup utility, 171-173
    Disk Defragmenter utility, 174-176, 181
        report, 175-176
    Error Checking utility, 173-174, 181
    Event Viewer utility, 179-180
        application log, 179, 181
        security log, 179, 181
        system log, 179, 180
    Scheduled Tasks, 177-178
Distributed File System (Dfs), 229-232
    cache timeout periods, 242
    common problems, 248
    domain-based (fault-tolerant), 231, 241
        configuration, 238-239

end user and network structure, 230
links, 235, 240, 242
   creation, 235–236
   security, 238, 241
replication, 236–237, 239
root, 234–235
stand-alone, 231, 241
   creation, 233–235
   limitations, 233
Driver, 6, 22
  for printer, 52, 58, 59, 61, 65
  signing, 17–18, 23
  tab, 14–15, 23
  troubleshooting, 185
  Update Device Driver Wizard, 15, 21
DTE rate, 26
Dual boot system, 101
Dynamic Host Configuration Protocol (DHCP), 44, 49
Dynamic volumes, 140
  Add New Volume wizard, 134
  common configuration tasks, 137
  mirrored volumes
    booting, 150
    breaking, 149
    configuration, 145
    creation, 145–148
    disadvantage, 153
    failed redundancy status, 187
    removing, 149
    repairing, 149–150
    resynchronization, 148
  properties, 137
    General tab, 138
    Hardware tab, 139
    Quota tab, 139
    Sharing and Security tab, 139
    Tools tab, 138
    Web Sharing tab, 139
  RAID-5, 150
    creation, 151–152
    disk requirements, 153
    failed redundancy status, 187
    repair, 152
  simple volume, 123
    Create New Volume wizard, 128–129, 133
    creation, 123–126
    extension, 129–131, 137
    mounting to empty folder, 127–128, 140
  spanned
    creation, 132–133, 140, 141
    FAT ineligibility, 132
    without fault-tolerant solutions, 132

states, 137
  failed, 138
  failed redundancy, 138
  failed redundancy (at risk), 138
  healthy, 138
  healthy (at risk), 137
  initializing, 138
  regenerating, 138
  resynching, 138
stripped
  creation, 134–136, 141
  without fault-tolerant solutions, 134, 144
see also Hard disk management

Encryption, 221
  see also Security
Ethernet adapter *see* Network interface card/adapter types

FAT(16/32) *see* Hard disk management file systems
Fault tolerances *see* Backup plan; Distributed File System; Hard disk management; RAID standard; Remote storage; Uninterruptible Power Supply
Fax
  Control Panel
    Advanced Options tab, 83, 84
    Cover Pages tab, 83
    Status Monitor tab, 83, 84
    User Information tab, 61
  device attachment, 90
  Windows 2000 capabilities, 81–82
File management, overview, xviii, 251
File Replication Service (FRS), 239, 241
File systems *see* Hard disk management
Flow control, 27, 39
Fragmentation, 174

Game
  controllers, 87
  playing, 67, 79
Graphics Device Interface (GDI), 52

Hard disk management
  adding a new disk, 118
  as an MMC (Microsoft Management Console) snap-in, 103, 107–108
  basic disk, 109–110, 182–183
    to dynamic disk upgrade
      considerations, 112
      steps, 112–114
  console, 102–106

disk partition information, 102–103
  graphic display, 103
disk properties, 119
disk quotas, 224–226, 228
  common problems, 246
  and compression, 224
  file restrictions, 224, 228
disk signatures, 115
dynamic disk, 110, 120, 123
  dynamic to basic disk return, 116–117
  foreign status, 117, 118, 121, 187
  no media status, 118
  offline status, 117
  offline/missing status, 117, 118, 187
  online (errors) status, 117, 118, 120–121,
    187
  online status, 117, 118
  selection criteria, 111
  unreadable status, 117, 118, 187
  unrecognized status, 117, 187
  see also Dynamic volumes
fault tolerances, 109, 110, 120, 132, 134, 143
file systems
  File Allocation Table (FAT32), 101, 107, 140
  File Allocation Table (FAT/FAT16), 100–101,
    107, 132, 140
    cluster size, 100
  NTFS, 101, 127, 139–140, 146, 163, 192, 217
  see also Compression; Remote storage;
    Removable storage;
    Security/NTFS permissions
formatting, 126, 137, 140
hard disk operation, 99–100, 107
  formatting, 100
limitations, 111
overview, xvii, 97
removing a disk, 119
SCSI problems, 184
terminology
  active partition, 110
  extended partition, 111
  logical drive, 111
  partition, 110
  system/boot partitions, 110
and Windows 2000, xv, 102
  mirrored volumes, 109, 120, 144, 145, 153
  RAID-5 volumes, 110, 120, 144, 150, 153
  spanned volumes, 109, 120, 132
  striped volumes, 109, 134, 144
  see also Disk tools; Windows NT Disk
    Solutions
Hardware Compatibility List (HCL), 5, 22, 28, 38,
  42, 53, 67, 80, 89–90, 91

Hardware installation and configuration
  new hardware installation steps, 4–5, 21
  overview, xvi–xvii
  Plug and Play, 1, 3–5, 21
    automatic adaptation to hardware changes,
      4, 5–6, 13, 22
    automatic driver loading, 4, 14–15
    automatic hardware resource allocation, 4,
      15–17
    see also Hardware Wizard
  Systems Properties Hardware Tab, 17–19
  using Device Manager, 11–17
  see also System resources
Hardware Profiles, 18–19
Hardware Wizard, 4
  Add/Remove Hardware Wizard, 22
    add new hardware, 6–8
    and legacy NIC installation, 42
    to install a new modem, 27
    troubleshoot a device, 9–10, 91
    uninstall/unplug a device, 10–11, 23
  and "legacy" device, 6
HyperTerminal, 37

Indexing Service, 271–272, 278
  catalog, 274
  configuration, 272–774
  full vs. incremental scan, 272, 279
  installation, 272
  and NTFS directory, 277
  performance check, 275–276
Internet
  connection sharing, 34
  printing *see* Printer set up
  Protocol properties window, 45
IP address, 44, 49
IRQ settings, 15, 20
  replaced by plug-and-play compliant system,
    3, 4

Keyboard configuration, 88
  Sticky Keys, 90

Laptop computers, using hardware profiles,
  18–19
"Legacy" device, 6
  modem, 27, 38
  NIC, 42, 44, 49
Libraries, 215–216
  cleaning, 206
  inventory creation, 206
  robotic/changers/jukeboxes, 193, 202
  stand-alone, 202

Line Printer Daemon, 62
LPRMON *see* Printer set up/standard port monitor

Macintosh printer support *see* Printer set up
Media
 logical, 202
 physical, 202
  configuring/managing, 208
 pools, 216
  application, 202
  configuration, 207-208
  system, 202
 states, 202-203
Microsoft Management Console (MMC) snap-in, 103, 107-108, 281-282, 290
 adding snap-ins, 283-285
  Action menu, 286
 MMC Mode selection, 287-288
 using multiple windows, 288-289
Microsoft web addresses, HCL copy, 5, 22
Modems, 25-27
 configuration via Control Panel, 30-33
  Advanced tab, 32-33
  Diagnostics tab, 30-32
  General tab, 30
 data compression, 26
 dial-up connection configuring, 33-37, 39
  Make New Connection wizard, 33-34
 dialing rules, 28-29, 39
 error correction technology, 26
 flow control, 27, 39
 hardware problems/solutions, 93-94
 and HyperTerminal, 37
 installation, 27-28, 38
  Install a New Modem wizard, 27-28
 legacy, 27, 38, 39
 and other "connection devices," 26
 plug-and-play, 40
 speed, 26, 39
 using Phone Dialer, 37
 see also Fax
Modulation/demodulation, 25
Monitors, age and refresh frequencies, 75
Mouse configuration, 88, 90
Multimedia system and Windows 2000, 76, 79
Multiple windows, 288-289

Netware, and network printers, 61-62, 65
Network adapter card *see* Network interface card
Network and Dial-up Connections window, 33-35

Network interface card (NIC), 41-42
 adapter types, 41, 44
 configuration, 42-44
 hardware problems/solutions, 94
 installation, 42
 protocol binding, 44-45, 49
NTBACKUP Command Line parameters *see* Backup/restore
NTFS *see* Hard disk management file systems; Security/NTFS permissions

Offline files *see* Synchronization Manager
Open Systems Interconnect (OSI) model, 42
Operator request, 210-211
Optical disk libraries, 192

Paperless office, 51
Phone Dialer, 37-38
Plug and Play
 and "legacy" device, 6
 modems, 40
 OnNow design initiative, 4
 problem minimization, 91
 and USB devices, 48, 49
 in Windows 95, 3-4
 see also Hardware installation
PnP technology *see* Plug and play
Port, remote/standard *see* Printer set up
Power Options
 Hibernate Tab, 88, 89
 power scheme, 88
 UPS tab, 88
Printer set up
 Add Standard TCP/IP Printer Port wizard, 53, 54
 and client computer access, 61
 configuration, 55
  Advanced Properties, 59-60, 65
  General properties page, 56
  ports, 58-59
  security properties, 60-61
  Sharing tab, 56-58
 and features from Windows NT, 51
 installation, 53-55
  Add Printer wizard, 53
 new features
  Active Directory, 53
  Additional User Settings, 53, 63
  Internet Printing, 52
  Macintosh and UNIX attached printer support, 53, 62
  Monitoring, 53, 63
  Remote Port, 52, 64
  Standard Port Monitor, 52, 64

print device, 52
        hardware problems/solutions, 94-95
print queue, 53, 63
printer, 52
        pooling, 58-59, 65
web browser printer identification, 62, 64
Protocol, 26
        and NIC, 42
        V.42, 26
        V.90, 26

RAID (Redundant Array of Independent Disks)
    standard
        RAID 0 (Disk Striping), 144
        RAID 1 (Disk Mirroring/Disk Duplexing), 144
        RAID 2 (Disk Striping with ECC), 144, 153
        RAID 3 (ECC stored as Parity), 144, 153
        RAID 4 (Disk Striping with Large Blocks), 144
        RAID 5 (Striping with Parity), 144
Remote Procedure Call (RPC), 52
Remote storage, 191-192
        application media pool, 193
        common problems, 243-245
        fault tolerances, 198
        and "free media pool", 192
        installation, 192, 199
        lower level (remote), 192
        media management and synchronization, 198
        NTFS formatting, 192, 199, 244
        set up, 193-195
                Wizard, 193-194
        snap-in, 203
        tape libraries, 192, 193, 199
        upper level (local), 192
        volume management, 195
                add file rule, 195-196
                add/remove volume, 196-197
                change file copy schedule, 198
                change/delete a file rule, 196
                file selection, 195
                reprioritize file rules, 196
                set free space, 197
                set runaway recall limit, 197, 244
                set validation, 197
        working with Removable storage, 193
        see also Removable storage
Removable storage, 201-202, 215
        cleaning libraries, 206
        command line, 213
                allocate command, 213
                deallocate command, 213
                deletemedia command, 213-214
                dismount command, 214

                help command, 214
                mount command, 214
                view command, 214-215
        common problems, 245
        library configuration/management, 203-204
        library inventory, 206
        media type changes, 205
        queued work, 209-210
        and Remote Storage, 193
        snap-in, 203
        security configuration, 212
        supported devices, 199
Resource tab, 15-17
Runaway recall limit, 197

Scanners and Cameras, 85-86, 89-90
Security
        and Dfs links, 238, 241
        Encrypting File System (EFS), 221-223
                common problems, 247-248
                file restrictions, 221, 227
                recovery, 222-223
                and Temp folder, 221, 228
                via command line/cipher command,
                        221-222
                via Windows interface, 221
        log, 179, 181
        network logon options, 35, 36
        NTFS permissions, 253-254, 269
                advanced access, 258-260
                assignment, 254-257
                inheritance, 255
                managing shared folders, 261-262
                moving/copying files, 255
        printer management properties, 60-61
        for Removable Storage, 212
Sound cards
        configuration, 76
                Audio tab, 77, 78
                Hardware tab, 77-79
                Sounds tab, 76
        installation, 76
        troubleshooting, 77-79, 95
Stop message, 75
Storage features, overview, xvii-xviii
Synchronization Manager, 263, 269
                computer configuration, 263
                file/folder availability, 264
                set up, 264-268
System resources, 20-21
                Direct Memory Access (DMA), 20
                Input/Output (I/O) port, 20
                Interrupt Request (IRQ) line, 20

Memory Address Ranges, 20
System state data, 157, 168
Systems Information tool, 20-21, 188

TCP/IP, 26, 42, 44, 49
  Printer Port wizard, 53-54
Token ring adapter *see* Network interface
    card/adapter types
Troubleshooting
  boot partition access, 185
  common problems
    configuration, 186-187, 249
      cannot create spanned, striped,
          mirrored, or RAID-5 volumes, 187
      change NT files to dynamic for more
          management features, 186
      NTFS vs. FAT/FAT32 features, 186
    disk quotas, 246
    Distributed File System, 248
    Encryption and Compression, 247-248
    modems, 93-94
      Diagnostics tab for modem testing,
          30-32
    Network Adapter Cards, 94
    printers, 94
    removable storage, 245
    sound, 77-79
  Device Manager properties sheets, 183-184
  Disk Management and volumes hardware, 139
  disk swap, 185
  driver check, 185
  dynamic disk status indicator responses, 118
  ESDI devices, 185
  Event Viewer utility, 179-180
  Game controllers, 87
  IDE devices, 185
  peripherals, 95-96
  scanners and cameras, 85
  SCSI hard disk problems, 184
  tape backup and floppy disk devices, 185
  tools
    Add/Remove Hardware Wizard, 9-10, 91
    Device Status window, 14, 92

System Information, 21, 92-93
USB devices, 48, 94
video cards, 68, 72, 95
Windows 2000 Troubleshooters, 188

Uninterruptible Power Supply (UPS) *see* Power
    Options
Universal serial bus (USB) devices, 41, 49
  bandwidth usage, 48
  hardware problems/solutions, 94
  "tiered" topology approach
    device, 46-48
    host, 46
    hub, 46-47, 49
UNIX
  printer support *see* Printer set up
  unrecognized disk status, 117

Validation, in Remote Storage, 197
Video cards
  configuring display settings, 69
    Adapter tab, 70-71
    color management tab, 72-74, 80
    General tab, 69-70, 80
    Monitor tab, 71-72
  installation, 67-68
  multiple and multiple monitors, 75-76, 80
  troubleshooting, 68, 72, 73
    solving problems, 74-75, 95
  VGA device selection, 68

Windows 2000 Professional, xv, 101, 110
  and dynamic disk features, 111
Windows 2000 Server, xv, 101, 109
  and Dfs, 229, 231
  Indexing Service, 271-272, 278
  remote storage feature, 191-192
  Windows Backup tool, 155-156
Windows NT Disk Solutions
  mirror set, 110
  stripe set, 110, 134
  stripe set with parity, 110
  volume set, 110, 132